*Acclaim for Florence King's* Southern Ladies and Gentlemen:

"It needs a warning on the cover, because if you rashly open it in a public place, you risk being carted off, giggling helplessly, in a padded van....It's the funniest book I've read in years."
—Jane Clapperton,
*Cosmopolitan*

"Polished...sophisticated....Only a Southerner could have written it. Nobody else could have pinpointed the charming paradoxes that make up Southern personalities."
—Anita Black,
*Milwaukee Sentinel*

"Florence King may well replace Alice Roosevelt Longworth as the last best hope of desperate feature writers in search of an outré quote to spark their jaded readers on a slow news day."
—Rod Cockshutt,
*Raleigh [NC] News & Observer*

"It's funny, satiric, ironic, sympathetic and from what I know of the South from a decade of living in its hospitable midst, graphically accurate."
—Larry Rumley,
*Seattle Times*

"Tender venom drips from Ms. King's portraits of the Good Ole Boy....Delightful humor tinges her discussion of the South's passion for genealogy....Accuracy of portrayal has been achieved before by Larry King, Willie Morris and Tom Wicker, all in dramatic narrative; however (a word Ms. King says a Southerner seldom uses), I think Ms. King is funnier."
—Murrah Gattis,
*Los Angeles Times*

"Ms. King writes about these [Southern] creatures with wit, sauciness, fascination and understanding."
—David Hershkovits,
*New Orleans Magazine*

# Southern Ladies
# and
# Gentlemen

*Also by Florence King*

Wasp, Where Is Thy Sting?
He: An Irreverent Look at the American Male
When Sisterhood Was in Flower
Confessions of a Failed Southern Lady
Reflections in a Jaundiced Eye
Lump It or Leave It
With Charity Toward None: A Fond Look at Misanthropy

# Southern Ladies and Gentlemen

Florence King

St. Martin's Press
New York

SOUTHERN LADIES AND GENTLEMEN. Copyright © 1975
by Florence King. Afterword copyright © 1993 by
Florence King. All rights reserved. Printed in the United
States of America. No part of this book may be used or
reproduced in any manner whatsoever without written
permission except in the case of brief quotations
embodied in critical articles or reviews. For information,
address St. Martin's Press, 175 Fifth Avenue, New York,
N.Y. 10010.

"The Good Ole Boy" originally appeared in the
April, 1974, issue of Harper's Magazine.

Library of Congress Cataloging-in-Publication Data

King, Florence.
        Southern ladies and gentlemen  / Florence King.
            p.      cm.
        Originally published: New York : Stein and Day,
    1975. With a new afterword.
        ISBN 0-312-09915-0
        1. Southern States—Social life and customs—
    1865-   —Humor.   2. Sex role—Southern States—
    Humor.   I. Title.
    F216.2.K56    1993
    975.04—dc20                              93-23126
                                                CIP

10  9  8  7  6  5  4  3

*For* MEL BERGER, *my literary agent*

# *Author's Note*

I am neither living nor dead, and being purely coincidental runs in my family.

When naming characters, a writer must choose names that fit the characters' ethnic identity, which is why Margaret Mitchell received a letter from a distressed Roman Catholic Bishop named Gerald O'Hara, whose calling did not permit him to win plantations in poker games.

Except for my late grandmother's full name, and certain of my family's surnames mentioned in passing, all the names used in this book were invented by me and checked against a list I made of all the actual Southerners I have known whom I was able to remember. In most cases, I followed the advice of Oscar Wilde (who picked the name "Windemere" from the map of England) and converted place names to personal ones.

I once found my own name in a book I happened to read, and it didn't bother me a bit, but to those more sensitive than I who might find their names herein, I offer my sincerest apologies.

6

# Acknowledgments

## or: "Belles vs. Lettres"

I did not interview anyone for this book, nor did I make a nuisance of myself at the public library, so I have none of the usual people to thank.

I would, however, like to express my gratitude to my editor and fellow Southerner, Mrs. Aldis Jerome Browne III, née Miss Jean Reynolds Dillard, a direct descendent of Governor Spotswood of Virginia.

Mrs. Browne, whose next-to-favorite word is "penultimate," knows 435 ways to get "because" out of a sentence, and she shared every one of them with her author.

Next to editing, her greatest service has been morale-building via that Southern custom, "passing the time of day." Hence I wish to thank my publisher Sol Stein for gallantly paying the phone bills. Transcripts will shortly be made available to the public in a fifteen-volume matched set tentatively entitled *Giggles Deleted*.

Thanks are certainly due my other publisher, Patricia Day, for her unflagging skepticism when confronted with authors who guarantee the accuracy of historical facts with: "I think I remember reading something about that somewhere." Ms. Day also served with honor in her official post of Yankee Crucible. Encountering such blithe regional assumptions as: "*Everybody* has a crazy cousin who hears

7

voices," Ms. Day somehow managed to find sufficient space in the margins to record her standard comment: ?

Thanks are also due to Stein and Day's sales manager and secret weapon, John Maclaurin, Scotland's penultimate intoxicating export, who has the power to make weak women weaker merely by rolling the *r* in Florence.

Finally, I would like to thank God for the use of His name, which I took in vain in the margins during the First and Second battles of Because.

# Contents

# Southern Ladies
# and
# Gentlemen

# 1

## "Build a Fence Around the South and You'd Have One Big Madhouse"

### or: The Tip of the Iceberg

I have good reason to know that the only way to understand Southerners fully is to be one. When I was in graduate school at the University of Mississippi, I found myself party to a drunken kidnapping and ended up in a rowboat in the middle of a lake at 2:00 A.M. with an hysterical Southern belle who kept hissing: "Kill him, Wade, kill him!"

Suddenly I wondered: How did I get into this? What am I doing here? How was it possible that a sane young woman like myself could merge so effortlessly into a situation that bizarre?

The answer came to me just as suddenly. I was not sane, I was a Southerner. It is interesting to speculate on the moment when a child first realizes that he or she is a Southerner. No one ever actually tells him he is one, but something always occurs at a very tender age that helps fix it in his mind. The moment of truth tends to arrive in a burst of comprehension, following an incident in which an important truth suddenly becomes perfectly clear despite the fact that it makes no sense whatsoever. Once a child successfully negotiates this psychological legerdemain and snatches chaos from the jaws of logic, he wins his crossed cavalry sabers.

My red-letter moment occurred in the Year Eight of Franklin D. Roosevelt as I stood in front of the candy counter at Woolworth's. The sign on the counter read: TAR BABIES 20¢ LB. Inside the bin was a

11

mountain of little licorice candies shaped like black children. Everyone privately called them "nigger babies," but my grandmother had taught me that using the word "nigger" was one of those things no lady could do and still remain a lady. Granny wouldn't even say "tar." And so, to avoid hurting the feelings of the blacks who were standing up at the end of the segregated lunch counter where she was seated, she swiveled around on her stool and called out to me:

"Do you want some babies to eat in the movies?"

As the blacks looked up and stared at her, everything fell into place. Granny was an arch-segregationist with perfect manners; it's all right to segregate people as long as you don't hurt their feelings. Furthermore it is much better to be known as a white cannibal than as white trash who uses words like "nigger," because to a Southerner it is faux pas, not sins, that matter in this world.

I bought a nickel bag of tar babies, and Granny and I went off to the movies. The film was H. Rider Haggard's *She*, which I assumed would be a newsreel about Mrs. Roosevelt. (I had grown up hearing: "It's not his fault, *she* made him do it. *She* got them all stirred up, *she* thinks they're just as good as *she* is.") I sat through the film waiting for the First Lady to appear. Finally, when the withered old woman died in the snows of Tibet, I asked Granny: "Is that Mrs. Roosevelt?"

She snorted and said: "Would that it were."

For the second time that day, I heard the click of regional identity in my brain. Now I understood how it was possible for my family to worship FDR despite all the things he had done during his administrations that enraged them. They had used Southern logic to "straighten everything out just fine." It was very simple: Credit Franklin, better known as He, for all the things you like, and blame Eleanor, better known as She or "that woman," for all the things you don't like. This way, He was cleared, She was castigated, and We were happy.

Once my regionalism was launched, there was no stopping the stockpile of Southern contradiction that built up in my mind. As we emerged from the movie, Granny was busy making a grocery list and did not notice that I was still eating tar babies. But suddenly she turned, looked down, and gave me the Southern woman's all-powerful silent reproach known as "freezing." This is a look that needs no words. It is an exercise in pained hauteur and courageous endurance topped off with flaring nostrils and a stiffening just this side of rigor mortis. Despite my tender age, I knew instantly what it meant without being told: Ladies don't eat on the street. Granny did not have to tell me why, because my burgeoning Southern instincts told me: It looked *trashy*.

I already knew that ladies did not smoke on the street. My mother, who smoked five packs of Lucky Strike Greens a day, was always announcing an oncoming nicotine fit with a fluttery moan, an unfinished gesture toward her handbag, and her favorite dire pronouncement: "If I don't have a cigarette, I'm goin' to fall down dead." Yet as much as she loved tobacco, I had never seen her smoke on the street. I had seen her shake on the street and I had heard her become incoherent on the street, but she had never smoked alfresco because it looked trashy.

No one ever told me what "trashy" meant, but I never asked because I can't remember ever *not* knowing. As any Southerner can verify, the definition of trashy is trashy.

Granny and I went to the Fourteenth Street arcade market after the show. It took us nearly an hour to make our way down the sawdust-covered main aisle—Granny had to stop and "pass the time of day" with everyone she knew, which was just about everyone in the market. She sailed in, a two-hundred-pound neighborhood chatelaine in a lace bertha, bifocals, and a ten-year-old Empress Eugénie hat tilted at a rakish angle.

Instantly, the air was thick with her Tidewater Virginia drawl and those view halloos worthy of John Peel that she emitted every time she saw a friend. Traffic in the aisle was soon backed up to the Bundles for Britain booth beside the front door, but Granny talked on, the spotted veil on her hat fluttering like an ensign in a high wind.

"Oh, look, there's Miz Whitmore! OOO-HOO! Miz Whitmore! You come right over here this very minute! I haven't seen you since the fall of Rome!"

She meant two Saturdays ago, but I suddenly understood the principle behind the Southern internal time clock. Granny, a genealogy buff, was sunk like a Wasp dinosaur in the muck of prehistory, in love with any bygone age she could lay her hands on.

Another regional click: What is past is perfect.

After Granny had finished making her gracious way down the aisle, we bought a "mess" of pickled pigs' feet, a "mess" of oysters in the shell, and a "mess" of Maryland soft-shell crabs. Then, laden down with enough unfit edibles to make us stagger, we stopped by the kosher deli for a "mess" of bagels, which Granny persisted in calling doughnuts.

"How do, Mr. Silverman! How in the world are you? Law, I haven't seen you since the Age of Pericles!"

"But you were here day before yesterday, Mrs. Ruding," Mr. Silverman pointed out. I looked at him strangely, realizing for the first time that he never picked up on Granny's figures of speech.

"Let me have a mess of your wonderful doughnuts, please, sir."

Again, he looked puzzled.

"How many?"

"Twelve," said Granny.

It was not the first time I had heard these two confuse each other, but now I gave some hard thought to their communication problem. How could anyone not know what a "mess" was? *Everybody* knew that it meant a dozen or a pound, unless, of course, it meant a bushel or a peck, or, in the country, a truckload. My maturing Southern mind conceived a clear, concise picture of a "mess." It was a neatly arranged and properly weighed collection of anything edible. If it was more than the usual unspecified amount, it was a "nice mess."

It was to be many years before I realized how Mr. Silverman must have felt. Day after day, he had to stand in his hospital-clean store and listen to Southerners order a mess of his beautiful, ritually slaughtered, and rabbinically approved foods.

It has been said that when two Greeks meet they will start a restaurant, two Germans will start an army, and two Englishmen will start a silence. It is not necessary for two Southerners to meet in order to start something because we have taken a little nervous problem called schizophrenia and raised it to the level of a high art. When one-half of a Southerner meets the other half, the result is folie à deux.

It is this simple fact that Yankees always miss.

The best-known Yankee who missed it was that nineteenth-century traveler, Frederick Law Olmstead. Judging from his journals, his mind was blown soon after he set foot across the Mason-Dixon line.

A much more recent casualty was one Dr. Jonathan Latham of Boston, who wanted to win the Pulitzer prize in regional studies.

It all began on a Southbound plane, in which Dr. Latham was contentedly sipping a Scotch-on-the-rocks as he planned his scholarly attack on bourbon country. He was headed for a small city in Dixie, armed with an attaché case filled with three-by-five cards, which no Yankee sociologist can live without, and a heavily underlined copy of *The Mind of the South*, by Wilbur J. Cash, which no Yankee sociologist can live with—because, after all, Cash was himself a Southerner and therefore incapable of cool objectivity, that quality which alone can solve the mystery of Southern psychology.

Dr. Latham, a wholehearted believer in the infallibility of the scientific method, was firmly convinced that his frequency charts and cluster-grouping graphs would triumph over the Southern penchant for irrational behavior and contradictory thought processes. He knew his forthcoming book about the South would be a brilliant success because he intended, with the aid of the objectivity for which he was deservedly famous, to drive the spike of logic through the opaque mist of contradiction and paradox that floats like a vapor over every Southerner's head.

Warmed by this pleasant thought, Latham took out his copy of *Gone with the Wind* and reread his favorite part, marked with one of his red plastic find-it-fast markers, about the second Mrs. Calvert, the Yankee governess who had married a widower-planter.

Mrs. Calvert seemed ready to weep. She had somehow made a blunder. She was always blundering. She just couldn't understand Southerners, for all that she had lived in Georgia twenty years. She never knew what to say to her stepchildren and, no matter what she said or did, they were always so exquisitely polite to her. Silently she vowed she would go North to her own people, taking her children with her, and leave these puzzling, stiff-necked strangers.

An amused smile played over Dr. Latham's mouth. He took out his slim gold pencil to make more marginal notes—a favorite activity of his—on the already crowded page. "Nonsense!" he wrote. *He* was not going to let the South upset him. . . .

The first thing that upset him was the political confusion that fills the polling booth in which the solitary Southern voter acts out his problems in multiple personality with the blithe confidence that characterizes Dixie's true child.

Latham discovered that the typical Southerner:

—Brags about what a conservative he is and then votes for Franklin D. Roosevelt.

—Or brags about what an isolationist he is and then votes for Richard Nixon.

—Or brags about what a populist he is and then votes for Barry Goldwater.

—Or brags about what an aristocrat he is and then votes for George Wallace.

—And is able to say with a straight face that he sees nothing peculiar about any of the above.

Next, Dr. Latham encountered Southern political morality in a typical tavern called Johnny's Cash 'n' Carry. He went there for the purpose of observing and taking notes, but when he took out his slim gold pencil and a three-by-five card, a potbellied beer drinker demanded in a hostile drawl: "Are you a member of the press?" Suddenly the paranoia in the air was so thick that it could have been cut with the knives Latham saw sticking out of several back pockets—which inspired him to pretend that he was merely writing down the phone number of a girl he had met. The angry man relaxed immediately and grinned.

"We fellas got to git our nooky," he said genially. "You like football?"

Latham felt that this was somehow a non sequitur.

The man invited him to join the group at the bar. Latham himself soon felt awash with beer, but there was nothing else to drink unless he wanted to travel thirty miles to a "wet" town. Wet? He was already beer-logged enough to sink the *Titanic* merely by stepping aboard; what could be wetter? But no, his companions said, this was a "dry" county. It all had to do with something called "local option," which meant, they explained, that anybody can do what he damn pleases as long as an election is held first.

"Local option is kinda like states' rights," one of them elucidated. "Only it ain't as much fun."

Latham stared at him. States' rights was *fun*?

Before long, they were waxing nostalgic about the good old days, when there had been no hard liquor at all and their beloved state had been empowered to collect a Black Market Tax from the bootleggers.

"A *what?*" Latham asked.

"Why, shore. Used to be, there weren't no legal hooch a-tall, so the bootleggers was makin' all this money, see? Waal, you got to have tax money to run a state, so the legislature passed the Black Market Tax on hooch so the state could git tax money from the bootleggers."

"You mean it was actually on the statute books?"

" 'Course it was," said Latham's informant. "You got to make it legal."

"But the legislature had also passed a law saying liquor was *illegal!*"

"Thass right. They had to please the Baptists," said the man, with a shrug that seemed to say he had now made everything clear.

Latham persisted.

"Didn't the Baptists object to the passage of the Black Market Liquor Tax?"

The men seemed too surprised to speak for a moment, but then one of them explained.

"Waal, don'tcha see? The Baptists and the bootleggers have always been hand in glove 'round here. Neither of 'em wanted anybody to drink legal hooch. It was bad for both their businesses, you might say. They was both afraid that the state would go legally wet, so they got together and pushed this bill through the legislature."

Latham shook his head in disbelief.

"Didn't anybody feel a sense of. . . of conflict?" he finally asked.

"Waal, I reckon the legislator who was both a bootlegger and a Baptist deacon had a right good laugh when he collected bribes from both sides."

The next revelation came to Latham during Homecoming Week at the state university. The sexual identity that Southern men drew from football boggled his mind. They could talk and think of nothing else but The Game, and although they were all planning bacchanal weekends with women, they got very anal with each other. There was a great deal of butt-slapping and goosing. It was all accompanied by detailed descriptions of their potency with women, of course, but it upset Latham nonetheless. Other American men weren't like this . . . were they?

The Homecoming Queen, a waxily ladylike creature with a perpetual sweet smile who reminded him somehow of Pat Nixon, made a speech in which she announced that her body was a temple and that she did not believe in premarital sex. When a reporter asked her what man she admired most, she replied, "Jesus." As Latham studied her, he knew with slow but certain recognition that she was the ideal wife/daughter for an American politician to drag out and plant on a platform while he made a speech to the assembled multitudes. Despite Women's Liberation, or perhaps because of it, there was still something about a woman who reeked of Pathood that soothed American voters everywhere and made them feel that all would be well if they elected a man whose wife could cross her ankles, say the proper thing, and keep a locked Wasp smile on her face.

Latham wondered: Had the Southern Homecoming Queen represented an image of women that non-Southern Americans of both sexes *still* secretly favored?

The question led him into a survey of Southern sociosexual mores. He had often heard that the South was a land where men were men and women were women, and certainly their names bore out this theory. Many men had virile first names like Vance, Lance, Chance, Slade, Cade, and Wade. As for the women, their names alone were enough to render Latham smitten. He met heartbreakingly sweet girls named Nell, Daisy, and Jennie; arch, saucy girls who had what the South called "fire" and who tended to have names like Nan, Rhonda, and Dana. He also met professional sexpots who had been baptized Solange or Désirée, and one delectable creature he would never forget named Royal Montgomery, who rode sidesaddle.

And then he ran head-on into the South's sexual no-man's land, where baptismal fonts go bump in the night.

—Three-hundred-pound Good Ole Boys named Vonnie, Lynn, Shirley, and Beverly, who hold forth about "what my daddy said."

—That fine old Southern custom of bestowing the mother's maiden name on children of either sex, resulting in women named Rand, Taylor, Prentiss, and Ewing.

—The large number of Southern women who are named after their fathers. Some of these patronymics were quite dashing— Blaine, Ames, Ramsey, Dorcas—but Johnsie and Charlsie got on Dr. Latham's nerves.

—Women who were *really* named after their fathers. The classic example in this group must ever remain Commodore Vanderbilt's Alabama-born wife, née Miss Frank C. Crawford.

Latham's most serious nomenclatural trauma occurred when, exhausted from hours spent poring over telephone books in search of a cluster-grouping, he took a Scotch break and read the local paper.

He opened to the woman's page, and there was the headline in all its glory.

MRS. BALL HOLDER SOLICITS
WOMEN FOR RELIEF WORK

Who in the name of God was Mrs. Ball Holder and what kind of cluster grouping was *she* working on? Latham read the article, which turned out to be a commendable plea for volunteers to aid the victims of a recent flood.

He reached for the phone to call the woman's editor, then stopped. Mrs. Holder might be a paragon of Christian virtues, but there was no way he could discuss her name in mixed company, much less ask the question that he wanted to ask.

Instead he called a professor he had recently met at the university, Dr. Dabney Darcy Dalrymple III, who had offered Latham his aid in the most hospitable terms.

"Call me anytime, I'll be more than happy to help you in any way I can. Now don't you hesitate a minute, you hear? No matter what it is, you just pick up that telephone right quick."

Dr. Dalrymple, who was about sixty, had also instructed Latham to call him "Little Dab." Everyone called him that, he explained, because he was the son of the still-living Dabney Darcy Dalrymple, Jr., who was called "Big Dab." Latham could not bring himself to call anyone Little Dab. He wondered, moreover, what Little Dab had been called while his grandfather was still alive. Tiny Dab? Dabby?

"Oh, Christ," Latham muttered as he dialed the professor's number.

Dr. Dalrymple answered the phone himself.

"Jonathan Latham here. I'd like to ask you about this Mrs. Ball Holder."

"Oh, yes!" said the professor. "A fine woman. I'm so happy you've had the pleasure of meeting her. A tower of strength, that woman. She's a rock!"

"I haven't met her," Latham explained. "I just saw her name in the paper. It's her name that I wanted to ask—"

"That woman has worked her fingers to the bone for this town," Little Dab said, whereupon he launched into a paean of praise that went on for five minutes, interspersed with that curious compliment, "She's a rock." Latham made a note to find out what a Rock was.

At last Little Dab stopped talking long enough for Latham to ask his question. He expected a hearty male laugh and a locker-room quip or two, but the professor seemed completely unaware of the connotations in Mrs. Holder's name.

"Mrs. Holder, née Mindy Lee Ball, married Houghton Grenier Holder," Little Dab explained. "They were divorced. There were no children, but of course Mindy didn't take back her maiden name and call herself Miss."

"Why not?" Latham asked.

There was a startled pause on the line.

"Why, someone who didn't know her might think she had never been married."

". . . Oh."

"Our newspaper, like all Southern newspapers, has very strict rules of etiquette. The proper way to refer to a divorced woman is to use 'Mrs.' and both of the surnames that she has carried in her life. It's incorrect to refer to a divorced woman as 'Mrs. Mindy B. Holder.' That would sound flippant and undignified. Down here we believe in tradition and niceties, so in order not to embarrass Mindy, the newspaper refers to her as Mrs. Ball Holder."

"I see," Dr. Latham lied. "But . . . couldn't they just call her Mindy Holder?"

"A woman without an honorific? Somebody might think she was single, dead, or even colored!"

Latham took a quiet trip to Richmond to see a psychiatrist whose name had been given to him by his own shrink in Boston. The Richmond doctor, unfortunately, was also a Yankee.

"Latham, I don't know what to tell you," he said in a comforting

New England twang. "I've been here five years and I don't understand Southerners. All I know is, there's a family tree under every bush. They lie here on my couch and tell me so much about their ancestors that I never hear about what's troubling *them*."

"Could you give me a clinical opinion on Southerners that I might quote in my book?"

"Sure. They're nuts."

Latham put away his notebook with a sigh.

"Well, then, could you give me some tranquilizers? I'm all out."

"Try these," said the psychiatrist, writing out a prescription. "They help me a lot."

On his way back to the Richmond airport, Latham shared a taxi with that species of elderly Southern woman known as a Dear Old Thing. A white-haired matchstick figure in a hat and white gloves, her timid wave made the driver stop so suddenly that Latham was thrown to the floor.

"Aw, looka there," said the driver. "The dear ole thang. Les' see iffn she's headin' anywheres in your direction."

She stuck her head through the window and gave Latham a twinkly smile as she launched into a monologue, oblivious to the backed-up traffic behind them.

" 'Deed I am so sorry to intrude on you, but if you don't mind, would you be kind enough to let me share your cab if I promise to dance at your weddin'? When I saw two such handsome men I said to myself, I said, 'Law, it'll just be the most wonderful treat if I could ride with those lovely gentlemen because it's been many a year since I was escorted in such style.' "

The wrinkled lids fluttered over her azure eyes. She tossed her head in sprightly little jerks from Latham to the driver and back again, then awarded each of them a denture-clicking smile.

Where in the world had the old biddy escaped from, Latham wondered?

"Now, ma'am," said the driver, "you're jes' havin' fun with us. You know good 'n' well you say that to every man what asks you to go fer a ride."

"Why, you wicked thing!" she giggled. "Upon my soul, I meant every single word I said, and now you're takin' me for a flirt!"

Latham looked first at the clicking meter, then at the pile of traffic behind the cab.

"Now don't you get het up, ma'am," said the driver. "You're jes' a ladybug. You know we'd be more'n honored to carry you wherever you're goin'."

"Where *are* you going?" Latham interrupted, and immediately noted the disappointment that flickered across both their faces.

"To the Richard Evelyn Byrd Flying Field," she said, cocking her head to one side.

Latham visualized a landing strip running through a cornfield for the convenience of people with very small private planes; or perhaps she was going to an air show of World War I antiques put on by an histerical society.

"I'm going to the Richmond International Airport," he offered.

"That's right, the Richard Evelyn Byrd Flying Field," said the Dear Old Thing as she climbed in beside him. "We old Richmond folks prefer the original name. It's so depressin to think that Richmond has an international anything. Why, I remember. . . ."

She talked nonstop all the way to the airport a disjointed potpourri of old blood, new blood, old money new money old blood and new money, new blood and old money; the "bohemians" who were ruining something called the "Fan District," where she had lived *all her life* the rotting tree that the City was trying to make her cut down, but which she refused to touch because it was a *dueling oak;* how terrible it was that the Episcopal church was allowing *morphodites* to hold meetings in the basement; the cobblestones in the Fan District which another old lady—they'd gone to school together—had defended *with her very life* by stationing herself in the middle of the street and *refusing* to let the construction crew work; and how horrified Mr. Tazewell, her late husband, would be if he could just see how Richmond was *growing.*

Once they arrived at the Richard Evelyn Byrd Flying Field, Latham found himself appropriated and turned into a lackey with a deftness that belied her fragile appearance and fluttery soft voice. He fetched and carried, checking her luggage buying her a "drink of Co'Cola," and scurrying around for a copy of yesterday's newspaper because she wanted to read the obituaries to see if anyone she knew had died. In response to "Oh, Law! I just can't read upside down! Why, I can hardly read right-side up!" he found himself explaining the airline schedule to her. All the while, she kept gazing raptly into his face and saying things like: "Oh, I just don't know how you can figure it out! You're just like Mr. Tazewell, so smart and so clever at explainin' things."

Next the screw came out of her eyeglasses, which brought on a stream of "Oh, Law's!" and a breathless plea to Latham to "Oh, please, do something!" He ended up on his hands and knees searching for the world's smallest screw. He found it, which meant that he had to put her glasses back together again. By this·time he was trembling so badly that he dropped the screw into his lap, which necessitated a search that the Dear Old Thing tactfully avoided watching by turning to comment on the terminal's hideous modern architecture, which the late Mr. Tazewell, an architect, would have deplored.

By the time Latham got her glasses back together, she had exactly five minutes to catch her plane. "Oh, Law! Whatever am I goin' to do!" she cried, whereupon she dropped her opened handbag. Latham found himself on his hands and knees once more, gathering up loose keys, packs of subscription envelopes stamped with a red Episcopal cross, a bottle of smelling salts, God knew how many prescription bottles ʻempty , wads of transfers from the Richmond Transit ʻunused), and a sheaf of engraved calling cards.

Latham stuffed everything back into her bag, commandeered a wheelchair and deposited the Dear Old Thing in it, then ran like hell down the ramp and across the field to get her into the waiting plane. She hobbled up the steps babbling: "You're just the sweetest thing I ever did see! I don't know what I would have done without such a charmin' escort because I've just been on the horns of a dilemma since Mr. Tazewell passed on and I haven't had him to do for me. 'Deed I just can't cope with the quandaries of life without a smart gentleman to turn to.ʻ

At the door, she turned around, gave Latham a twinkly smile and a pert wobble of her head.

"You come see me, you hear?"

The exhausted Latham found that he had missed his own plane. He couldn't take it anymore; he felt his mind slipping away.

"I'm getting just like them.ʻ he muttered. "Nuts!"

A vision, dearer than Tara, rose in his mind: Joy Street, complete with dog droppings. Home! He was going home!

To hell with the book, he decided. Then he spoke those famous lines from the Yankee Swan Song: "Build a fence around the South and you'd have one big madhouse!"

Yankees always make the mistake of going home the moment they realize they are going mad, which is why they have never understood the South. They do not grasp the simple fact that losing one's mind is the most important prerequisite for fitting in with Southerners. Sanity has never held any charms for us; in fact, we're against it. We long ago realized that madness was the only weapon we had: if you're crazy enough, people will leave you alone. Madness has also helped us survive the rigidly stratified, comformist society that our fear of change forced us to build around ourselves.

Southern madness is marked by a devotion to the Very Old Math: two plus two equals five, and any psychiatrist who tries to tell us it doesn't ought to have his head examined.

America could use a little Southern madness right now, for it is the sort that stands like a stone wall against the onslaughts of creeping technocratic sanity. Ours is the kind of madness that psychiatry has ruined, that the boys in the blue suits have white-papered to death.

It enabled us to start a war without owning a single cannon factory, secure in the belief that such things are of no consequence to aristocrats. Thanks to our mad decision, we became the only Americans to know military defeat—an experience that made us America's cinder blocks: Once you have been through fire, you can never burn again.

The psychology of defeat has been bad for Southerners in many ways, but it has also been good. Being the product of a region that was once collectively guilty of high treason has its advantages: gloomy contemplation of the national navel is simply un-Southern. Knowing, alone among our countrymen, what it is like to lose a war has made supposedly hokey Southerners America's true sophisticates. We may not know wines or gourmet cuisine, but we are chefs of survival who have learned to emerge from sad and disgraceful events with courage and humor intact.

Every good recipe has a secret ingredient. Ours is a blasé acceptance of contradiction and . . . well, "colorful" behavior.

# 2

## Thou Shalt Be Kings
## No Matter Who Begat Thee

### or: I Dreamt I Dwelt in Marble Halls

In the North, where many people have recently discovered it, the name of the game is "ethnic awareness." In the South, where many people have been at it for so many years that they don't even think of anything else, it's known as genealogy, or Tombstone Twitch.

Southerners offer an ideal control group for sociologists who want to study the effects of ethnic awareness. A lot of Southerners have traditionally been so obsessed by their lineage that they have preferred to marry people to whom they were already related by blood. Nor does devotion to respectability necessarily preclude pride in incest. A friend of Granny's made a great show of addressing her mother as "Cousin Lydia," as if anyone who could not claim such dual kinship must be the product of a mésalliance. I have known several Southerners who were kin to themselves. Whatever else was wrong with them, they were remarkably free from the tortures of identity crisis—which may help explain why judges so readily released them in their own recognizance.

When confronted by strangers, the Southerner's first question is, "Who *are* they?" The stress we give to the "are" is a well-known Southern code indicating that we really mean, "Who *were* they?" The best people have been dead for centuries; the longer they've been dead, the greater their social prominence.

The Southerner paying a psychiatrist fifty dollars an hour to be cured of some present-day neurosis indeed may never get around to talking about it. For *one* Southerner to be crazy *now* is a shameful thing; parvenu nuts are nothing to brag about. Being able to say, "It runs in my family," on the other hand, lends a fine glow of continuity to individual emotional problems.

The psychiatrist Dr. Jonathan Latham visited in Richmond was not exaggerating when he diagnosed Southern insanity as a family tree under every bush.

A Virginia friend of mine arrived at the shrink's office for her very first session. She lay down on the couch and politely waited for the first question.

"What seems to be troubling you?"

"Well, Ah'm a direct descendant of James Radcliff, the Fourth Earl of Derwentwater."

My cockney father could never comprehend the obsessive interest in our ancestors manifested by my mother and grandmother. He always referred to Granny's genealogical charts as "yer kennel papers," "the stud register," or "the book of the dead." Whenever things got too much for him, he would yell, "I'm sick of 'earing about yer bloody blood!"

Shortly after he and Mama met, she invited him to the house for dinner. He had no sooner gotten in the door when Granny hauled her huge leather scrapbook, gold-stamped with her maiden name, *Lura Virginia Upton*, from its special resting place in a shrinelike cabinet that also contained bits and pieces of faded yellow silk—those mementos that every cavalry-crazed Southerner cherishes.

She plunked the book down in Herb's lap, thereby ensuring his inability to move, and began to unfold it. As she unearthed section after section of Daughters-weight parchment, his eyes widened in disbelief.

"Crikey, hit looks like Burke's *Peerage!*"

Mama and Granny seated themselves on either side of him and explained the meaning of the colored zigzag lines. Green was for Upton, red was for Ruding, purple for Whittaker, blue for Givens, brown for Fairbanks, and black for Codrick.

At the very top of the chart, like the angel on a Christmas tree, sat the name "Nathan Upton" in a neatly ruled, rectangular box. This was our patriarch—an indentured servant.

"He was the first Upton in America. He was a colonizer," said Granny.

Granny raised me on the Southern idée fixe that ladies do not lie except in the interests of tact, so I suppose she was merely being tactful when she tampered with our ancestral charts. Shortly after we saw *Gone with the Wind*, I noticed a telltale smear of ink eradicator on our kennel papers. The word "colonizer" had been removed from under Nathan Upton's name, and the angel box now read:

SIR NATHAN UPTON, BART.
LANDOWNER

Thanks to its genealogy fetish, the South often seems like one vast laboratory full of drawling technicians typing blood. Historical societies, quiet enough places in other parts of America, do a land-office business in Dixie, where hordes of dusty-fingered women can be found poring over tomes, trying to figure out what section of Interstate 50 was once "Tyler's parcel, claimed in curtsy right by Robert Nelson of Nottingham, being a houfe, outhoufe, servaunts' houfe, as wyll as a chicken houfe."

The Southern woman often conducts her own genealogical research. Her devotion to this task, and the high esteem in which she holds aristocratic lineage, have earned her the status of supersnob. If she plans a fifteen-country tour of Europe, she spends much of her time looking up ancestors. Sometimes she never gets out of England; she will choose to stay in that green and pleasant land because she has unearthed a real find—a pamphlet entitled *The Pathetick Historie of Sir Guillaume de Fornays, Who Was Hanged, Drawed, and Quartered, With a Comment on his Colonial Descendants in the Carolinas, By Bishop Fornay of Pluckley*.

The older a Southern woman gets, the more time she is likely to spend in the bowels of her local archives, where she is occasionally locked in for the night because it is hard to see little old ladies crouched in the stacks behind a black-bound copy of Governor Spotswood's household accounts.

Little-old-lady archivists tend to arrive at their local historical societies the moment the doors are opened, armed with a picnic lunch and the biggest magnifying glass they can find.

I once had a beau who worked in the genealogy room of the state archives. I began to notice that he had started to drink a good deal, then I noticed that he had become impotent. It turned out that he was on the verge of a nervous breakdown thanks to the inquiries put to him every working day by little old ladies who were looking for somebody to be descended from.

Among the facts he was asked to unearth:

—The maiden name of the wife of the illegitimate son of Thomas Jefferson's bricklayer.

—The wedding date of Lady Tryon's dressmaker.

—The whereabouts of the work orders of William Byrd's ironsmith.

Hardly a week went by without a wrangle about the eight Marys who served as ladies-in-waiting to Mary, Queen of Scots. These women, all named Mary and two of them surnamed Beaton and Seaton, were highly popular with the senile historians.

They would have loved being descended from Mary Stuart or Bonnie Prince Charlie, but this is hard to manage because the Queen of Scots had only one child and the Young Pretender was a little funny. So the Marys-in-waiting were the next best thing for the little old ladies who tottered down the steps of the sub-sub-basement to drive my beau to drink.

He invariably ended up in the middle of a dozen of them. They were all as deaf as a post and got into fights over the only copy of Stefan Zweig. "Hah? Hey? Mary who? Seaton? Beaton? I'm descended from the one who laid out the Queen. Did Seaton lay out the Queen, young man? Speak up, I can't hear you, young man. Did Beaton take her prayer book, young man? Why doesn't that boy stop mumbling? I declare, all the young people mumble nowadays. The Queen's head talked for fifteen seconds after death, and it talked to Beaton! Young man, what did the head say? Well, can't you look it up somewhere? Oh, Law! Young man, young man! I've broken my glasses!"

Young Man went on a three-day binge every time Anya Seton published a new historical novel containing those genealogical charts she always provides so that her readers can find out *which* Percy of Northumberland is ripping up the bodice of *which* Lady Twittingham. The charts invariably launched the old-lady historians on yet another treasure hunt. When *Katherine* came out, they all decided that they were descended from the generous supply of bastards produced by John of Gaunt and the luscious Lady Swynford, which meant, of course, that they could claim direct descent from John's father, Edward III.

The ancestors most favored by the Southern genealogical buff are the Stuarts, because the House of Stuart, like the Confederacy, was a Lost Cause. After years of research, a certain cracked doyenne named Mrs. Caroline Jarvis Montague set what has to be the South's unbreakable record for Stuart search-and-seizure when she decided that she was a direct descendant of the illegitimate child sired by Bonnie Prince Charlie upon the sacred body of North Carolina's own Stuart princess, Flora MacDonald.

There is only one thing wrong with this story. There was no child —nor, as far as we know, did any activity likely to produce one ever take place between the principals. But legends like this have a way of springing up and lingering despite any historical evidence to the contrary.

After Charlie lost the battle of Culloden in 1746, the Stuart cause was finished. The distraught Pretender was in a terrible state after the battle and according to some accounts had to be carted off the field by one of his aides. (Little-old-lady researchers always want to know the maiden name of this aide's wife.)

The Jacobites had to get Charlie out of Scotland and into France before the English could capture him, so they took him to the MacDonald family, who hid him before rowing him over to the Isle of Skye from which he would embark for the Continent. It was thought best to disguise him, so the young lady of the family, Miss Flora, gave him some of her clothes. That's all she gave him. The hysterical, grief-crazed prince, who was none too stable at best, was hardly in the mood for bed sport—which would in any case have been difficult to manage in that wee hut crammed full of MacDonalds, aides-de-camp, and Jacobite operatives who sat up all night keeping an eye out for the English.

There is only one other time that Charlie and Flora could have become one flesh, and that was in the rowboat, with Charlie in drag and Pappy MacDonald manning the oars. This is something that could happen only in an unpublished novel, but little old ladies throughout the South, who never canoodled except in a bed with their legally wedded husbands, are convinced that Charlie and Flora had at it in a wave-tossed rowboat headed for the Isle of Skye. They want that wee Stuart bastard for their ancestor.

A few years later, Flora did something that has made hypertension

the number-one health threat to anyone who works in a Southern ar-
chive. She emigrated to North Carolina. She should have had an hysterical bonny toddler with her, but she did not. She lived for a while in
the colony, until the Tory sympathies she developed during the American Revolution inspired her return to Scotland.

Her brief stay in North Carolina has enabled all those Southerners
who want to be descended from a Stuart to convince themselves that
Flora was in such a hurry to leave that she forgot to take her bonny toddler with her. Thus an unstable little royal bastard was left roaming
around in the piny woods, ready to grow up and become somebody's
ancestor.

So it was that the septuagenarian Mrs. Caroline Jarvis Montague
decided that this child had reached down through the centuries and
fingered *her*. To prove it, she wrote a genealogical monograph, but because it ran two hundred pages longer than this book and made no
sense whatsoever, I will summarize Mrs. Montague's claim in one
clear sentence:

It had something to do with a man in an iron mask, a set of
switched twins, a premature burial, that eighteenth-century dental
problem romantically known as the Hapsburg jaw—and a changeling
corpse.

Mrs. Montague concluded that a certain long-dead individual in a
certain mold-encrusted tomb in her churchyard was not the individual
that the nameplate claimed, but was none other than the missing link
in the chain of evidence she had built up for her Stuart-blood stake.
There was just one problem: The only way she could prove it was to
check the corpse's teeth for the Hapsburg jaw, which is how she nearly
got arrested for grave-robbing when she was discovered trying to pry
open a vault with her cane. "All" she wanted to do, she explained to
the terrified sexton who found her, was to see if she was kin to the contents of the vault—surely a perfectly acceptable reason for breaking it
open, no?

Southern ancestor worship enrages or amuses other Americans,
who take it as a sign of snobbishness and xenophobia. Such pat inter-
pretations are both unfair and untrue. The genealogy fetish is much
more complex than that, and, moreover, it has resulted in several admirable Southern virtues.

The South was never the aristocrat-crammed region that many Southerners would like to believe, but the very first settlers were a good deal classier than the average immigrant of other times and places. They formed what Wilbur J. Cash has called "pocket aristocracies" in the camel's hump of northern Virginia, along coastal South Carolina and Georgia, and in southern Louisiana. Cash estimates that the total number of these bona fide aristocratic families never exceeded two hundred, but although they were a small group, they were choice. Otherwise, the great majority of people in the seventeenth- and eighteenth-century South were quite ordinary, and many, like Nathan Upton, were a menace.

This sharp class difference was exacerbated by slavery. The caste mentality, leisure, and immense farming potential that slave labor created in the South lent upper-class life a Babylonian aura, so that when nonaristocratic Southerners dreamed of improving their lot and raising their status, their dreams tended to run riot. Unlike the poor but ambitious New Englander, who merely wanted to have the best farm in the county, the poor but ambitious Southerner merely wanted to be a belted earl.

As the South entered the nineteenth century, many such extravagant dreams came true. The South we call the Old South, the antebellum South that fought the Civil War, was a region of nouveau riche frontiersmen not long out of backwoods cabins who had worked hard enough to realize their elaborate ambition. If they had simply built the best farm in the county, they would have prettied up their backgrounds just a bit. Every nouveau riche does; it is thoroughly human and understandable. But the nineteenth-century planter achieved far more than the best farm in the county. He found himself with endless acres and numberless slaves; he was master of all he surveyed—animal, vegetable, and human. In a single generation he had become landed gentry, and he needed the sort of ancestors and background that would justify and give credence to his dizzying rise. Nothing would do but the most patrician noblemen, a long line of quivering Anglo-Saxon thoroughbreds going as far back as possible. Respectable bourgeois antecedents were not enough; he had to have baronets, earls, dukes, or—best of all—kings.

The Southern personality was particularly prone to colorful ancestor hunts. What Cash calls "frontier brag" and a capacity for romance encouraged the storybook leanings of these easily stirred people. The popular literature of the day further fired their dreams—it was the era of Sir Walter Scott's swashbuckling novels and Lord Tennyson's epics. Northerners also read these works, but they were immune to their effect because the North was committed to progressive politics and the industrial revolution. It dreamed of more factories and more money, and its hope lay in the future. But the South was inextricably trapped in the past; geographical conditions had enabled it to create a medieval barony in a fast-buck nation, a rigid caste society that was doomed to yield eventually to the press of modernity that surrounded it. Perpetually on the defensive in the political arena, the Southerner at bay took understandable comfort in dreams of marble halls—in short, he was indulging in a nostalgia kick, a hobby that many hard-pressed Americans are presently cultivating like the finest of orchids to help them make it through the night of a rapidly changing and ever more threatening world.

The Southerner's fierce pride also encouraged the growth of ancestor worship. Even the most hotheaded antebellum chauvinist secretly realized that the South's days were numbered, but he was loath to admit it. He preferred to hide his fears under swashbuckling boasts like: "One Southerner can lick twenty Yankees!" And what made the difference in this numerically uneven battle? Why, the fact that "gentlemen fight better than rabble." It therefore became necessary to prove beyond any doubt that every Southerner was a gentleman, and so everyone searched high and low for the passenger lists of William the Conqueror's rowboats.

As civil war loomed, the image of the aristocratic Southerner became a valuable psychological weapon to use against the Yankees. It was the only weapon the unindustrialized South really had, and so Southerners flung accusations of commonness and mongrelism in the North's face until many Yankees half-believed it. Certainly every Southerner believed that gentlemen fought better than rabble, which made finding or imagining noble antecedents a matter of self-preservation, at least on a subconscious level.

The defeat of the Confederacy was a blow to the Southerner's ego, so to bolster his pride anew he embarked on another round of ancestor-hunting calculated to help him ignore the heel of the conqueror's boot. After 1865, having ancestors who had fought at Agincourt or

Marston Moor was not enough; the Southern genealogist set his sights on the very bogs of time and, as Cash points out, tried to prove his descent from quasi-historical or even mythological figures such as Scota, the pharaoh's daughter who was said to have drifted somehow out of the bulrushes and straight up to what is now Scotland—hence, "founding" it. Also popular were Helen of Troy, Cleopatra, and anyone from the Agamemnon clan. My grandmother remembered a charmingly psychotic dowager from her childhood who had developed an especially interesting theory: She decided that Jesus had married and produced children, traced herself back to one of His progeny, and was thus able to claim that she was a direct descendant of God.

Thus did go-for-broke Byzantine status-seeking take root in the Southern psyche. It hit the nouveau planters first, and then, as such things tend to do, it filtered down into the minds of lesser folk—like Granny.

It has had a beneficial effect, though: Southerners are less prone to plastic, garden-variety status-seeking than any other Americans. The tiresome game of keeping up with the Joneses via bigger and better refrigerators and automobiles exerts a limited appeal to most Southerners. We would much rather prove descent from Alfred the Great and lord it over the Joneses, who can go no further back or up than Guy Fawkes.

Our genealogy fetish has been contemptuously called "mythmaking" by many commentators, yet what is mythmaking but another word for imagination—a quality sadly lacking in our present era? To the Southerner, a tree cannot simply be an ordinary tree, it must be a dueling oak. The Confederate Army was no ordinary army: We had no enlisted men whatsoever and no infantry or artillery, only cavalry, and our field-rank ancestors who rode in it all wore plumes in their hats and led charges. Just who followed the commands to charge is a minor point in the fevered Southern brain; it is the fine warmth cast by a good story that matters. In the midst of our dull gray technocracy, Southern mental life is a Cecil B. DeMille screenplay sired by a Sir Walter Scott novel.

The fusty Southern Dowager bent on conserving anything with a history behind it has long been a target of ridicule to Yankee sophisticates, who have scorned her for living in the past because she belongs to organizations such as "Save the Cobblestones!" "Save the Carriage Blocks!" and "Save the Trees!" Yet what is this but ecology?—that "new" movement that Southerners have been involved in for years, thanks to their ingrained pride and sense of self.

The Noblesse Syndrome imbues Southerners with standards that the rest of America would do well to adopt. I recently told a Richmond friend about a woman who stuck drip candles directly on the surface of an expensive marble-top table. Naturally when the dried wax was scraped off, the marble was scratched.

My friend's face twisted in horror.

"Is she *trash?*" she asked incredulously.

Snobbish? Perhaps. But, thanks to Noblesse in all its vainglory, Southerners have a sense of fitness that is sadly lacking in our rude country. People with a sense of the past do not snap aerials, slash tires, or break windows just for the hell of it. One form of respect leads to another.

Perhaps the greatest virtue in ethnic awareness, Southern-style, is a freedom from the worst kind of snobbery of all: that based on money alone. The Southerner's preference for heredity over environment as the answer to the mystery of human nature enables him to ignore outward trappings and symbols and base his opinions of others on invisible, inborn traits that mark the aristocrat of the spirit. The quick Southern instinct can spot the one illiterate mountaineer out of a hundred who possesses an elusive quality of homespun grace. To us, he is a gentleman, and that's that. The vulgar rich man is not.

The obverse and contradictory side of the Southerner's Noblesse coin is a proneness to make snap judgments about people. We are dedicated to the mystique of "good blood," and we firmly believe that it both shows and tells. Furthermore, nothing will ever make us change our minds.

I grew up hearing about "that trashy look" as opposed to "that quality look." According to Granny, the family arbiter in all such matters, a trashy look ranges from ferret-faced, predatory sharpness to the heavy, bovine face with undefined features that look as if the Lord had smeared them while they were still wet—the opposite of what Granny called "chiseled" features. Also beyond the pale were beady eyes, shifty eyes, slack mouths, weak chins, and something she called "that pink-eyed look."

This is not the disease called "pinkeye," nor does it have anything whatsoever to do with eyes or the color pink. Rather, it refers to a kind of pale, watered-down-blood look that often goes with poor posture and missing front teeth. Males of this species tend to have inordinately unruly cowlicks, which is why they wet their hair to slick it down so often that it always looks wet, even when it is dry. Comb tracks are always visible, and *everybody* knows a man with comb tracks in his hair is the scum of the earth.

"That pink-eyed look" is also called worthless, shiftless, no-count, and, sometimes, "garfish." To elucidate: A gar, by Southern definition, is a shiftless, worthless, no-count fish that evolution bypassed. It is no good to anybody because it is full of tiny, vicious bones that not even a cat could negotiate. Gars can eat anything and thrive, but nothing can feed off them. They are a betrayal of nature's cyclical prudence.

In other words, they're trashy fish.

The Southerner's devotion to outward manifestations of gentility caused even the highly professional Margaret Mitchell to slip up and commit that bane of every writer's existence, unconscious humor. In Rhett Butler's introductory scene, she describes his appearance in detail, starting at the top and ending with a description of his feet, which she calls "absurdly small."

This has to be the epitome of a throwaway line. The size of a fictional hero's feet makes no difference whatsoever unless the work is a mystery novel with a clue that involves a pair of shoes. Unfortunately, Miss Mitchell's remark about Rhett's feet evokes old jokes about certain other dimensions that men with small feet are likely to have. Any suggestion that the virile Rhett might be cursed with manhood's most shameful lack is unthinkable, yet I have always wondered about it. Miss Mitchell had undoubtedly heard the jokes, so why did she risk Rhett's image by giving him "absurdly small" feet?

My own guess is that the author of *Gone with the Wind* was being more Southern than female when she wrote that line. Southerners associate graceful physical features with gentility. Small feet, long, tapering fingers, delicate bones, high cheekbones, and chiseled features are immediately noticed and forever praiseworthy.

Judging people too quickly by their physical appearance is one of the worst effects of too much ethnic awareness. Most Southerners do it —it was one of Granny's chief faults and remains one of mine—but there is something to be said for it. Very young people, filled with commendable ideals about spreading love and treating all with equal respect, refuse to "size up" others. They feel that it is snobbish and undemocratic, and while they may be right, it is also necessary at times. A hitchhiker or a motorist whose nose is rotting away from cocaine and whose arm is tatooed with "Born to Kill" stands an excellent chance of being a mite trashy.

Whenever anything traumatic happens to the proud South, the ancestor fetish receives another shot in the arm. Populism, the Great Depression, the civil rights movement—all these shocks to the Southern psyche encouraged genealogists to reach for their magnifying glasses. If we have another Depression, I predict that another epidemic of Tombstone Twitch will sweep Dixie. Anyone in the Daughtersweight parchment business will make a fortune, and I daresay I will be one of his best customers.

LORD NATHAN UPTON
EARL OF ARLINGTON

Observe that I am not dwelling in the past, I am thinking ahead

# 3

## "Would Youall Be Good Enough
## to Excuse Me While
## I Have an Identity Crisis?"

### or: The Cult of Southern Womanhood

Novelists prefer complex women for their protagonists, which is why the Southern woman has been the heroine of so many more novels than her Northern sister. The cult of Southern womanhood endowed her with at least five totally different images and asked her to be good enough to adopt all of them. She is required to be frigid, passionate, sweet, bitchy, and scatterbrained—all at the same time. Her problems spring from the fact that she succeeds.

Antebellum Southern civilization was built upon the white woman's untouchable image. In order to keep her footing on the pedestal men had erected for her, she had to be aloof, aristocratic, and haughty. These qualities have always been required of women in societies based upon vast, entailed estates, but they were especially necessary in the South. They enabled the white woman to maintain her sanity when she saw light-skinned slave children, who were the very spit of Old Massa, running around the plantation. By being sufficiently frosty and above it all, she was able to ignore and endure the evidence of intercaste sexuality that surrounded her.

When the disregard she cultivated was mixed with the inevitable disgust she felt, the result was often frigidity. Southern men have actually been known to drink a toast to women's sexual coldness. The best of these florid paeans has been recorded by Carl Carmer in *Stars Fell*

37

*on Alabama:* "To Woman, lovely woman of the Southland, as pure and chaste as this sparkling water, as cold as this gleaming ice, we lift this cup, and we pledge our hearts and our lives to the protection of her virtue and chastity."

Southernese loses a great deal in translation. Here's what the toast really means: "To Woman, without whose purity and chastity we could never have justified slavery and segregation, without whose coldness we wouldn't have had the excuse we needed for messing around down in the slave cabins and getting plenty of poontang. We pledge our hearts and our lives to the protection of her virtue and chastity because they are the best political leverage we ever did see."

As male propaganda continued through the years, Southern women came to believe these fulsome testimonials to their purity and tried to find a middle road between their normal desires and their male-manufactured image. Anything can happen in a land where men drink toasts to frigidity, so the Southern woman often decided to enjoy sex as much as possible while remaining a virgin—a compromise that won her a reputation as a sadistic flirt.

More time passed, and other American women gained greater sexual freedom, so the Southern woman evolved another compromise. It was easy for her to do this sort of thing because she was the product of a region that had spent two centuries justifying itself to the rest of the country. After performing the kind of mental gymnastics it takes to prove that slavery is God's will, rationalizing mere sexual peccadilloes was child's play. She hit upon another modus vivendi, a much more swinging one this time, that would permit her to lose her virginity, enjoy a regular sex life, and yet soothe her male-induced guilt. She would throw away her hot pantalets, do as she pleased, and convince herself that her hymen was still intact.

She became a self-rejuvenating virgin.

To recycle her pearl beyond price, certain ground rules had to be established. First, premeditation was forbidden. The self-rejuvenating virgin never planned ahead, she was always "swept off her feet." If she could not make herself believe this, she engineered bizarre sexual encounters that were never quite the real thing, so that the next morning she could tell herself, "It didn't really happen because . . ."

1. I was drunk.
2. We didn't take all our clothes off.

3. We didn't do it in a bed.

4. He didn't put it all the way inside me.

5. He didn't come inside me.

6. I didn't come.

7. . . . Well, not really.

The self-rejuvenating virgin never bothered with contraceptives because that was premeditation. If her date wanted to use one, that was *his* business. They might drive past two dozen drugstores on their way to the woods, but she never said a word until the very last minute—at which point she shrieked: "Do you have something?" ·He nearly always did.) Thanks to the self-rejuvenating virgin, the wallet of a Southern man in pre-pill days was likely to contain more condoms than money.

The woods, of course, was the only place a respectable self-rejuvenating virgin could go to earth. The very idea of making love in a bed threw her into conflict—it was too official, too premeditated, and too comfortable. She preferred to mortify her flesh in the woods, where she could count the chiggers and ticks as punishment.

When I was at Ole Miss in 1958, the boys were so used to self-rejuvenating virgins that they automatically headed for the woods even when a bed was available. Every car trunk contained both a blanket and the most Southern of all contraceptives, a bottle of warm Coca-Cola, because the self-rejuvenating virgin would walk over hot coals before she would ever buy a douche bag.

If her date failed to use a "precaution" and if the douche-that-refreshes did not work, the self-rejuvenating virgin could claim the best excuse in her rule book:

"It didn't really happen, because I'm pregnant."

This is the webby Southern mind at its best. Translation: "I let him do it to me and I enjoyed it, but now I'm being punished, which wipes out the pleasure and therefore the entire act."

Some self-rejuvenating virgins behaved themselves at home but went into a sexual frenzy on holiday trips. Their lovers were men they met in hotels and resorts. Thanks to this vacation psychology, they were able to go home and tell themselves: "It didn't really happen because . . ."

1. I'll never see him again.

2. I don't remember his name.

3. He never told me his name.

4. I didn't tell him my name.

5. It happened in New York.

The self-rejuvenating virgin might fondle a man's privates as he drove to the motel, but when he pulled up to room 102 she refused to go in.

"Let's just sit here a minute," she said, and the next minute was all over him. A steamy petting session ensued, but when they became excited to the point of adjourning to the paid-for room, she said, "Let's go somewhere!" Meaning, of course, the woods.

Sometimes she was drunk enough to enter the motel room, tear off her clothes, and fall backward onto the bed. She landed in the missionary position and promptly passed out—or pretended to. The next morning she awoke naked, next to a naked man, stared at him in horror, and then shook him awake: "Did anything happen? Tell me the truth."

Southern men always knew what to say.

"No, honey, nothin' happened, I swear it didn't."

The self-rejuvenating virgin always had a ladylike orgasm, a pelvic legerdemain that she infused with fey girlishness. When she felt it coming on, she giggled—a feat that ought to be worth an Oscar or two —and when it hit she trembled prettily in the zephyr range. Afterward, she registered an awesome combination of astonishment and innocence: "Ohhh, what happened to me?"

The birth-control pill has all but wiped the self-rejuvenating virgin and her plea of crime passionnel from the face of the South. She must now own up to the fact that she is guilty of canoodling in the first degree.

I am glad she is passing into history, but I will miss her, because she made life, particularly dormitory life, most lively and interesting. The self-rejuvenating virgin I will never forget was a Mississippi girl who, without a doubt, had the most active sex life of any woman since Pauline Bonaparte—and, of course, convinced all of her lovers that she was a virgin. Her secret weapon was an alum-spiked red mouthwash that assured her of having pucker-power.

Readers of those moonlight-and-magnolia historical novels so popular in the Forties quickly became accustomed to certain words used to describe the patrician heroine. Somewhere around midbook she hauled off and melted, becoming: *languid, voluptuous, sinuous, sultry, abandoned,* and above all, *wanton.*

"Isn't that what you want? Wanton?" she breathed, her hot, *tremulous* lips moving against the hero's ear. *Suddenly,* she became *insatiable* and *demanding,* and, what's more, she started to *pulsate.*

The motivation for her startling change was usually a last-ditch attempt to drag a Southern gentleman from the arms of another female character called, invariably, "the insolent, sloe-eyed Zerline." Zerline was a slave—but always a high-yellow one—to whom the hero had turned for affection after Miss Lily had gone as stiff as a board on him for the four hundredth time. She went so stiff on her wedding night that he could have picked her up by her feet; she assumed this military posture every time he approached her bed, naturally driving him into the arms of Zerline.

Underneath the thesaurus style of plantation novelists lay a basic truth: Being "good in bed" is the Southern woman's specialty if not one of her most cherished arts. The novelists were also correct about her original motivation for taking up the sensual arts: competition. The nineteenth-century South Carolinian and enthusiastic diarist Mary Boykin Chesnut hints at this motivation in her angry comment: "Mrs. Stowe did not hit the sorest spot. She makes Legree a bachelor." Mary Chesnut stated bluntly that she hated slavery, but it was a selfish hatred. What really bothered her was not so much the misery of the slaves but the provocative ways of the slave women.

All Southerners are easily challenged, and pride is never far below the surface. When the plantation novelist's well-bred heroine made her inevitable decision to "fight back," she was simply being Southern. Gentlemen danced attendance on her, showered her with extravagant gallantries, and generally egged her along the road to narcissism and boundless conceit. The easy sensuality of slave women, for whom sex was life's only pleasure, became an ever-present challenge to the white woman, whose ego had been engorged by the code of chivalry.

A further puff for her ego—but really intended as a defense of slavery—was the Southern gentleman's boast that black men had to be kept in chains lest they make a beeline for the inordinately desirable Miss Lily, the mere sight of whom was enough to drive all males mad.

Being human, Miss Lily reveled in such compliments, whether direct or implied, and soon came to believe them. Once the twin gaunt-lets of the black woman's competition and the white man's press agen-try had been flung down before her, she responded in predictable ways. Most Victorian women did not become wanton—that had to wait for a later day—but they did take up arms in the cause of sensual allure. The cult of the delectable belle was born. Her motto was: "Promise him anything." She may have delivered nothing except sidelong glances, but it is on such propaganda that images are built, and it is in the nature of Southerners to believe their own propaganda. When the passage of time brought greater sexual freedom to women, Miss Lily indeed be-came good in bed. Northern soldiers stationed in the many Army camps in the South licked their chops the moment they received their orders and said: "Oh, boy, Southern girls!"

Even when Miss Lily did not actually come across, she performed all the preliminaries with a fiery abandon that many Yankees, es-pecially those with immigrant Catholic backgrounds, had never before encountered. Living in the myth-drenched South had made Lily a fine actress, and she had the Southern gift for playing to the galleries; she did more moaning, writhing, and scratching than Salvatore and Patrick had ever seen nice girls do. There was no doubt that Lily was nice, for in her nonsexual moments she danced the measured ballet of Southern life with exquisite propriety. She was a *hot lady*, a con-tradiction guaranteed to intrigue all men.

The Southern woman's sensuality is aided by her Anglo-Saxon heritage. Being Protestant, the Southern woman does not grow up un-der the shadow of Virgins, Madonnas, and saints. She might be a rock-ribbed fundamentalist, but old-time religion contains a great deal of sensuality, especially when the preachers let loose and everyone starts swaying and rolling. If the Southern woman is an Episcopalian, as many are, the battle of being good in bed is half-won by definition; Episcopalians, especially in the South, pride themselves on their so-phistication. They also drink.

Healthy sexuality is easier to come by in rural areas. The Southern woman has an earthy streak that serves her well. If she belongs to the horsey set, loss of hangups is almost certain, because horsey people are constantly talking about mating.

Living in the South would make anyone sexy. The long-hot-sum-mer tensions of Southern life create an aura of *waiting*, a perpetual alertness, and a sensation that something is about to happen. Such a mood turns people's minds to sex because it is the only form of release available. Quite often something does happen, and the ensuing excitement also stirs sex drives.

Finally, the Southern woman's sensual talents can be traced to her relationship with her father. Southern fathers behave very seductively around their daughters. Southerners in general tend to be physically affectionate, and in addition, the Southern father is obsessed with sexual differentiation. He wants his sons to be manly and his daughters to be womanly, with no shades of gray in between. Subconsciously he begins, early in her life, to ensure her proper development by training her to respond to men. His modus operandi includes a great deal of hugging, kissing, and lap-sitting, which launches a little girl onto the path of sexual response. She grows to like the way men smell, the feel of whiskers and hard muscles, and connects these things with the security of father's love. *Provided this love affair does not go too far,* the Southern daughter emerges from it as a very fortunate young woman. She is used to men, and she has also practiced her flirting on her father. Since she is the "apple of his eye," he always responds with elaborate fervor to her techniques, which instills supreme confidence in her and makes it virtually impossible for her to doubt her womanly charms. Used to a steady stream of male approbation and blandishments, she can hardly wait to get more of the same. The best way to get them is to be good in bed, and so she sees to it that she is.

Some Southern women love sex so much that they appear to be near-nymphomaniacs. Actually, they are not so passionate as they seem, for their attachment to bed sport is mainly an ego trip. Sex as ego-satisfaction is a pratfall that looms before all women in a man's world; much female sexuality is a substitution for success, money, and fame, a way to become a VIP without endangering one's femininity. The Southern woman is more susceptible to this psychological transference; she frequently throws herself into a virtual debauch simply because she has a human need to excel.

The Hollywood casting office has done its part in promoting the near-nymphomaniac to almost legendary heights, but she is a bona fide fixture of Southern life. I knew one, whose problems sprang from her father's Miss America complex.

She was his youngest child and only daughter. Overjoyed at her birth, he insisted upon giving her a name that, he felt, represented the sultry sensuality of the Southern woman at her tempting best. He called her Velvet, and she was baptized with this symbolic moniker in the poshest Episcopal church in town.

In case Velvet missed the point of Daddy's christening caper, he drummed it into her head that she was supposed to "grow up and become Miss America," "grow up and break men's hearts," "grow up and be a beautiful movie star."

What Velvet did was simply to grow up—in record time. As soon as she could walk, she put on her mother's high heels, smeared her mouth with filched lipstick, and sashayed down the street like a half-pint hooker, with Daddy behind her calling: "Hold on! Say I'm a little lady that behaves myself, say butter wouldn't melt in my mouth 'cause I'm so fine and sweet, say I'm just a little princess!"

He tried to ensure her fastidiousness by telling her the story of "The Princess and the Pea," but all Velvet got out of it was a fondness for lots of mattresses. From the age of fourteen, she oozed musk and wreaked havoc throughout a five-county area. Wives shot husbands, husbands shot wives, and private detectives made a fortune, all because Velvet devoted her every waking moment to living up to her name.

At no time in her nefarious growing years did Daddy speak of college, future careers, or constructive ambitions. The only time he mentioned Velvet's future was the day he made vague allusions to the fact that young ladies who become professional corespondents in divorce cases might hurt their Miss America chances.

Velvet did go to college, but only because it provided a happy hunting ground, and because Miss America contestants who are coeds are better representatives of the American dream than those who never go beyond high school. She became a dilettante, dabbling in writing, acting, sketching, and modern dance, and showing some talent for all of them. She especially liked art and drew very well. In one of her rare nonsexual moments she expressed a desire to go to art school in Chicago, but Daddy would not hear of it, and Velvet eventually forgot about her ambitions.

The urge to excel remained, however, and Velvet turned her energies to sex "showings" instead of art showings. She craved recognition and exposure; she wanted to be caught in the act, and, not unsurprisingly, she got her wish most of the time.

Like the good artist she was, Velvet was discovered by none other than Miss Lulugrace Tewksbury, Clerk of the State Senate, who barged into a young legislator's office and found Velvet and the statesman locked into a complicated cubist posture on his desk. Miss Tewk, as she was affectionately known throughout the state, took one look, screamed, and ran down the hall of the statehouse in such hysteria that she forgot about the lovely antebellum staircase at the end of it. She rolled like a ball down the entire flight and, thanks to the lovely thick carpeting, she arose unhurt, just like Vivien Leigh's stunt girl.

She was barely on her feet before she was telling everyone what she had seen, which was just what Velvet wanted.

The conflict between ice maiden and pulsating temptress often rages in the Southern woman's breast. The Miss America contestant is a case in point: She parades before crowds of strange men in a bathing suit and sings a torch song, but when she wins the crown, waves of guilt and confusion rush to the surface and cause her to make statements to the press like: "God is not dead, he's alive in my heart."

Movie bills of the Thirties and Forties left no doubt what the Southern woman was like.

She was Jezebelle.

"Drusilla was a clawing cat! A hot-tempered virago! Spoiled, self-centered, she always got her way!"

In the middle of this splash of words stood Drusilla herself, ready to burst a blood vessel. Here was your true Southern vixen, full of sound and fury, her mouth twisted in a red wound of rage, and a vase or a riding crop in her soft, dimpled hand. "No man had ever mastered her until. . . ."

Enter the hero on another movie bill.

"Trask Fontaine was all MAN! A ruthless riverboat gambler, Trask tamed his women the way he tamed his horses—with a firm hand, a curb bit, and if necessary a WHIP!"

In addition to being as cold as a witch's tit and pulsating with passion, the Southern woman is expected to behave in a manner that warrants commitment for observation. In Jezebelle novels and movies all she does is fight, fight, fight. The battle royal begins the moment Drusilla and Trask meet. She flays him with her crop, rakes him with her nails, hurls priceless objets d'art at his head (she always misses), and destroys the pianoforte with a crashing two-fisted discord.

Throughout her uninterrupted attacks of grand mal, Trask remains unmoved—even amused. He grins at her, "undresses her with his eyes," and says: "You look mighty pretty when you're mad."

It all ends with a spanking, or with a knock-down, drag-out struggle in which Drusilla suddenly relaxes and stills her pounding fists. Helplessly, her arms rise to encircle Trask's neck in a sinuous embrace. The shrew is tamed.

A professional bitch does the Southern man proud. If she is skittish, high-strung, and easily upset, that means she is a thoroughbred with good blood as opposed to a sluggish peasant. Good blood became very important in a region where white men were busy mixing theirs with blacks, so the Southern woman was given the job of proving how aristocratic everybody was. Whenever she shied violently, showed the whites of her eyes, and laid her ears back, the South could feel superior to the egalitarian North.

For a woman who does not know whether to be hot or cold, temper tantrums are a convenient compromise. Men find it very easy to translate female rage into female *genital* rage. She indeed looks mighty pretty when she's mad; her cheeks flame, her eyes glitter, and she trembles uncontrollably. It looks like an orgasm; it even sounds like one. The Southern woman at last found a way to indicate her hot blood without doing anything unladylike. All she had to do was throw things, keep her riding crop at the ready, and foam at the mouth a little. She learned to use bitchiness for the same reason that she used glycerine and rose water—it made her feminine and lovely so that men would WANT her.

Any woman who gets mad becomes a Southern belle in the minds of male witnesses. Angry feminists who have been the target of that famous diagnosis, "What she needs is a good screw," can thank the Jezebelle novelists and the cult of Southern womanhood.

"She was the only completely kind person I ever knew," sighed Rhett Butler of Melanie's death, and with that eulogy, the image of the Southern woman as a gentle, self-effacing comforter of the afflicted was assured.

The specter of unflagging virtue has haunted all women since time immemorial; the angel in the house simply will not leave, she hangs around like the last drunken guest who keeps saying: "Just one more cigarette."

The Southern woman's problem with the virtuous image has been intensified by constant articulation. One minute she is called a "ladybug," the next minute a "heartbreaker," so it is not surprising that she behaves like Scarlett O'Hara for a month and then puts in a week as Sweet Melanie Wilkes.

The Melanie Syndrome is responsible for those trumpet blasts of self-effacement that Southern women emit and which sound to the Northern ear like an insufferably hypocritical game of Alphonse-Gaston. Saucy belles, who have the instincts and ethics of a cobra, break down from time to time and hunt themselves to earth with protestations such as:

"You dance so much better than I do! Why, I just have two left feet compared to you!"

"You'd look better in rags than I would in a Dior!"

"Oh, I wish I had your hair! Mine is just so ugly!" (It's strawberry blond and naturally curly.)

It sounds catty, but it isn't. It's just Melanie trying to get some fresh air after being walled up in the belle's psyche for the past two weeks.

The Melanie Syndrome is responsible for the Southern woman's fashion "look," which is somewhat less than chic. The compulsive need to *be* sweet is often translated into an attempt to *look* sweet that results in "busy" ensembles. A little more lace here, a few more tucks there, something "cute" pinned on the waist of a svelte dress, or even today, a flower garden of a hat.

The Melanie Syndrome is also responsible for the inordinate amount of home sewing that goes on in the South, most of which is done by mothers of belles who want to make sure that Daughter looks just darlin' no matter what she does on those nights when she returns home with liquor on her breath and her pants in her pocketbook. The Southern mother is no more able than her daughter to cope with the intricacies of the cult of womanhood; she "would rather not know" what her daughter is up to because such knowledge might unearth some conflict of her own and cause her to have one of those Southern nervous breakdowns known as "going to pieces."

The Jewish mother snoops to keep her daughter in line; the Southern mother sews. Permissive because it is too disturbing to be otherwise, she tries to exert some control over her daughter by "running up" sweet-looking dresses for her in a spirit of genteel compromise: If the dress her daughter pulls up in the back seat of a car is made of dotted Swiss, then surely virtue cannot be far behind.

In addition to being cold, hot, bitchy, and sweet, the Southern woman is required to be something called "pert."

Pertness grew out of psychological and political necessity in the Old South. The slaveholder, secretly guilty and doubtful of his clout, needed to feel that the medieval fief he had created produced delirious joy in those who lived on it. It was only logical that he turned to his slaves and his women for reassurance on this score.

Blacks played the banjo for him and grinned or giggled whenever he caught their eye. His women did even better. They tinkled with insouciant gaiety and became saucy, piquant, lively, merry, sparkling, vivacious—in a word, "pert." The Southern woman did everything but lead a Virginia reel between labor pains; as secession and conflict loomed, her spirits rose higher and higher, keeping pace with her laughter. By the time Old Massa went off to war, he was certain that he could lick the Yankees in a month.

He lost, which meant that he needed pertness more than ever to bolster his fallen ego. It did not matter that his war had brought poverty and Reconstruction down on everyone's head; Miss Dixie could be happy no matter what. To prove it, she followed the first commandment of pertness: *Thou shalt have the time of your life.* She detonated into a flurry of excitement over the slightest thing, bubbled with ecstasy at every gathering, and ran up and down the floor in her patched party dress, shrieking: " 'Deed I'm just havin' such a wonderful time I don't know what to do!"

The second commandment of pertness is: *Thou shalt entertain.* People forget their troubles when they're being entertained, so the Southern woman learned the art of being onstage at all times, performing like Dr. Johnson's dancing dog no matter how she felt. She had to sing, play the piano, and tell clever stories with the expert timing of a stand-up comedian.

The third commandment of pertness is: *Thou shalt play dumb.* Men who have lost a war must feel superior to someone. Dumb women cannot tell clever stories, however, so dumbness had to be mixed with pertness to achieve a brew that suited Southern tastes. Since under no circumstances could Miss Dixie grow logy with stupidity, she chose an energetic form of dumbness that involved a lot of haphazard motion. She became scatterbrained, empty-headed, helpless, doe-eyed, forgetful, confused, and simpleminded. Men delighted in her arch panic, especially when she threw herself into their arms and screamed: "Oh, I just don't know what to do!"

Being pleasant and agreeable is one thing, but the Southern woman overdid it until pertness became an ingrained habit. She could not stop giggling, any more than she could lower her voice. She became an irretrievable victim of the Pert Plague, that hyperkinetic frenzy that still exists in the South.

Simulating convulsive mirth is an exhausting business. The Pert Plague has affected the Southern woman's habits and priorities to an inordinate degree. Our friend Dr. Jonathan Latham encountered one of its chief effects on his first visit to a Southern home.

Aware of the Southern woman's hospitality and her fondness for antiques and other "fine things," he assumed that she would be a superb housekeeper, the kind of whom it is said, "You could eat off her floors." But the moment he entered his hostess's house, he realized that it would take a strong man even to eat off her table. It was piled high with weeks' worth of undiscarded newspapers, an overflowing sewing basket, hair rollers, and a cluster of grape seeds.

In horror, he looked down at the exquisite Persian rug and saw thereon a clump of something that he associated with the sidewalks of Beacon Hill. Balls of dust lay everywhere, like gone-to-seed dandelions, and the unwashed windows were caked with grime. And what was his elegant hostess doing when Dr. Latham arrived? She was seated at her sticky groaning board polishing her silver, or, as she took pains to point out, her great-grandmother's silver. Latham watched in amazement as she dug down carefully into the elaborate curliques with a gauze-wrapped toothpick: the silver, shining to begin with, was the one thing in the house that didn't need cleaning.

Dr. Latham did not remain in the South long enough to learn about the Pert Plague: many Southern women are simply too tired to clean house. Their silver is kept spotless because it's *silver* and because this is one housekeeping task that can be done while sitting down.

The Pert Plague also takes its toll outside the home. An enormous amount of time is wasted in Southern offices by otherwise capable and intelligent women who simply cannot calm down. If someone brings a woman a file, she will not say "Thank you," but: "Oh! You've rescued me from the horns of a dilemma! Whatever would I do without you!"

After such a metaphorical litany, a simple "You're welcome" would sound painfully inadequate if not downright rude. The proper Southern reply? "Oh, I'm more than happy to do it for you! It was no trouble whatsoever, 'deed it wasn't!"

Northerners living and working in the South, impatient with these matins and lauds, often voice that well-known Yankee criticism: "Nothing ever gets done!" There is some truth in this because Southerners use up so much of their energy simply being nice that they have to take work home—which never gets done there, either, because they spend the evening being nice to their guests.

The Pert Plague is not only a spectacle for men; Southern women also pull out all the stops for each other. When two of them meet, whether they have been separated for years, weeks, or days, they immediately begin to shriek—literally. The decibel level has to be heard to be believed, but it goes something like this:

"Yeeeeeeeeeee! Oh! I'm just so thrilled to see you again!"

"Yeeeeeeeeeee! It can't be you, it just can't be! I just don't believe it!"

At which point they fall into each other's arms.

The Pert Plague is responsible for the general confusion in which so many Southern women dwell, known as being "on the horns of a dilemma." They are so busy talking, flirting, and laughing that they create an aura of turmoil in which they lose things, drop things, and spend a great deal of time rooting in their handbags like pigs at a trough, wailing: "Oh, I've lost my ticket! . . . Oh, I can't find my baggage check! . . . Now where's my wallet? I had it just a minute ago, and now it's gone!"

Sometimes they even lose people. Prearranged meetings get snarled, itineraries are misread, someone misunderstands or never hears an instruction about time and place. . . . Soon it's all hopelessly snafued and everybody gets on the telephone to everybody else: "Have you seen Mary Lou? No, she's not here, I thought she was *there!*"

When the Southern woman's hyped-up nervous system is unleashed, it is not long before a simple misunderstanding becomes a federal case. Thanks to every Southerner's tendency to exaggeration, when nobody can find Mary Lou the verdict is:

"She's just vanished into thin air!"

When I was a little girl, we lost Mama somewhere on the boardwalk at Colonial Beach. Granny immediately set up an outcry and churned up the atmosphere with melodramatic allusions to foul play.

"She's disappeared! She was here just a minute ago, and now it's like she never was. It's like somebody snatched her up and took her off!"

Instead of staying put and waiting, Granny added to the confusion in true Southern style by organizing a search party and sending people hither and yon, with the result that my aunts kept finding each other and my father was nearly beaten up by the husband of a woman who looked like Mama—from the rear. (We finally found her crouched under a slimy pier like a troll in a fairy tale, desperately puffing away on a Lucky Strike because ladies do not smoke on boardwalks.)

The Pert Plague takes a heavy toll from Southern men, whose gallantry can be strained to the breaking point by Miss Dixie's spirited frenzies. In a letter to me, a Southern man had this to say about his former wife:

> She had that maddeningly imprecise quality of mind that made her sure no plane would dare leave without her no matter how late she got to the airport. She thought it was "cute" to rush through the terminal, giving voice like a hound on the scent, and that I would be charmed by this evidence of her femininity and feel more masculine thereby. At first I was charmed—but then I started having chest pains.

Many Southern women subconsciously use the Pert Plague as revenge on men. When a woman approaches the ladies' room at an airport, some man will buttonhole her and say: "I beg your pardon, ma'am, but my wife is in there someplace. Her name is Cindy Lee MacIvor. Would you be good enough to tell her to hurry up or else we're gonna miss our plane?"

When the messenger enters the rest room, she calls out merrily, "Cindy Lee MacIvor? Your husband's outside. He says for you to hurry," whereupon all the women shriek with laughter.

It was the Pert Plague that led many Americans to think that Martha Mitchell was insane when she first told her kidnapping story. From the beginning of the dull Nixon administration, Martha was a classic example of Southern vivacity, famous thanks to her spontaneity and her sometimes calculated wackiness. Compared to the dark-suited Nixon crowd, her colorful behavior made her seem more or less crazy by default.

To make matters worse, the kidnapping incident occurred during America's obsession with Zelda Fitzgerald. The analogy was too much for many people, who decided that Martha was just another one of those bananas belles. Later, of course, crazy Martha was redeemed in all her glory. Thanks to her, pertness was displayed at its best on the Mike Douglas TV show, when she told the entire Watergate saga, complete with hilarious imitations of the principals. Whatever else it has done, the Pert Plague has made the Southern woman a most delightful raconteuse.

Every great civilization has had its courtesans, witty women who reigned in salons and enchanted men with their conversational powers. The Southern woman's lively charm has made her the last of America's courtesans.

# 4

## "I'd Be More Than Happy to Carry You Upstairs, Ma'am."

### or: The Cult of Southern Manhood

Nay, he would be more than *honored*, which is where the trouble lies. To understand the Southern man, one must first understand that the South is a gynecocracy. In a way it is like pre-Christian Britain, a primitive land full of wildly romantic Celts who worship goddesses. The Southern woman is the ancient Hibernian goddess Brigantia before Christianity reduced her power and changed her into the drab St. Bridget. Giddy belle, submissive wife, or bustling DAR, every Southern woman is to every man Queen Boadicea, a strawberry blonde in full armor, borne on a chariot and waving a spear. She is thrilling, fearsome, and totally sensual.

All of this is, of course, the result of the worship of white women that Southern men instituted for political purposes, but, like the original Pygmalion, they discovered that inspired creations can be dangerous business.

I first became aware of Southern gyneolatry at the age of five during a telephone call. The catalyst was a matter of honorifics, or, as Southerners put it, "callin' customs."

Our family was much more heavily supplied with women than with men, and they all tended to live forever, which meant that we had a great many female relatives who had to be differentiated with titles that were both clear and respectful.

My grandmother's aunt was still alive at ninety-some, and because she had raised Granny, Granny had always called her Aunt Mama. This is the sort of confusing, conflicting mess that warms the Southern heart, so naturally we all picked up the title and used it, too, except that we called her Great-Aunt Mama.

I had only one grandmother, so I called her Granny, but my cousin, who had two, called our mutual grandmother Big Mama (black English that white Southerners have borrowed). I called my mother Mama, but my cousin called her mother Little Mama.

One day, I delivered the following telephone message to my cousin, taking care to use her calling customs so that she would be sure to get everything straight.

"Big Mama and Mama just called from downtown, and they want to know if Little Mama bought nightgowns for Great-Aunt Mama yet."

From the next room I heard my father moan.

"Crikey! All these bloody women! I feel like I'm married to the 'ole lot of them!"

Suddenly I realized, with that visceral instinct that children have, that I lived in a goddess world in which women reigned supreme according to a carefully worked out hierarchy. The various titles that came so naturally to my cousin and me were like the graduated obeisances of royal protocol; more, they were *heavenly* titles. If we had been well-to-do enough to have had black servants, I might also have grown accustomed to that well-known distaff triumvirate that has long abounded in upper-class Southern households: Old Miss, Young Miss, and Little Miss.

As I put down the phone, I remembered my kindergarten classmate who had recently showed me his penis in the cloakroom. The next day I stuck my tongue out at him and said: "You're just a *boy!*"

Southern men, black and white alike, are affected throughout their lives by the Big Mama Syndrome. The black woman's strength has been moral and quite often physical; the white woman's has been primarily social, but in their men's minds they both symbolize on an unconscious level an ancient matriarchy in full tilt.

The many sexual conflicts that plague Southern men can all be traced back to the goddess world in which they live. Chief among these conflicts is the Blue Angel Syndrome.

The Southern man has heard so much about ladies that he periodically gets sick of them. The untouchable pristine creature whom he himself placed on a pedestal for his own political expediency has long since turned into a specter that haunts him with clocklike regularity, and so he must rebel against woman-worship by seeking out the tawdriest woman he can find.

The Southern male's *nostalgie de la boue* superficially resembles satyromania. Men climb into cars and go on the prowl more in the South than in any other part of the country. These street harassments and attempted pickups invariably astound Northern women living in the South, several of whom have asked me: "Are they that horny?"

No, they are not horny, they are haunted—by the perfect-lady image in which they long ago clothed the Southern white woman. When they simply cannot take it anymore, they go out "looking for slash," as they are likely to call it among themselves. These reconnoitering movements invariably take place on one of those hot, sticky nights now associated with Rod Steiger movies, a race-riot sort of night in which not a breeze is stirring, a night so airless and hot that you can even smell the cockroaches that no Southern household can keep away during such weather.

A woman who goes to the corner mailbox to post a letter is almost certain to encounter a reconnoitering slash hound. It is possible to spot them from the way they drive. The car moves slowly and ponderously; even if it is a VW bug, its heavy, laborious movement always reminds me of a Packard. It seems like a tank rolling over enemy terrain, yet there is nothing of the tank's grim tenacity in its motion. There is more of a wavering uncertainty reminiscent of the student driver, because the slash hound behind the wheel is *undecided*. He wants desperately to convince himself that the woman on the way to the mailbox is a slut, he wants to convince himself that all women are sluts—yet he is not quite sure, because another part of his mind tells him: "She must be a lady, she's white."

He pulls over to the curb and leans across the seat to speak to her. His face and voice are tinged with panic, and his pleas are the plangent sort guaranteed to provoke every molecule of bitchiness in a woman's soul.

"Can I talk to you?" he says, immediately placing her in the position of a queen granting favors. "Hey, look . . . please . . . wait a minute . . . I just want to talk to you a minute . . . look, please, I . . ."

His sexual tension is almost tangible; there is a quality of morbid desperation indicative of sexual compulsion that marks neither healthy lust nor true ardor, and no woman can mistake the difference. She feels like prey, a doe in the forest, and she is repelled. No man, whatever his region, can ever understand how enraging these attempted pickups are. Men think that a woman is flattered by such approaches, but nothing could be further from the truth. Her only instinct and wish is to strike out, to hurt, to insult.

The Southern woman wisely refrains from doing so. Predictably, her regional antennae guide her response—she pulls her best Southern "freeze." Hauteur is the quintessence of the lady on the pedestal; the sniff, the offended nose in the air, and the stiff, retreating back are the weapons that work on Southern men because they thrust him into deepest guilt. You *are* a lady after all, not a slut who can be picked up. He was wrong, he made a mistake—and because he is, at the moment, filled with self-hate, he is only too happy to be both wrong and mistaken.

The very worst thing a harassed woman can do—as many stunned Northern women have discovered—is to lash out with a stinging insult, a curse, or, worst of all, a cutting allusion to his potency. Any woman who responds this way is not a lady, and is therefore a slut. The slash hound, knowing that he has struck out and therefore has nothing to lose, will reply with an obscenity so withering that the Northern woman asks her Southern female friends: "I thought Southern men were supposed to be such *gentlemen?*"

The Blue Angel Syndrome is responsible for that aura of tension that strangers in the South mistakenly attribute to purely racial causes. It is actually the tension of men waiting to see which women will fall off the pedestal—and the corresponding tension of women who are trying to maintain their balance. Race enters into it only insofar as race enters into the Blue Angel Syndrome; the combination of a white woman and a black man has traditionally been "proof" of her sluthood, and the combination of a white man and a black woman has always been, by definition, an incidence of *nostalgie de la boue*—the white man's ultimate wallow always occurred in the slave cabins, or, in more recent times, in "niggertown."

So when the non-Southerner tests the air of a hot summer night and says, "I get the feeling this place is about to explode," the tension he senses is not necessarily burn-baby-burn; more probably it is jump-baby-jump—off the pedestal.

The more admired and respected a man is, the more susceptible to the Blue Angel Syndrome he is likely to be. The need to shore up unnatural façades of social behavior causes his nerves to give way; a craving for bawdiness comes over him, and with it an unconscious wish for self-immolation. He will tempt fate and invite public exposure because he *wants* to be caught. Next to death, disgrace and ruin are the best means of escape from his gyneolatrous world, for once he is no longer acknowledged as a gentleman he will not need to trouble himself about ladies. It is a case of social secession via debauchery.

Next to the respected man in susceptibility ranks the *respectable* man, the type who has spent a lifetime "doing right" and going to church. It is men such as these—nice, ordinary, decent men—who plague a woman traveling alone and staying in hotels and motels in the South. They literally sniff like hound dogs after a bitch; they trail you down hallways, are perpetually sending over drinks, and in general drive you insane. Sometimes they even show up at your door with a bottle in a brown bag, introduce themselves with elaborate formality, and then come out with: "How's about you and me. . . ."

The contrast between the introduction and the invitation is proof of the conflict raging in their minds. One-half of the brain is saying: "She's a lady"; the other half is saying: "She's a Blue Angel."

It does not matter in the least how you comport yourself; the mere fact that you are staying alone in a rented room is enough: This is the whore's traditional pied-à-terre. I have been through this countless times in the South; my most recent bout occurred less than a year ago. I possessed the necessary qualifications for a potential slut: I was alone, and I am in possession of "one of those li'l ole thangs." The Blue Angel boys were saying, in effect: "You too can be a fallen woman."

If the Southern woman often seems prissy and sniffs a lot, it is not so much that she is conceited and spoiled but that she is forced to engage in a perpetual balancing act.

When the Southern man finds his trashy woman he will, like Maugham's Philip Carey, endure anything she does because he craves her trashiness, just as Baudelaire craved the animalistic qualities of his slatterns. The original Blue Angel as played by Marlene Dietrich threw her pants in the professor's face. The Southern man who has had all he can take of ladies wants nothing so much as to "wipe his face in it," as it were; to be humiliated and brought low by femaleness. The more depraved the woman, the better she can accomplish his destruction.

Ashley Wilkes represented one tragedy of the Southern gentleman, but the victims of the Blue Angel Syndrome represent a far more common one—one with which non-Southern men can empathize. There are few lofty Ashleys, but every man in the world has some of the Southerner's Blue Angel Syndrome in his makeup.

The Southern man is always pitting himself against something. Forces of nature are his favorite test; any act of God will do. If he cannot find fire or flood, he will settle for a bear fight, as did a former beau of mine. I will never forget the night I heard about the bear fight. We were, at the moment, enjoying what is poetically called the "afterglow," and on this particular occasion it was *le mot juste* . He was whispering the usual sweet nothings—which, of course, I was enjoying thoroughly—when suddenly out of the blue, he said:

"Did I ever tell you about the time I was in hand-to-hand combat with a bear?"

So help me God, that's exactly what he said, which ruined the rest of the evening because I did not show the proper respect. The mental picture was too much for me. I laughed in his face, then I blurted out: "Did the bear have *hands?*"

There followed one of those interminable monologues that Southern men so love, full of field-and-stream vocabulary. It included something about a thirty-oh-six rifle, whatever that is, a rambling analysis of firing pins, whatever they are, and several verbal sorties into things like coveys; what he had "treed" and what he had "bagged" plus a who-struck-John involving a lost Bowie knife, a drunken farmer with a broken arm, a fish, and a setter bitch. By the time I realized that this was some sort of hunting trip, and that he had met this bear in the woods, I was numb with boredom. I also wanted nothing so much as to make love again, but he had to finish telling me his story.

It was his way of restoring to himself the male vigor that he felt I had drained from him.

Every Southern man harbors a certain resentful fear of the Southern-gentleman image. It smacks of the drawing room and the dancing master; it suggests that he hovers in attendance upon women (which he most certainly does); that he is overcivilized, overhousebroken, even foppish. One part of him wants to squire the ladies in style, and another part of him wants to get away from them and take to the woods—where no woman can rob him of what he calls "jism."

The symbolic qualities of seminal fluid are as old as humankind. Primitive warriors and Roman gladiators refrained from sex before battle for fear of being drained of the manliness that could make the difference between life and death, and abstinence before the big game is still an ironclad rule laid down by most football coaches.

My bear-battling lover was not a Good Ole Boy; he was, au fond, an intellectual, and a Southern gentleman in the best tradition of the breed. Yet despite—or to spite—these qualities, he showed a Deliverance Syndrome as well. I sensed that periodically something came over him that compelled him to shut me out, and I eventually became alienated by the mighty-hunter side of him that he let me see with increasing frequency.

The Deliverance Syndrome hits at fairly regular intervals, and its absence or presence affects a man's sexual desire. Every Southern woman is familiar with the signs that one of those famous weekend hunting trips is imminent.

First comes the gun-cleaning, which, considering the number of guns most Southern men own, can go on for days. It is hard to miss the symbolic rejection exuded by a man cleaning out a gun barrel—an activity invariably followed by rubbing and caressing the gun's stock, on which he manifests a tenderness that is both endearing and maddening. Often the entire Smith & Wesson petting party gets on a woman's nerves so badly that she slams out of the room.

Next come the nostalgic reminiscences about the individual designated in Army terminology as an "asshole buddy." The Southern man tends to have at least one of these friends; they have usually grown up together and often have gone to war together. "I wonder what ole Ed is doin'?" muses the mighty hunter—before launching into a story about Ed that his Southern wife or girl friend has heard six dozen times.

As luck would have it, ole Ed isn't doing a thing next weekend. In fact, he just happened to be wondering what ole mighty hunter was doing, so they plan to go out in the woods and bag something—whereupon the Southern woman begins to notice that something has happened to her beloved's grammar. He starts to say "he don't" instead of "he doesn't." I heard these lapses from a professional writer: less literary and articulate men can come up with mind-boggling syntax when they hear the call of the wild, because a large part of the Deliverance Syndrome involves a rejection of culture and intellectuality.

As John Erskine put it in his essay, "The Moral Obligation To Be Intelligent": "The disposition to consider intelligence a peril is an old Anglo-Saxon inheritance." The Southern man is a fighter by nature, heritage, and training. He is not cerebral; he has inherited the philosophy of the gentleman's C and the feeling that it is the playing fields of a school and not the classrooms that really count. Aligned with this genetic tendency is his heritage—culture in the Old South was given over to women, who were required to have what were called "accomplishments," to which the hard-riding, hard-drinking gentlemen paid polite attention. The average Southern man still feels that intellect and culture are vaguely tainted by effeminacy, which is another reason he must escape to the woods from time to time. Even the most exalted Southern men of letters have harbored this discomfort; William Faulkner made a great show of hobnobbing with his fishing buddies, and James Dickey has made much of his bow-and-arrow hunting in the pages of *Playboy*.

The Deliverance Syndrome is not a fear of homosexuality, as many non-Southerners are all too quick to charge. It is a fear of the drawing-room society that the Southern man himself created, combined with a deep-seated male instinct to avoid the enervation that overcame the courtiers of Versailles. For the Southern man knows that he is, in truth, a courtier, a knight who waits upon the favor of his goddess lady. His multiple identity problems are as troublesome as hers, for he both loves and hates his gentlemanly image.

As dawn rises on the morning of the great hunt, the Southern man experiences a form of male ovulation. Hormones flow through him and turn him into a bull in the china shop. There is an enormous amount of thumping and bumping; he stamps about the house, happily banging into everything he touches—which, if possible, he will also manage to drop. Any woman who expects to sleep through this is living in a fool's paradise. She has no choice but to wait until the asshole buddies drive off into the sunrise together and then go back to bed.

In 1898, the phenomenon that surprised Americans nearly as much as the explosion of the battleship *Maine* was the vast number of Southern men who answered the call to the colors. It was America's first war since Appomattox, and Southern loyalty had been in question for thirty-three years. No one expected the sons of the Confederacy to fight under the flag that had conquered them; bitterness against the Yankees still rankled in the South and was to continue for many years, but suddenly there were the boys in gray, chomping at the bit and raring to go to war against Spain.

The Southern man's intense national patriotism frightens, surprises, and occasionally disgusts many Americans. They cannot understand why he is so ready to wrap himself in Old Glory, the Yankee flag from 1861 to 1865. It does not seem possible that men who still feel a vibrant love for the Confederacy can, at one and the same time, feel an equally intense emotion for the United States.

There are several reasons for the Southern man's patriotism, the simplest of which is idiosyncratic: To the Southerner, self-contradiction is more fun than hand-to-hand combat with a bear. Dual citizenship is bound to appeal. The most admirable reason is that the Southerner is a good loser. As an Anglo-Saxon, he has inherited England's most valuable export: character. The English character can be maddening, as Margaret Halsey tells us in *With Malice Toward Some*, but at its best it comprises simple decency and great respect for a good and fair fight.

The most hostile motivation behind the Southern man's patriotism is that, again, it is a means of shutting women out and escaping from gynecocracy. There is a certain kind of Southern man to whom every war, justified or otherwise, is actually a battle of the sexes. Most of the time he is an adder-mean Good Ole Boy who is neither a good loser nor a good American. Moreover, he is not even a good Confederate. To him a defeated nation is a feminized nation. Because he belongs to the only region of America that ever lost a war, he secretly hates his "effeminate" Southernness and wants to go to war—with anybody—to prove his masculinity.

This kind of man has given Southern patriotism a bad name and a very simplistic interpretation. He actually seeks sexual potency in the cannon's mouth; the only thing that would give him an erection is rigor mortis, and so he wants to die.

The patriotism of the vast majority of Southern men is not necrotic but ultimately life-giving, a healthy primitivism that often has beneficial effects on their sexuality. Essentially, it is panache, based on a self-image that Cash calls the *beau sabreur*. It masquerades as anti-Communism or as a hot-eyed love of country, but it is really self-love. Shot through with peacockery, it goes back into the mists of time in a quest for male plumage and titivation, to an uncivilized era when sexual superiority was a simple matter, based on male beauty and female drabness.

Many men today, having lost domination over women, have begun to seek via sartorial display the kind of male domination that has always existed in the animal world. In this endeavor the Southern man emerges as definitely avant-garde; long before the relatively recent burst of color and style in men's fashions, he was dreaming of beautiful uniforms. Southern men wore America's last really dashing one. The gray Confederate uniform was elaborately filigreed with gold braid and hung with sashes and epaulettes, yet even this was subdued in comparison with the brilliant red leggings of the Louisiana Zouaves or the hussar designs that predominated in socially élite troops at the beginning of the Civil War.

Like the Northern man who buys a velvet suit, the Southern man also yearns to reestablish himself as a member of Nature's favored sex. The difference between them lies in their respective heritages; the Southern man is drawn more to uniforms than to civvies, a preference that enables him to come closer to the core of this male fantasy and hence derive more satisfaction from it. He wants a lion's ruff of gold braid and the proud feathers of chanticleer for his campaign hat.

Most Southern men, however, are reluctant to acknowledge the real lure of the beau sabreur image: self-adornment. Governed by the South's commitment to polarized sex roles, they fear that an interest in personal display would be interpreted as an effeminate wish to primp, so they redirect their dreams from the vanity of militarism to militarism itself. The resultant bellicose patriotism that so worries urbane liberals is nothing more than a twisted version of the same emotions that send the liberals into Brooks Brothers. The long-overdue and very healthy burst of narcissism in the human male is readily acknowledged by the Northerner. He wants to be the "master mold of fashion and the very glass of form." The Southerner wants to be swashbuckling.

Viewed as vanity and panache, Southern patriotism has an antiquated quality that women who are hungry for the sweep of old-fashioned romance find exciting. The Southern man has a certain swagger about him that every woman craves in a man, whether she is willing to admit it or not. In this depressingly utilitarian age, when young lovers remove identical faded jeans and pea jackets before getting into bed together, the thought of a beau sabreur lover is not unappealing. Neither the overbearing male chauvinist nor the supportive gelding are capable of stirring the female blood, but a dashing cavalier *is*. Such a man has always appealed to women because he is basically androgynous; his idea of warfare is not the grimly masculine one of Calley and Medina mumbling on walkie-talkies, but of a bugle calling a charge; of brilliantly colored flags unfurling in the wind. Once understood, the Southern man's patriotism ceases to be threatening and becomes, instead, a reaction against technocracy's victory over the human heart.

This kind of Southern male will admire and respect any man who exhibits beau sabreur swagger. One of the most startling phenomena I ever witnessed occurred in the South after the Arab-Israeli Six-Day War. I doubt if the world has ever seen such a rapid cease-fire in anti-Semitism. I heard one Southern man after another say in tones that I can only describe as gleeful: "By dern, those Jew boys sure can fight!" One man seriously recommended that Congress pass a special act making Moshe Dayan an American citizen so that he could become Secretary of Defense. He had obviously found a new hero; as he put it: "That one-eyed bastid would wipe anybody offn the map whut gave us any trouble."

The Southern man's beau sabreur leanings often make him refreshingly simple in our era of identity complexes. The real Southern gentleman knows who he is because his self-image is made up of unshaded qualities: duty, honor, loyalty, old friends, old places, and old ties. He does not sit on the floor and fret about what is "relative" because to him so many stars are unalterably fixed. The firmament may be so small that it resembles a compression chamber; he may well be paleolithic in his stubborn refusal to expand it. He can be a slave to the Southern "niche"—the place that was carved out for him, or that he thinks was carved out for him, by forces beyond his control. One of these forces is his father, and so he tends to be a Daddy's boy in a country of Mama's boys. He perpetually measures himself against his father, and because Daddy's views are usually carved in marble, the Southern man seldom uses qualifying words or phrases like "however" or "on the other hand." The last thought in his father's head is whether or not something is "feasible," and so his son does not make feasibility studies, either. Neither father nor son "deplores"—they hate.

His opinions are calcified, and he tends to be rockheaded, but this too can be a virtue. As a Southern woman who has lived in the North, I have discovered what every woman discovers: I neither like nor trust men who are too quick to profess intensely profeminist views. They remind me of the flaming pseudoliberal of twenty years ago who slithered up to blacks at cocktail parties and said: "I've always been for the Nee-grow."

The Southern man makes no secret of his antifeminist views; you can count on him to be dead set against any newfangled ideas that creep into your sweet, pretty little head. His "supportiveness" will generally run a short gamut between two statements:

1. "Well, for Chrissake . . ."
2. "Go ahead and do it, but you'll be sorry."

There are only two ways to handle him, and neither is exactly calculated to make one feel like a brave New Woman:

1. Cry.
2. Refuse to sleep with him until he gives in.

(Both work.)

I do not like male chauvinism any more than any other woman, but I do like masculine pride, and thanks to the beau sabreur dream, the Southern man has it. It imbues him with that fast-vanishing, raw manly courage that makes a woman feel secure. He does not try to reason with a mugger out of a smug conviction that everyone is potentially cerebral—he mugs back.

The Southern woman has an advantage over other women in coping with male chauvinism. Gifted at working around male neuroses (practice makes perfect), she acquires an understanding of the male mind that comes close to empathy.

If you can catch a Southern man between syndromes, he is terrific in bed. Affection-showing and talkativeness are Southern traits, after all, so with certain Good Ole Boy exceptions, the Southern male is not your grim, silent lover. He tends to be quite a kisser, and his kisses last as long as the average Southern conversation. He may be the only man left in sexually revolutionized America who still indulges in long necking sessions on a sofa. This may be sneered at by some as a teenage habit, but it infuses his romancing with a salad-days fervor guaranteed to make any woman feel desirable as well as desired—and much younger than she actually is.

The combination of his kissing tendencies and his d'Artagnan-swath heritage makes him a hand-kisser and even a foot-kisser. For that matter, when he gets going he's an anything-kisser. The reason he labors so long and so well is that he longs to melt a woman's ladylike mask and make her turn "wanton" in the manner of Frank Yerby heroines. This is the bright side of the Blue Angel coin; he is powerfully stirred by the dichotomy of a woman as a lady in the parlor and a whore in the bedroom. Nowadays many men, in the name of liberation, are gritting their teeth and permitting women to be whores in the parlor; they feel that it would be sexist to object to women using four-letter words in mixed company or appearing braless at a party, wearing a see-through blouse. The Southern man will have none of this; he does not like blended women any more than he likes blended whiskey.

He does not like blunt boldness even when he gets you alone, so in the beginning of a romance or on the night of the first intimate encounter, the wise Southern woman lets him think that he has to break down her resistance. It is not necessary to stage a mock rape; simply walk around the room with a drink in your hand and let him follow you. He also likes a few seconds of hesitation or stiffness, followed by one of those Frank Yerby turning points, which means that the Southern woman must learn to master the Suddenly-Slowly Axis.

"Suddenly she relaxed and . . .

1. melted slowly."
2. slowly made herself small in his arms."
3. slowly twined her arms around his neck."

Making oneself small in his arms is dear to the Southern male's heart. It involves a kind of scrunching down followed by a kittenish wriggle. He likes to loom over a woman, and he relishes the thought that she is huddled against him. This stage of Southern lovemaking involves a lot of sliding around on a sofa, where it usually takes place.)

Southern men love long nails on a woman—the better to scratch him with because he is motivated by the Wildcat Syndrome. Also by the Jeannie-with-the-Long Syndrome. He adores long hair and loves to stroke it and run his fingers through it. Even better is long hair that has to be taken down first. The thought of a woman who still, praise God, uses *hairpins* thrills him down to his brogans, and the thrill will be revitalized the following morning if he finds one that got away lying on his lady wildcat's rumpled pillow. Finding a hairpin in a well-used bed in the cool light of day makes him feel like a Victorian seducer.

He is turned on by any and all evidence of daintiness and femininity in a woman's bedroom and bathroom. He will love her if she has a vanity with matching bench; on it should be decanted perfume in stopper-topped bottles, with brush, comb, and mirror in a matched set nearby. Should you not possess the matched set, he will buy you one— a nice gift and a rare one nowadays. If you want to score a real coup, display one of those little glass caskets known as a hair receiver, made especially for lady wildcats with long hair who brush it at vanity tables.)

Most Southern men do not like a lot of obvious makeup on a woman, but you should have plenty of it sitting around anyway—they love the sight of jars, bottles, and tubes. It looks so feminine, and they like to pick the bottles up and sniff at them. The Southern man is a great sniffer and uses his sharp olfactory sense for sexual stimulation and general appreciation. He loves what he calls a "woman smell," a mixture of hair, soap, skin, and the mild saltiness of female perspiration that, especially after sex, contrasts so noticeably with the brassier aroma of maleness. He talks a lot about the woman smell and makes a great show of inhaling it. This touch of earthiness in the Southern man can be very pleasant and flattering.

He is also something of a fetishist. A discarded stocking lying across a chair stirs him deeply; he will pick it up and study it, caress it, and run it through his fingers. (This is impossible to do with panty hose because they curl up into oval knots that look like what the pioneers called "buffalo flop," and so the Southern male hates panty hose.)

He also likes to touch soft leather gloves that a woman has just removed. Since most Southern women use hand lotion and put perfume on their wrists, he also smells the gloves.

He hates pants on women, but because he realizes that the pantsuit is here to stay, he prefers pants that look like long skirts. He is forever after a woman to wear more long hostess gowns, and the sound of a rustle will stir his lust.

In general, his preferences indicate an overwhelming appreciation of femininity, and elements of envy and worship as well. The artifacts of a woman's vanity table become sacred relics in the temple of Isis, and he touches with awe the things that have touched her.

# 5

## "You Can Tell She's Got Good Blood. She's Delicate."

### or: Pelvic Politics and Bad Nerves

Gentlemen planters do not take sturdy women of the people to wife. And so, in addition to being frigid, wanton, bitchy, virtuous, pert, and stupid, the lady of the manor had to have trouble whelping. This was not hard to arrange. Her "delicate parts" had long been at the mercy of the whalebone corset, and when she was not sunk in languid inactivity in the drawing room, she was twisted like a corkscrew and listing to starboard on a sidesaddle.

It was not long before "female trouble" became a status symbol. The ever-resourceful Lucinda, haunted by her multifaceted image— no one could decide what sort of woman she ought to be—went for the jackpot. She became, simply, a woman in the most literal sense. She started to have trouble with her "parts."

There being nothing more feminine than female trouble, every-body was happy. The Southern man could take one look at this pale, wan creature and tell himself that aristocratic women were too delicate to lift a finger—and that slavery was therefore necessary. The Southern woman could enjoy one clearly defined image, at least, and rest as-sured that nobody would ever question it.

Since so much depended upon Lucinda's female parts, it was not long before she became obsessed with them. Obsession was not hard to arrange, either, considering how much time she spent surrounded by other women in that Victorian gynoecium, the parlor. As tea and cakes were passed, the gynecological hoedown began. Someone related the horrendous details of her "lady's complaint," when she took to her bed of pain and spent the better part of a day screaming. Being doubled up with cramps was a regular occurrence that sent wilted ladies to their rooms and servants in search of hot bricks and hot toddies.

Victorian women did not know much about ovaries, tubes, or cervixes, and they would never use the word "vagina," but the Southern ones all knew about the womb. It was respected as the Peck's bad girl in the female system, an agony-control-central that lurked in every well-bred lady's belly like a bad-tempered octopus, capable of making illness strike any part of her body.

At least one member of Lucinda's circle could be counted on to have that Southern ne plus ultra, a "tilted" womb. This awesome malady was good for at least three hours of self-absorption. Another status symbol was a "descending" womb, which "hung by a thread." Descending wombs were caused by having too many children too fast, and many Victorian women actually had this ailment, but many more *thought* they had it. Once they got the bit in their teeth, their wishful thinking intensified until there evolved a blood-chilling Southern pronouncement that I grew up hearing: "She lost all her parts. They just fell right out."

Spontaneous hysterectomies are said to run in my family. In the summer of 1943, Cousin Evelyn Cunningham tried her best to have one during our vacation at Colonial Beach.

The moment she arrived, she rushed over to our cottage to tell Granny all about her latest visit to the gynecologist, in whose office she spent the better part of her days.

"Oh, Aunt Lura, you'll never guess what the doctor told me!" she cried, throwing herself into Granny's arms. "It's a miracle I'm not in bed. I was for two weeks, but I struggled up so we could all be at the beach together."

"Coo lumme," said Herb, who couldn't stand her.

Granny's eyes gleamed, for this was her favorite subject.

"I just want to hear every word," she said, patting the sofa. "Now, you sit right down here and tell me everything. Is it that tube again?"

"No, I've got something new!" Evelyn exclaimed. "It's truly the vex of Venus, Aunt Lura. It's my womb! It's started to descend! The doctor said it's a miracle it's still up there, it's hangin' by a thread, just a *thread*! It was the last baby that did it, I should never have had another child. I'm just too weak down there."

"Female trouble runs in our family, honey," Granny assured her.

"I should have gotten into bed the minute I suspected I was pregnant," said Evelyn. "But I didn't, and now I'm paying the horrible price. Yesterday when I was carryin' the picnic basket to the car, I felt it descend. I just went to pieces when I felt it. My womb could go at any time, Aunt Lura, at any time."

My mother, not to be outdone, mentioned *her* female trouble.

"My womb flutters whenever I have the pip."

"That's an Upton womb," Granny declaimed. "The Cunningham womb descends, the Fairbanks womb tilts, and the Upton womb flutters."

"I 'ad an auntie wot was born in Dundee. 'Ers did the 'ighland fling."

The defense plant at Dahlgren was testing shells that summer, and at regular intervals deafening explosions would split the air. After one such blast, Herb turned his poker face toward Evelyn.

"Hit wud be a 'orrible tragedy hif that bloody noise jarred yer poor womb loose."

Evelyn, used to solicitous Southern men like her husband, beamed at Herb and nodded violently in agreement.

"Truly, it's dangerous. You're so sweet to worry about me."

One lazy afternoon as we were all rocking on the porch . . .

KAAA-VOOOOOM!

"There goes some poor gel's womb," said Herb.

"You know, I just bet you're right," said Evelyn. "There are Cunninghams all over this part of Virginia, and they all have my female trouble because it's *inherited*."

One day, she had a violent choking fit and lost her breath. Everybody except Herb rushed to slap her on the back, and her terrified husband fetched her a glass of water and patted her hand.

"Oh, Law," she gasped. "That was the most terrible feeling, like something fillin' me up inside."

"It was your womb," said Granny.

"Hif I 'ear another word about—'ow the bloody 'ell did she choke on 'er womb?"

"It sent a signal of distress to her poor throat."

"Is that what caused my toothache, Granny?" I asked.

"Don't *you* start!" Herb yelled.

That Sunday, we invited Evelyn and her family to dinner at our cottage. Granny fixed her famous fresh cherry pudding, and Evelyn brought it in from the kitchen. Midway across the floor, one of her boisterous children bumped into her; the pudding slid off the plate and landed with a splat at her feet. Because it had happened so fast, and because her mind was so fixated on her womb, she misinterpreted the incident.

"Oh, Law! It's happened! It's fallen out."

Herb bolted from his chair and threw down his napkin.

"We 'aven't talked about anything else for a 'ole bloody fortnight except that woman's privates! So 'elp me God, I'm going to Australia!"

As he stalked out, Evelyn's husband gathered up the pudding and tried to show her what it was. He needn't have bothered, Cousin Evelyn, who had both hands over her eyes, refused to look.

The Southern woman is the world's foremost practitioner of pelvic politics. She has more power over men while she is sexually hors de combat than other women have in the middle of intercourse, for the Southern man's socioeconomic identity and masculine image are trapped in her bonny blue box. Being delicate means that she is both aristocratic and feminine—which means that he is both aristocratic and masculine. This is pussy power in the most literal sense.

Her obsession with her body is by no means limited to her pelvic region. She is launched on the road to self-absorption early in life because the notion that she has the power to drive men crazy is constantly drummed into her.

"I can't wait till I get bosoms, can you?" my girl friend said when we were ten years old. "You can bump men with them and just drive them crazy."

"You have to make it look accidental, though," I pointed out. "Or they'll think you're not nice."

"Accidentally on purpose," she hissed, giving me a wicked grin. At which point we both collapsed into hysterical gigles, and, clapping our hands to our mouths, rolled around on the bed in truly demented fashion.

As far back as we could remember, we had heard all about driving men crazy. We knew that merely touching a man's sleeve could reduce him to mindless lust.

"Don't be a lint-picker," Granny warned me—when I was five. "A woman's touch makes a man go crazy."

When I got a little older—eight—she told me what sitting in a man's lap could do.

"He can feel the whole shape of your body, and he just goes crazy."

My girl friend's older sister filled us in on what happens when a woman blows into a man's ear.

"He starts to breathe real fast, his eyes glitter, and he just loses his mind! You have to be real careful around a man's ears," she warned us. "And the back of his neck, too. Just trailing your *fingernail* across his neck will turn him into a wild man!"

My girl friend and I both recognized these warnings for what they were: not warnings, but instructions. The Southern girl is usually an unsalvageable narcissist by the time she gets to junior high school because she has grasped the charming fact that her body, especially its exclusively female parts, has the power to make strong men weak—and strong governments fall.

Toppling a government was an easy thing to dream about when I was a little girl because that famous Maryland lady, the Duchess of Windsor, had actually done it a few years earlier. She had accomplished what we were all taught to do: Cause trouble.

"Isn't she wonderful?" we breathed. "She just got everybody so upset! Wouldn't it be just the most fun to upset a whole country? She almost caused a war—she *must* have bumped Edward with her bust. Oh, I'd just love to cause a war, wouldn't you?"

As preparation for the future abdications and parliamentary crises my girl friend and I planned to instigate, we practiced bust-bumping. The only problem was, neither of us as yet had a bust to bump anybody with, so we used oranges, which we tied on our chests with the net bags in which they were sold.

"When you pass him, you accidentally brush his arm with one," my girl friend said and demonstrated. We jousted with each other until we had perfected this, then pressed on to the art of bending over a seated man and letting him have it with an orange to the back of the neck.

We slung those four oranges around until we considered ourselves experts, then sat back and waited for the real McCoys to grow. We sat in math class doing long division with one hand and pulling down the collar of our blouses with the other so we could peer in and see if anything had begun to sprout. Alas, things were such that we worried about a future populated with nothing but sane men.

"If they don't hurry up, I'll never be able to drive anybody crazy!" my girl friend said, stamping her foot in good Southern belle fashion.

We took deep, deep breaths, especially when there were boys around, and then cut our eyes at them to see if one of them had noticed. Making him "look" and catching him in the act would have been triumph indeed; instead, the boys stared not at our chests but at our beet-red faces and bulging eyes. This at least gave us our first opportunity to voice the Southern woman's contemptuously affectionate philosophy: "God, men are dumb!"

It never occurred to us that we were the dumb ones for trying to suffocate ourselves; we thought we were perfectly wonderful, rosebuds in a world of tempting blossoms. Males were our satellites, spear-bearers in the wars we would someday cause. To us, the male's sole function on earth was to "like" you. We wanted to attract them, not because we wanted them but because we wanted them to want us. Attracting a man was not an end in itself but the prerequisite for driving him crazy. You had to get his attention first.

While we waited for our bosoms to appear, we planned our wedding nights. We assumed that we would be "in love" because one was supposed to be, but we really did not care about our own emotions. What absorbed us was the idea of somebody being in love with *us*. The Southern girl is the shining star in her wedding night fantasy, a radiant vision in a white negligee who "floats" out of the bathroom and into the arms of her audience-husband. In our minds, "he" was whoever we happened to think was cute at the moment; most of the time it was Cornel Wilde, but it really did not matter. Needing a face to put on the man in our mental images, we chose the most likely face around. We cast a suitable supporting actor in the role of husband; then we hurried back to the important character: the star. We were madly in love with ourselves, but neither we nor the adults around us viewed our behavior for what it was: colossal egotism at the very least, and classic egomania of textbook proportions at worst.

Around age eleven, most of us noticed that our nipples were enlarging, so we did the proper Southern thing and stared at them for hours on end with the aid of two hand mirrors. We measured the are-olae and talked incessantly about our "pink parts." It was the era of strapless formals, and we could not restrain our eagerness to pour our lovely selves into one because:

"If you accidentally-on-purpose let a little of the pink part show, it drives boys crazy."

Southern contradiction never lies far below the surface, however, and we had regular attacks of it. We wanted "nice" bosoms—i.e., a whole handful—but we did not want to be too big because that was trashy. The specter of the peasant woman haunted us, along with the specter of the black wet nurse with mountainous breasts who took over Miss Lucinda's lacteal duties because Miss Lucinda was too delicate to have any milk.

Fragility was our ideal when it came to nonsexual parts of the body, and we kept examining our hands to make sure they "tapered." Those of us who actually had long, tapering fingers were horrified to discover that we also had long, tapering feet. Feet, of course, were supposed to be "tiny." No one ever pointed out to us that hands and feet tend to match up, nor did this obvious bit of anatomical common sense ever occur to us. We already knew what was supposed to taper into infinity and what was not.

"Fineness" was another goal, and this one, too, was shot through with contradiction. We wanted thick hair—i.e., what our grandmoth-ers called "a good head of hair"—but each individual strand of it had to be fine and silky. Because we were all products of the Shirley Temple era, we also wanted beautiful curls. Here again, no one told us that thick, fine hair is one of the worst troubles that can afflict a woman; it is usually as straight as string, and when it is naturally curly it tends to friz. Nor will it take a body wave properly, nor can anyone except Sassoon himself even *cut* it. But no matter; we were Southern, and ev-erything we had was supposed to be "fine." We pitied the girls who had coarse hair, who could make it do anything they wanted—and were miserable because it was coarse and, therefore, trashy by definition.

We forgot all about hair when we started to get *hairs*. We locked ourselves in the bathroom and counted them, every one of them, and then compared scores. Those of us who were blond from the neck up were puzzled and distressed to discover that we were not quite so fair from the waist down. "It's black!" we wailed. Of course it wasn't but we panicked anyway. There were no skin magazines around to enlighten us, and we all had modest mothers; having never seen a nude adult woman, we had no idea what we were supposed to look like down there, so even more shocking was the discovery that our new growth was also *kinky*. . . .

By now we were at the acne age and could worry about skin (as opposed to acne, which we didn't have). A true sign of delicacy and good blood was "sensitive" skin. Once more, our etymology triumphed over common sense. We wanted skin that was so sensitive that a mere half hour in the sun would send us to bed with chills and fever. "Fainting from the sun" appealed to us, and though none of us had nerve enough to pull a mock faint, we all wished that we would just happen to keel over when there were lots of boys around.

That would have been hard to manage, since we did not really want suntans. We were torn between the desire to look like the bronzed beauties we saw in the movies or ads, and the desire to be on the receiving end of the prized compliment: "You're so fair." All of us had grandmothers who spoke fondly of So-and-So, who was so fragile that "she looks as if she's going to break in two." So-and-So invariably had that bluish tinge of translucency because she was so "thin-skinned." Her veins showed, however faintly, and visible veins were proof positive that one was a lady. Because our self-worship knew no bounds, we promptly compared veins.

The one area of our bodies that did not hold us in thrall was teeth. No one ever even hinted that bad teeth were aristocratic, and our parents saw to it that we went to the dentist when necessary, but somehow we got the impression that teeth were not in the running. Perhaps it was because we had heard about black people's teeth; how white, strong, and beautiful they were. Perhaps, too, it had something to do with the fact that we associated beautiful white teeth with "swarthy" people like Italians and Gypsies, on whom beautiful white teeth are more noticeable. *Straight* teeth weren't even in the running. The orthodonture bills that descend like snowflakes on the Jewish family are not so common in Southern families—not because Southerners need orthodonture less, but because nobody is obsessed with teeth.

Braces simply do not turn on a Southern mother. They are too functional, and they are metal. She is not going to get excited about braces as long as there are such things as brassieres to get excited about. Teeth, after all, are not a secondary female sex characteristic. Nor an erogenous zone. It's true that Southern women are supposed to smile a lot, but the important ingredients of a Southern smile are not teeth but dimples, tremulous lips, and a crinkling around the eyes that we call "devilish." Teeth, the most vital characteristic of a smile, somehow get lost in the Southern shuffle.

The young Southern girl doesn't dread the onset of menstruation, she looks forward to it. For on that glorious day when she has her first period, she becomes eligible for membership in the United Daughters of Delicacy, free to mantle herself in female glory and lord it over men.

Northern girls of my vintage, particularly Catholic ones, would have died before letting boys know it was "that time of the month." Southern girls did everything but issue a public statement. Of course, we couldn't tell outright, but we found ways to let them know.

The best way was to ask the teacher for a pink infirmary slip and "float" wanly out the classroom door. We lay on our beds of pain in a curtained-off area of the infirmary, and whenever we heard a boy's voice asking for a Band-Aid, we groaned. We could see their silhouettes through the curtain; they turned around and stared at the sickbed area, and sometimes, when the nurse went to the supply closet, they peeked around the barrier at us. This was pure gold. When we knew they were looking at us, we put our hands over our faces and groaned louder. No matter how sick we were—and I, for one, had terrible cramps every month—we were never too sick to put on a little show. The idea was to *make him feel sorry for you.*

Another gimmick was the mysterious—and constant—allusion to the fact that you could not go swimming. Southern girls could find ways to make mention of swimming in the dead of the winter. When we got to high school, where swimming was offered in phys ed class, we made a great show of being "excused." We made a grand entrance into study hall by "floating" through the door, then we sat near some boys and whispered loudly about "not being able to go in swimming today."

Walking home from school with a boy offered endless possibilities.

"It's so cold. . . . I can't get a chill today."

"No, thank you, I can't stop at the drugstore. I feel weak today."

"I'm not well today."

Our moment of victory came when the boy frowned, was silent for a moment, then said: ". . . Oh."

It was all an updated version of the mock swoons that Mammy

urged on the disgracefully sturdy Scarlett, not that any of us ever made the connection.

My girl friends and I were all fortunate enough to have mothers or grandmothers who were self-appointed film critics. To them, the best movies were the ones in which: "She dies in the end." Thanks to their Camille complexes, we gave every evidence of dying in the beginning.

Lucinda the Frail gets a lot of mileage out of her pelvis because Southern men gladly dance attendance on weakened women. That doubled-up bundle of aristocratic pain is *theirs*, by God, and they will brew tea and mix hot toddies until they drop. Unfortunately, she has them so well trained that the moment she gets pregnant her life becomes unbearable. A healthy girl at heart, she is forced into the role of Sacred Vessel: In addition to keeping a beatific smile on her face for the better part of a year, she has to live virtually without sex.

The moment a Southern man finds out his wife is pregnant he becomes a monster of solicitude. He, the brute, has "made her this way." To punish himself, to ensure a well-born child, and to protect the Virgin Mary Lou from any and all strain, he waits on her "hand and foot" until she is wild. He inquires after her comfort every two minutes, will not let her lift a box of chocolates, and shows the greatest reluctance, even in the early months, to "go near her." If the Virgin Mary Lou happens to like sex—and she usually does—the most she can hope for are infrequent sessions of love made porcupine-style because her gallant husband has miscarriages on the brain. He is afraid that if he "lets himself go," at worst, "it will all fall out"; at the least, he will damage the baby, or Mary Lou, or both.

The Virgin Mary Lou, heretofore the vainest of the vain, finds that she has lost both her figure and her husband. He takes a masochistic pleasure in "holding himself back" from her until she feels even less lovely than she actually is. Southerners are always good at "sitting around," but now Mary Lou must sit around and *smile* like a Madonna for months on end. The scintillating sex goddess who likes to "float" around in front of an adoring male audience is now crying and complaining that she is *not* delicate, but it does no good. The only area of her person in which her husband takes any interest is the small of her back, and the only thing he thrusts her way is a pillow.

Lucinda's delicacy can also backfire on her in a more serious way. Her husband may decide to satisfy his baser nature with someone who is not a sacred vessel but simply a vessel, or even a human spittoon. The Blue Angel Syndrome strikes, and off he goes with Linthead Lil who works at the mill. At such times, the Southern husband finds it very easy to convince himself that he is merely being "considerate." In a way, and according to his lights, there is some truth to his claim, but the specter of the delicate wife, who is now even more of a lady because she is carrying his child, can often trigger a *nostalgie de la boue* so compulsive that his wife cannot help finding out about it. His anxiety state becomes so intense that he loses all sense of proportion and does something foolish that blows up in his face. The scandal comes to his wife's attention at a time when her vanity is at its lowest point, and she spends the most uncomfortable weeks of her pregnancy crying herself sicker.

Her problems are intensified if she has any older female relatives around, because Southern women tell bloodcurdling childbed stories. The older the women, the worse are their stories. With grim pride they relate terrifying sagas of lacerated vaginas, breech births, hemorrhages, and labor that went on for four, five, six days. Their favorite lying-in stories concern home births because more suffering is involved. The fact that Mary Lou plans to go to the hospital ceases to matter after she has listened to a few of these ancient mariners describe what it's like to bleed to death, split in half, and scream yourself mute for life.

I heard such stories from childhood on. My grandmother's favorite one concerned her own suffering: "I strained so hard that the blood vessels in my eyes broke and I cried tears of blood."

By the time Mary Lou enters the hospital to drop her thoroughbred foal, she has a bad case of nervous prostration.

Northern women have the menopause; Southern women have the Change. If they are really delicate, they have the Early Change, because aristocrats don't "keep on" as long as hoi polloi. Anything under age forty-four is considered a pelvic coup, and if they can manage a hot flash before their fortieth birthday, they will talk about it until the day they die.

When a Northern woman has a hot flash she will say: "I had a hot flash."

The Southern woman describes it this way:

"My brain was on fire! It was as if the gates of Hell had opened and I'd fallen right in the fiery furnace itself!"

By the time I was twelve, I knew all about "that time of life." My education began during a performance of *Macbeth*.

"*Out, damned spot! Out, I say! Hell is murky!*"

Granny stirred beside me and sighed.

"She's havin' the change."

"*All the perfumes of Arabia will not sweeten this little hand. Oh, Oh, Oh!*"

"*What a sigh is there! The heart is sorely charged.*"

"I had sighin' spells. It runs in the family. I started sighin' at thirty-nine, and I just sighed and sighed for ten years."

"*This disease is beyond my practice.*"

"Hmmmph!! That's what they always say."

"*What is that noise?*"

"*It is the cry of women, my good lord.*"

"I had screamin' fits so bad they had to tie me to the bed. Your grandfather didn't leave my side for a whole week. I can see him now, I can see the tears rollin' down his cheeks as he knelt beside the bed so he could feed me."

"*The queen, my lord, is dead.*"

"She did away with herself, just like Cousin Rosalie."

Our family excursions into culture never got out of the pelvis, for no matter what we saw, Granny had but one interpretation.

*Antigone*: "Some women get a bee in their bonnet at that time of life."

*The Necklace*: "You always get forgetful then."

*Phaedre*: "My mother had terrible tempers when she was changin'."

*Jane Eyre*: "Cousin Fannie Lovejoy got so bad they had to keep her up in the attic, too."

The Southern woman is threated by those cheerful books with titles like *That Wonderful Time of Life*. In the first place, she doesn't want to have the menopause, she wants to have Oh-God-the-Change. That being her last opportunity to exercise pelvic politics, she vows to milk it for all it's worth.

It is also her last opportunity to be delicate, to suffer, and to take to her bed of pain with an ailment that is connected with sexuality. Hot flashes and crying spells are feminine, and ravaged "parts" are quintessentially female. In a last-ditch attempt to hurl her organs around as prehistoric goddesses hurled spears, she will either have a hysterectomy of her own and recite every detail, or garner every smidgin of information about the hysterectomies of her friends and talk about them.

The Northern woman who has a hysterectomy says: ·

"I had a hysterectomy."

The Southern woman puts it this way:

"I went under the knife! They took it all, cleaned me right out. My womb is in a jar at Johns Hopkins, the doctor said he never saw one like it."

When the Jewish woman wants to use physical weakness as a weapon against men, she has migraines. This is all very mental and thus calculated to appeal to Jews. But the Southern woman is a primitive.

The Southern woman never relinquishes her absorption in her body, even when she is in her dotage and no longer has any living, breathing female organs left. Her parts and her breasts may be withered, but her custom never goes stale. At this stage of life, she often begins to consume port wine, which she decants drop-by-genteel-drop into what everyone keeps calling "lovely old glasses." The glasses are very important in establishing a general aura of fragility, so that when she announces: "Wine makes blood," everyone will get a mental picture of the attractive droop of anemia.

This mental picture is necessary for the story that she is getting ready to tell: about how sick she was the day she got married.

The number of elderly Southern women who were "run down" on their wedding day boggles the innocent Yankee's mind. Not only does he wonder why a woman in such a weakened condition did not postpone her marriage, but he is further perplexed by the similarity of statistics these dear old things recite:

"I only weighed ninety pounds."

"My husband could span my waist."

"I could hardly stand up."

"The wind could have blown me away."

"The doctor said he never saw anybody so *narrow*."

One old lady I know got so carried away that she wrapped up this tale of hymeneal despair with: "I was so weak that my husband had to carry me around in his arms like a baby the whole first year we were married."

The Northerner wonders: What, pray tell, was the matter with her? But he wonders in vain—the only piece of information these garrulous matchsticks withhold is the name of this mysterious wasting disease. If anyone asks her, she replies with the vague explanation: "I was run down."

Even more intriguing is another question: Did her husband consummate the marriage during that moribund first year? Surely not, for no gallant Southern man would force himself on a bride in extremis. Besides, Southern men are known to have high standards of feminine pulchritude; they would hardly find wasted-away, ninety-pound weaklings desirable . . . would they?

Thus, the Northerner is forced to conclude that Southern women really are more delicate than the sturdy North Country lass—which is precisely what he is supposed to think.

I recently returned to the South after a three-year absence. One of the first people I met was a Northern woman who is now an interviewer on a North Carolina TV station. As we were discussing what we would talk about on her show, she frowned quizzically and said: "I have *never* heard women talk so much about their . . . er, organs, the way Southern women do. Do you think they'll stop it as Women's Lib gains strength in the South?"

I rather doubt it. After my interview, I met an old girl friend for lunch. As soon as we had gotten through screaming and hugging each other, she took a deep breath and said: "Oh, there's just so much news I don't know where to begin. Let's see. . . . Gerry had a hysterectomy, Ramona had her tubes tied, and Alicia lost an ovary. And you'll never guess what happened to me! I missed a period, and I'm only forty-one! Wait'll I tell you about my night sweats!"

Clearly, the Southern woman's obsession with her "parts" is with us yet. But what if she never has menstrual cramps, whelps babies like a cat after one hour of labor, and breezes through the change of life with nary a hot flash? How can she prove that she is aristocratic and quintessentially feminine? What viable alternatives are open to her?

She can go to pieces, because thoroughbreds are high-strung and so are women.

In the Southern subconscious, "walking up and down the floor wringing your hands and crying" is a status symbol. Upper-class women in the Old South did it quite often because the combination of their multifaceted image and their boredom was enough to make any-one have a nervous collapse. People got the idea that this was just an-other "lady's complaint," and it took on a certain fey charm that, when combined with the Gothic thread that runs through Southern life, emerged as good theater. The Southern woman was supposed to have an audience, and once again, she had one.

The American public has bought the saga of the Southern shaky lady time and again, which suggests that there is something appealing about the combination of bad nerves and female sensuality. In movies like *Raintree County* the Southern heroine is of a type: She's nuts. She is also devastatingly pretty—in this film she was portrayed by Elizabeth Taylor—and so sexy that the hero cannot resist her even though he knows that there is something a little funny about her.

Part of her appeal is that she is so endearingly childlike. She keeps two dozen dolls on the *lit matrimonial* and takes turns playing with them and playing with the hero. The only aggressive act she commits in the movie is setting fire to the house during one of her "spells," and she gets caught in the conflagration because she cannot find her male doll, already blackened from an earlier fire but treasured nonetheless. Her death frees the hero to marry the second female lead, who is pre-sented as the fine, upstanding, and sensible girl he should have mar-ried in the first place, yet the audience is left wondering. . . . Like an underground stream, the idea flows on that there is nothing quite like fey fucking.

When I was growing up, I kept hearing women say: "When I had mine . . ." i.e., their nervous breakdown. The curious note of pride in their accounts gave me the idea that all women were supposed to go to pieces at some time in their lives. When, I wondered, would I have mine? My easy assumption that I, too, would break down was aided by the colorful stories I heard, especially the ones about Cousin Olive Fairbanks, whom my father called "the skellington in yer family closet." Cousin Olive always baked her husband's favorite cake every Sunday, then took it to Congressional Cemetery and left it on his tombstone. When she returned the following Sunday and found an empty plate, she assumed that her husband, never the grave-diggers, had eaten it.

My father could never understand why everyone dined out on Ol-ive Fairbanks stories, saying: "Hif I 'ad any barmy relatives, I'd keep quiet about it." The Southerner's Kook-in-the-Attic Syndrome invariably astounds those outside the fold; cutting a wide swath through life —no matter how—is dear to the Southern heart because it is dashing, and that, too, is a sign of aristocracy. Whenever a Southerner smiles fondly and says, "I'll never forget the time Cousin Mary Ellen . . ." any Yankees present would be wise to hold their breaths, because there is no telling *what* is coming.

I know a Tennessee girl who actually stated that she was *descended* from four generations of institutionalized women, adding: "I haven't had mine," in a tone that left little doubt that she felt like a bend sinister on her family's escutcheon. (I know just how she felt, because I haven't had mine, either.)

Thanks to our quality-folks hangup, the South has evolved a colorful female type known as the in-and-out-patient. A North Carolina lady of my acquaintance was a prime example of the breed. She kept everyone thoroughly confused because we never knew whether she was what we tactfully referred to as "in," or whether she had done what we called signing herself "out."

The least little thing would set her off. Perhaps her *Atlantic* was late arriving the month she expected to see her letter to the editor in print. On the way to the newsstand to buy a copy, she scraped a fender or broke a heel, and then returned home to find that she had left something on the stove. The combination of everything made her go to pieces, so she would drive over to "the hill" and sign herself in.

One day a mutual friend called me and said, "Yolanda's back in," so I sat down to compose a cheering note. As I was gazing out my window, trying to think of some news to tell her, who should come waltzing down the street in fine fettle but Yolanda. Instead of sending a cheer-up note to the hospital, I sent her an invitation to an upcoming party, which, of course, I addressed to her home.

Three days later, my phone rang.

"Hey, honey, ha' you? This is Yolanda. 'Deed you are the sweetest thing to invite me to your party. I just now got the invitation, it was forwarded to me. Can you hear me? There's so much bangin' goin' on in this place. I'm in occupational therapy class, and we're makin' ashtrays. If I'm out in time for your party, I'll bring you one."

# 6

## The Good Ole Boy

### or: A Prince among Men

Like the French concierge and the cockney costermonger, the Good Ole Boy is such a recognizable phenomenon that he almost defies definition, but to say that he is simply a bigoted, uneducated Southern white male is comparable to summing up Genghis Khan with the statement: "He rode horseback well." As we all know, this is true, and, as we all know, there is a great deal more.

The song "American Pie" intrigued everyone because of its allegorical lyrics. No one knew what it meant, and even the composer, when asked to interpret it, indicated that he really was not sure himself. Whether or not this is true, it was a wise piece of press agentry because the question: "What do you think it means?" swept the country. I dined out on this parlor game in Boston because the mystery was buried in the rocky soil of idiom, and my Yankee friends did not know what a Good Ole Boy is. As a Southerner, I understand the term all too well, but my definitions were not exactly known for their clarity. I usually ended up waving my hands and saying, "A Good Ole Boy is . . . well, you know, he's . . . well, he's a Good Ole Boy."

During the heyday of the civil rights movement, the Northern press began to refer to sheriffs, prison guards, and anyone with either a bullhorn or a German shepherd as a Good Ole Boy. Thus our hero received a great deal of publicity and found himself elevated to national fame, something he had never before enjoyed. Suddenly there was *something* called a Good Ole Boy, instead of men who had always been called Good Ole Boys. The idiom went awry in foreign mouths, and the casting-office mentality took over, until non-Southerners came to believe that the Good Ole Boy was an exclusively low-class type, a tobacco-chewing Grand Klutz of the Ku Klux Klan, a redneck, or even a poor white.

While this is often true, it isn't always. I knew a practically illiterate Southern plumber who looked up from my dismantled sink when I put *Tristan und Isolde* on the phonograph and said, "By dern, ain't that the purtiest thang?" He listened to the love duet with an expression on his face that I have looked for but haven't found on the faces of far more elegant and sophisticated men when we were listening to music that I loved. He asked me for the name and record number, and the next time I saw him he told me that he had bought it. He also bought *Die Walküre*, which I have never been able to listen to without going mad.

The plumber and his friends undoubtedly called one another Good Ole Boys, but to me he was that find, a Southern gentleman.

On the other hand, I have known Good Ole Boys who were journalists, lawyers, college professors, and state legislators. They can be found in any social stratum; they are formed not by class but by the extent to which they have been confused by the contradictions of sex, Southern-style.

Since the casting-office mentality has done its work, we might as well take a look at the rushes and examine the really classic Good Ole Boy before we get into subcategories.

Because the Good Ole Boy is a Southern Wasp phenomenon, he has a broad, fair-skinned face that gets easily rubicund from the sun or drink and tends to go jowly under the influence of the latter. Because he lives in a rural, conservative state with indulgent gun laws, he has a callus on his trigger finger that never seems to heal, holes in his thumbs from fishhooks, and—souvenir of his regular manly crew cuts—boils on the back of his neck from the barber's clippers. He is a sartorial disaster, clad in baggy suntans, a white shirt open at the neck with the cuffs rolled back one turn, an enormous carved belt buckle of the *Gott und Reich* variety, decorated with horns or antlers, white socks, and Marine Corps-issue shoes with thick soles and cleats.

He is between forty and fifty years old. Forty is the high-water mark of Good Ole Boyhood; by this time the requisite beer belly and bar stool spread are coming along nicely. He always says "sports jacket," never simply "jacket." He will not wear shoes that slip on, because this is the way women climb into their shoes. His must tie, and he likes leather shoestrings. During the time that I covered the North Carolina Debutante Ball, I seldom saw the correct patent-leather slippers with faille bows, de rigueur for white-tie affairs. The debutantes' official escorts (their "marshals") usually wore plain black shoes, and I saw plain black leather shoestrings on quite a few Good Ole Boys who were socially prominent enough to kick their daughters out in style. I once mentioned patent-leather slippers to a Good Ole Boy who was scheduled to present his daughter, and his eyes flashed raw panic.

The Good Ole Boy will not drive with two hands. He keeps his left arm propped vertically in the window frame in a perpetual right-turn signal. When he approaches a bar stool he does not sit on it. He leads with his crotch, opens his mighty thighs, and slides forward onto the seat.

I first tilted with the Good Ole Boy when I went to graduate school at Ole Miss. More specifically, the first tilt came the moment I got off the bus in Memphis and walked through the waiting room.

Benches always draw Good Ole Boys; any long seating arrangement is bound to be full of them. Courthouse railings are their favorite hangout, but a row of anything will do.

As I walked past them it began.

"Shore would like to have that swing in my backyard."

"You want me to help you with your box, li'l lady?"

"Hesh up, Alvin, that ain't nice. Don't you talk to her like that."

"I just want to help her with her box, thass all."

An explosion of mirth followed this brilliant riposte, but it was quickly shushed by the man who had appointed himself my protector. There is always one Good Ole Boy in the lineup who takes on this role. Just as the minstrel show has an end man and a vaudeville team a top banana, any collection of Good Ole Boys has a Shucks Ma'am.

"Shucks, ma'am, he didn't mean to insult you. He just thinks yore mighty sweet, thass all."

"Thass right, li'l lady, I just want to help you out."

"Well," said another, "I just want to take her out."

"Don't you pay no mind to him, ma'am," said Shucks Ma'am. "He's just foolin'."

I checked into what I thought was a respectable hotel. No sooner had I started to unpack than the desk clerk was at my door.

"I just wanted to see if you were aw-right. It's too late for room service so I just thought you might like a Co'Cola."

I told him I didn't care for anything. He looked at the cascade of underwear that was spilling out of my open suitcase and got a glazed look in his eye.

"I just wanted to check yore air conditioner to make sure it's workin' aw-right."

The room was freezing, but he fiddled with the knobs and then turned around.

"Well, I just thought I'd better check, thass all."

As he was leaving, the door across the hall opened and a jowly, rubicund man of forty in suntans, white shirt, white socks, killer belt buckle, and thick-soled shoes poked his head out and grinned.

"I just thought I'd say hello, li'l lady. Felton, whatchoo doin' in this li'l lady's room?"

"I'm just seein' she's comfortable, thass all."

My neighbor winked at me.

"I'm just funnin' with you, ma'am. Felton's aw-right, he wouldn't bother nobody, he's a Good Ole Boy."

"Git on outta here, Raiford," said Felton. "Leave this li'l lady alone. If Raiford pesters you, ma'am, you just call down to me and I'll take care of him."

Raiford walked on down the hall. Felton watched him for a moment, then stuck his head back in my door.

"You don't really have nothin' to worry 'bout with Raiford, ma'am. He's a Good Ole Boy."

When he left I pushed the bureau up against the door and got into bed. A few minutes later I heard a thundering stampede of drunken men, and the hallway erupted with Rebel yells.

"Hey, you goddamn sumbitch, how are you! I want you to meet this here ugly-lookin' critter, this here's Pearl Hicks. Pearl's a Good Ole Boy, I wanna tell you. Ole Pearl knows where we can rustle up some women, don'tcha, Pearl?"

The elevator door clattered open, and suddenly a woman began to scream bloody murder.

"Hey, Pearl! Hey, come on now, you leave that lady alone! Don't you cry, ma'am, he didn't mean no harm, he's just friendly. Pearl, you wanna get us thrown outta here? This lady's a guest at the *hotel*. Now, ma'am, you don't have to be scared, I won't let him hurt you none. Lemme pick up yore things. This here yore earring? Wait, I see yore other shoe. There, now we got evrathing. Shucks, ma'am, I'm just as sorry as I can be."

"I just wanted to ask her in for a drink."

"Shut up, Pearl. You done 'nuff already."

There followed the muted shuffling sound of Good Ole Boys wallowing in guilt. Tendrils of their self-loathing seemed to penetrate my door, and I tried to analyze this fierce Angst.

The name "Good Ole Boy," while very male in a hail-fellow-well-met way, lacks virile masculine imagery. It suggests a man both fat and fatuous, yet the Good Ole Boy is more than a locker-room jock or a Babbitt with a Southern accent; his Sturm und Drang is much more complex because it is unique, peculiar to him alone and unshared by his fellow countrymen.

Men who consistently suffer military disaster, like the French, or who are simply uninterested in soldiering, like the Italians, tend to compensate with high levels of sexual ardor. As I see it, the Civil War is the cause of the Good Ole Boy's need to act out his shaky, klutzy, superstud role. Everyone knows what happens to the women of a defeated nation when the victorious army marches through. Southern women are the only American women who have experienced the fate of the Sabines in the course of a war, and the Good Ole Boy cannot get this out of his mind. Though he is a consummate womanizer and would, as the saying goes, hump a rock pile if he thought there was a snake under it, he feels an inordinate pull in the opposite direction and harbors a conflicting need to protect women from any conquering male, including himself.

This is why there is a Shucks Ma'am apologist perched on every railing when the Good Ole Boys line up in what is obviously an unconscious military formation. The Shucks Ma'am is a collective conscience, a salesman of guilt who reminds the others that sex and masculine aggression must be fought and defeated.

The Good Ole Boys' guilt accounts for the Just Syndrome. All

Southerners use "just" very often out of an unconscious feeling of free-floating guilt, but the Good Ole Boys use it the most often of anyone. They have a habit of saying: "I just want to hold you," when they really mean they want to go to bed. Sometimes they vary it with: "I just want to love you," but in any case they never fail to include the "just." This qualification also appears in their general conversation, and in mind-boggling ways such as: "Raiford just chased Sally Ann with a hatchet, ain't like he done any real harm," or "Darcy just shot that nigger in the ass, he didn't kill him."

He "just" wants to hold (protect) you, not prong (conquer, as in Yankee) you. He "just" wants to give you a Co'Cola, nothing more. To identify completely with male aggression would be, in effect, high treason. This psychological shell game puts the Good Ole Boy's sexuality on a now-you-see-it-now-you-don't basis; his virility is constantly being passed back and forth, bestowed and withdrawn by an internal gyroscope subject to capricious fluctuation.

My next tilt with a Good Old Boy occurred at Ole Miss, where I managed, with no effort whatsoever, to stir the Fascistic passions of one Calhoun Lee Creech, who was said to be a spy for the White Citizens Council. Calhoun's duties supposedly included lurking around the TV lounge in the student union building to eavesdrop on any pro-integration statements made by viewers when the civil rights bulletins came on.

Because I am a Capricorn as well as a Wasp, I give a false impression of aloof *froideur*, and because Calhoun was a Fascist as well as a Good Ole Boy, he was enchanted. My demeanor appealed to his Fascistic side because he craved conquest, and it appealed to his Good Ole Boy side because he dreaded conquest. In other words, he developed a crush on me for two reasons:

1. I looked as if I couldn't be had.
2. I looked as if I couldn't be had.

For a long time I did not realize that he was staring at me in lust because on Good Old Boy faces there is no discernible difference between expressions of desire and expressions of hatred. The eyes glaze once, as Emily Dickinson said.

Each time Calhoun telephoned me he opened with: "Betcha don't know who this is." But of course I did. I suppose being a spy leads to obfuscatory speech habits and a reluctance to reveal one's name, but considering how long he kept up this guessing game and the obvious pleasure it gave him, I tend to think that he himself was not sure who he was.

His conversations revolved around three statements:

"You look mighty good to me."

"You 'n' me's got to get together."

"I'd kill for you."

I refused to go out with him, so he decided to rape me.

One night quite late I was coming out of the graduate building where I regularly studied because the dorm was too noisy with the Pert Plague. When I got to the foyer, there was Calhoun, drunk.

We struggled, and Calhoun kept up a running commentary about getting six boys to swear on the Bible that they had had me, and various other threats all centering around my inevitable impeachment. He got me into an office and gave me a push; I fell backward onto a desk, in a perfect position for what Calhoun had in mind but also a perfect position to give him a good ole Fifties spike heel to the eye. He staggered backward, howling, and I made my escape.

I did not see him at all the next day. That evening, my buzzer rang, and when I went downstairs, there he was. He had a cut under his eye, but otherwise he looked better than I had ever seen him. He wore a coat and tie, and his hair was damp. He reeked of Old Spice, and he had shaved so closely that he had razor scrapes. He looked like a little boy freshly scrubbed by his mother and sent off to Sunday school. He held a dozen pink carnations.

He proffered the flowers shyly, and with his internal gyroscope tuned to Shucks Ma'am, he spoke.

"I'm mighty sorry 'bout last night. I didn't mean no harm, I just wanted to love you, but I was drunk and a li'l crazy, thass all. But I wasn't gonna rape you, 'deed I wasn't. I just wanted to hold you a li'l, thass all."

Suddenly I felt terribly, horribly sorry for him. For a moment, I wanted to go to bed with him; I contemplated it, then decided not to do it. I imagine he would have been impotent with me anyhow, after an attempted rape followed by flowers from Shucks Ma'am's florists, but every once in a while I still wish I had.

Any woman involved with a Good Ole Boy quickly discovers that her ashtrays and drinking glasses are never big enough for him. This is the Little Dinky Syndrome. Everything is "little dinky this" and "little dinky that," but he is good-natured about these complaints because he is so unsure of his masculinity that he overcompensates by cultivating an oxlike placidity wrapped in a shroud of inexhaustible patience. This, he feels, is very male and godlike.

He gladly replaces the little dinky items with unwieldy gargantuana, nice big masculine things that soothe his self-doubts, but it never stops there—which brings us to the Little Dinky Woman Syndrome.

Sexually threatened men must find or create as many differences between the sexes as possible; the *petite différence* is not enough; he needs all the *grandes différences* he can get. Here the Good Ole Boy nails his flag to the mast and navigates the treacherous straits of Scylla and Charybdis with a nightmarish cargo of diametrically opposed idées fixes.

Because men and women are different, his preferred physical type is the tiny, fragile, dainty, weak, delicate epitome of femininity who is forever getting lost—he has to "shake the sheets to find her."

However; because men and women are different, his preferred physical type is the soft, pleasingly plump, curvaceous epitome of femininity with a good rump on her, who inspires his gallant compliment: "The more there is, the more there is to love."

The Good Ole Boy cuts this Gordian knot by picking out a billowy girl friend and then buying her lingerie that is at least two sizes too small.

My Good Ole Boy beau, Skeetmore, once showed up wearing a roguish smile and bearing gifts. When I opened the box I found a black nightgown size 8, a black bra size 32A, and a pair of black bikini pants size 4.

I am five feet six and weigh 130 pounds, which Granny always called "wholesome."

I couldn't get the bra around my rib cage, and the pants jammed at midthigh. When I told Skeet my actual sizes he was astonished, and when I told him my height and weight he refused to believe it.

"I thought you weighed 'bout a hunnerd-five, and I know dern good and well you're not more'n five-three."

To win this argument, he picked me up. Or rather, he tried to. He staggered, groaned, and then we both went hurtling down into the coffee table. Everything on it was totally demolished except the twenty-five-inch-diameter birdbath ashtray he had bought me the week before.

I realize that I am weakening my argument by admitting that I accepted black lingerie from Good Old Boys, whom I seem to hate. In answer I will say that I do not hate Good Ole Boys, I just can't stand some of them, and that furthermore, weakening my arguments is a habit of mine. Try to think of it as part of my charm. In any case, hope springs eternal in the human vagina.

Like anyone who harbors a great deal of sexual fear, the Good Ole Boy seeks someone on whom he can project it. An unfailingly good way to find a psychological punching bag is to create an ideal to which no mere mortal woman can possibly aspire, and then, when the inevitable happens, cast blame upon the waters.

As far as women are concerned, all the Good Ole Boy demands is an oversexed Melanie, thass all. She must be so voluptuous that it requires no effort, talent, or knowhow to satisfy her, a woman so perpetually ready to pop that she will have an orgasm if he merely looks at her crooked. At the same time, she must be sweet, demure, passive, submissive, self-sacrificing, with a yen to be dominated. He burdens the Southern woman with her famous bête noire, the multi-faceted image, but because he has a low tolerance for frustration, he suffers more when women inevitably fail to meet his demands—hence the Good Ole Boys in country-music lyrics who are always crying their eyes out. Other Southern men would prefer a woman with a multiple personality, but they will settle for less. The Good Ole Boy insists on a package deal. He knows unconsciously that women who are good in bed tend not to be sweet and submissive, and that women who are sweet and submissive tend not to be good in bed. He sets himself up for inevitable disappointment, which is exactly what he wants, because then he can flee from the female entirely.

As the Irish girls who follow each other in a lemminglike migration to America will so readily attest, the romantic Irishman of song and story does not exist. The carefree minstrel boy is in reality a guilt-ridden, sex-dreading, forty-five-year-old bachelor who lives with his mother and prefers the company of the other lads down at the pub.

So, too, does every Southern woman know that the Good Ole Boy, like the Irishman, dreads the feminine and prefers to escape to the great outdoors with his camping equipment or go down to the pub with the other lads.

An excursion to Johnny's Cash 'n' Carry tavern is an experience in living sociology that should not be missed. It is always full of Good Ole Boys, a whole line of them all in a row. Our hero, Beverly Lee Tiddywell, is overwhelmed with joy and relief to see so many males all in one place, and they are equally glad to see him, but neither must show it. Instead, they exchange the South's only taciturn greeting: "Hey." It travels down the line: "Hey . . . Hey . . . Hey." Then Beverly slides crotch-first onto a stool. Once on it, he keeps sliding back and forth, up and down, to and fro, caressing the memory of many another pair of suntans. The squirming movements of Good Ole Boys on barstools and motorcycle seats must be seen to be believed.

With a walloping punch, Beverly Lee greets his ole buddy, Alva Lee Hicks, and they discuss their unfortunate fellow townsman, Shirley Lee Crouch.

"Waal, s'a cryin' shame if you ask me, the way they got ole Shirley down in the jailhouse. Shirley ain't so bad. He couldn't help it 'bout what happened. It wuz his property, and evrabody in town knows he got that big ole Army surplus bazooka. They shoulda had better sense than to trespass. 'Sides, they wuz comin' to get a piece o' Tilly Mae's tail, so it wuz really her fault. He wouldna been lickered up if it hadna been fer her and the way she done him. That gal dern near broke his heart, handin' it out lak she done, to anybody what asked fer it. Just as well he blew her head off, too, 'cause she weren't no daggone good nohow. But what beats me is the way they's fussin' 'bout him settin' fire to the house. It wuz *his* house, and 'sides, the county already condemned it and wuz gonna tear it down anyways. Looks to me lak Shirley saved 'em some trouble. He couldn't help it if the wind blew the flames over to the oil company. Can't blame a man fer the way the wind blows. Nope, Shirley's aw-right, he's a Good Ole Boy."

The sobriquet of Good Ole Boy is always spoken in such a way that it becomes a verbal passport, the only intrasexual endearment he dares permit himself, a code for the brusque tenderness that he cannot otherwise show. It is oddly reminiscent of shy, whispering nuns calling each other "Sister."

The Good Ole Boys have thus cleared Shirley of mass murder and arson and pictured him as nothing more than a put-upon cuckold thwarted by the vagaries of the weather.

They stick together against the women, these Good Ole Boys. Solidarity forever.

A good man is hard to find—now more than ever. A good Good Ole Boy is ever rarer, but they do exist, and the woman who runs across one finds herself having a surprisingly good time with him.

The *good* Good Ole Boy is named Earl, and the nicest thing about him is that he can cut the mustard. His lovemaking is not polished, but it's vigorous and there is plenty of it. Earl does not have "problems," he has erections. He is simplistic and uncerebral, and his work does not drain him dry. He already has an erection long before you hit the bed, and he can maintain it for as much as half an hour. After it is finally expended, Earl rests awhile, has a couple of beers, and then gets another erection. Earl's girl friend doesn't have to do a thing except *be* there.

For a woman who has spent five years on college campuses and dated a string of tormented intellectuals, there is nobody quite like Earl. There are times in a woman's life when she does not give a hoot in hell whether a man has read *War and Peace* or not. Earl's motto is: *Dulce et decorum est in medio coitu mori*, and he doesn't lose a thing in translation.

Earl's lovemaking is also normal. He is not interested in doing arcane things to the bend of his girl friend's elbow, nor will he invite her to stand on her head wearing crotchless bikinis.

When Earl takes a girl out for a special date, he will do what he calls "treat her right." He picks the most expensive restaurant in town, where, with touching magnanimity, he tells her: "You get anything you want, you hear?" Not for him one of those dark, atmospheric "in" places like Hindu Burpee. Earl would be horrified at the very thought of taking a girl to such a place. To him, it's a dump, and if he likes a girl, he considers her a jewel worthy of a proper setting. He may not know how to act in an expensive restaurant, but he doesn't care—he has the courage to go anyway, and muddle through.

Any woman who has sat silently by while a self-proclaimed wine aficionado tasts his ritual drop and then nods meekly to the snide and knowing sommelier should go on a date with Earl. He does not put on airs, and he cannot be cowed. I had given up all hope of actually being out with a man who sent back the wine, but then I met Earl, who slapped his mouth, shuddered, and said:

"This diddly-squat stuff tastes like vinegar. Ain't you got nothin' better 'n 'at?"

It was one of the finest nights of my life.

Earl is a prime example of Southern contradiction, for though he himself is not an intellectual, he takes fierce pride in a girl friend who reads books and does something interesting for a living. He will take her around to his favorite tavern and brag about her to all his friends. He thrusts her into their midst, saying: "She works on the newspaper, she writes pieces. Gets her name in the paper nearly evra day. . . . She speaks French. Hey, say sumpin' in French. . . . Hear that?"

Male chauvinist pig? I think not.

I was once in a crowded suburban drugstore with Earl shortly after vaginal sprays came out. We found ourselves in the feminine hygiene aisle, and Earl studied the labels on the aerosol cans with an expression of shocked disapproval. Then, oblivious to the crowds around us, he turned around and asked:

"What's wrong with pussy?"

Earl is a gallant man.

# 7

## Sex and the Good Ole Boy

*or: Bad Good Ole Boy, the Good Ole Boy*
*Dagwood, the Good Ole Boy Jock, the Haut*
*Good Ole Boy, and Good Ole Boys*
*Who Are Not*

It is not necessary to be Southern to be a Good Ole Boy. Richard Nixon is one. Warren Harding was one. So too, I suspect, were Marc Antony, the Earl of Bothwell, Rudyard Kipling, Edward VII, Hermann Göring, Nikita Khrushchev, and Ernest Hemingway.

Certain men seem to be Good Ole Boys but really are not. Into this category I would put Robert Burns, Andrew Jackson, George S. Patton, Theodore Roosevelt, and Harry Truman.

A Good Ole Boy is not simply a man who makes a to-do out of his masculinity—most men do a little of that. He makes such an incessant fetish out of it that he becomes gamy, or pitiful, or both.

The Bad Good Ole Boy is the mean adder with beady eyes, of moonlight-and-murder fame. He was the backbone of the Ku Klux Klan in the days when they still threw necktie parties, and he still attends their parades and lectures.

In Mississippi during the summer of 1964, when civil rights workers Schwerner, Goodman, and Chaney were killed, it was easy to spot the adders. Whenever violent death is in the air, they surface with the speed of sound and hang around in randy groups to stare at women with the stony-faced lust that is their trademark.

Lynching and murder are their ideal aphrodisiacs, but any kind of violence will do. After a hard night of tavern fighting, the adder likes to go out and get some "gash." Although this name for the female genitals is almost obsolete, he clings to it—just as he clings to "cut" to describe what he will do with the gash he gets. He seldom uses the two most common words for coitus and doesn't even know the more lighthearted ones.

When a woman walks past, he appraises her with gelid eyes and announces to no one in particular: "I'd like to cut her."

He uses his knife whenever he gets a chance. His standard threat during tavern brawls is: "I'm gonna cut you to ribbons!"

He takes the loss of the Civil War more seriously and personally than any other Southern man. To him, losing a war is like losing a fight: It means he has been dominated by another male, which reminds him of the passive feminine role in sodomy. He dreads femininity in any form, and since it manifests itself most thoroughly in the female sex, he harbors a vicious loathing for women. Their very existence threatens him.

This sexual psychology was illustrated to perfection in a scene near the beginning of *Midnight Cowboy*. Before leaving home, the sweet-natured Joe Buck had fallen in love with the town slut. He treated her with tenderness and true manly ardor and became the only man of her vast acquaintance to kiss her on the mouth. This humanizing caress enraged the pack of adders who sat behind the couple necking in the movies. They taunted Joe: "He's kissing her! Hey, he's *kissing* her!"

To them the girl was nothing but "gash," something less than human—a hair-covered opening obviously missing from their own bodies and therefore no threat to them at all.

But to Joe she was much more: a love object. He not only acknowledged her femininity, he also acknowledged his own feminine component by being gentle and loving with her. The adders could not endure the sight of a man who so readily exhibited softness; Joe had broken their Hotspur bond, and so they had to punish him. How? Why, treat him like a woman, since he's behaving like one.

In a scene so brief that many viewers missed it, they threw Joe face-down across a car hood and sodomized him.

The bestial mountaineers in *Deliverance* were adders, and their sexual attack on the weekend campers was typical—the adder is so terrified of homosexuality that he may indulge in it to calm his fears. If he does, he always plays the masculine, aggressive role: if it is masculine to take a woman, it is even more masculine to take the larger, stronger male.

The adder uses his analism as a means of humiliating women.

One day a few years ago, a friend and I were on our way to the Raleigh airport when we got caught in the middle of a Ku Klux Klan parade. The Klansmen had been drinking all day, of course, so something was bound to happen. We got pinched, goosed, and propositioned in barnyard terms. The perpetrators were happy drunks, but the bona fide adder is always a *mean* drunk, and we encountered two of them standing alone on a corner we had to cross.

We were both dressed to the nines for a very special occasion — two-hundred-dollar suits, wonderfully glamorous hats, kid gloves, and expensive handbags. A well-dressed woman feels absolutely marvelous. The knowledge that she looks smashing does magical things to her walk, her carriage, the way she holds her head, everything. She feels rich and aristocratic, confident and indomitable.

To adders, such a woman looks unattainable. This is the most dangerous demeanor a woman can present to a latent homosexual man, because every woman he cannot have pushes him closer to the front of the closet. The only way the adder can regain the masculinity that her aloofness has shattered is to humiliate her so thoroughly that her remote mask cracks.

As we approached these two, I had a flash of déjà vu that told me what was going to happen, and it did. One of them broke wind—loudly—as we passed, then both of them burst into laughter.

My friend and I instinctively reacted with the "freeze." We stiffened and gazed straight ahead, determined to remain unruffled. The adders only hated us more for that, and as we walked on, they discussed us in loud, snarling tones: "Who do they think they are? Goin along with their noses in the air. They got the same thang between their legs as evra other Goddamn woman."

The adder has an active sex life with women because what passes for his sanity is dependent upon heterosexual performance, but his worship of maleness makes him the world's worst lover. He is convinced that a penetrating penis causes actual shocks, like a cattle prod. The vagina is the socket and the penis is the plug; the instant they meet, everything is supposed to blaze into blinding light for the female. Certain that any woman goes mad the moment he enters her, he sees no need to indulge in foreplay, which is sissy anyhow. In a nation of breast men he stands alone in his utter lack of interest in these beloved female appointments, which he uses only as handles by which he can grab hold of a woman and yank her to him.

He does not kiss anything at all—especially the mouth, a horizontal version of the vertical vulva. All he wants to do is get in, get off, and get out as fast as possible. He accomplishes this feat by throwing his 250 pounds on top of whatever lucky girl he has picked up. (He never has any trouble getting an erection for these grand entrances because he has been hard as a rock ever since he opened Slade Gilette's scalp with a beer bottle earlier that evening at Trask's honky-tonk heaven.)

He makes his grand exit seven seconds after the grand entrance, heaves his 250 pounds to the clean side of the bed, and when he catches his breath, murmurs: "I sure pleasured you, Velma Lee, dint I? You know you had a real man, sure 'nuff."

Velma Lee's motto: It wasn't God who made honky-tonk angels.

He loves to tell women horror stories about the size of the black man's genitals, explaining that she "needs" to know these things. Thus forewarned, she presumably will develop the eternal vigilance any white woman needs in order to avoid the spontaneous episiotomy that awaits her in the black man's bed.

It is a well-known fact that no man, not even the most sexually well-adjusted one, likes to talk about big penises, because no man, not even the most sexually well-adjusted one, is ever satisfied with the size of his own. The adder is anything but sexually well-adjusted, so why does he dwell on this subject so much?

Perhaps because he wants to be sodomized by the black man, whom he looks upon as the archetype of maleness, since blacks were the only Southern men who won the Civil War. He sees the black penis as Excalibur, whence all male power and excellence spring. Subconsciously he feels that the victorious black man's semen contains magical properties that will somehow "rub off " on him; that the seminal elixir will seep into his system and, like a hormone shot, overwhelm and stamp out the femaleness that haunts him.

Conversely, woman's love juices are a contaminating poison to be avoided, which is why he will not remain inside a woman one second longer than necessary.

The adder is the only Good Ole Boy I hate. Whenever I see one I always wonder: What does Robinson Crusoe want from Friday on Saturday night?

The Good Ole Boy Dagwood is the white-collar type whose wife is always kicking him under tables and saying, "For heaven sakes, Wesley, stop making a fool of yourself!"

Wesley spends a lifetime making a fool of himself, until it becomes an unbreakable habit. A lower-echelon managerial employee who hovers somewhere around assistant bookkeeper, he is the man who makes the clumsy pass at the uptight Miss McIlhenny at the office Christmas party and can't follow through because at that precise moment he starts to get sick from the liquor he has drunk. He ends up with Miss McIlhenny holding his *head*—not quite what he had in mind—and someone has to drive him home to For Heaven Sakes.

The Southern woman is especially sadistic with the Wesleys of Dixie because this pitiful excuse for a man, merely by being male, is granted automatic perks and privileges. As bad as Wesley is, he still commands a higher salary than she does, and he can still get a certain amount of deferential, unthinking respect from other men—whereas she gets an unthinking: "Now, little lady," a dozen times during the course of a day.

Wesley is the eternal cartoon man with a lampshade on his head on New Year's Eve, which may explain why he is a lodge-joiner. Any kind of silly hat seems to comfort him: It is a symbol of a band of men who are as lonely as he is. He does not fit in with Southern gynecocracy and cannot hold his own in female-dominated society. He is ingenuous, lacks polish and sophistication, and he never catches jokes unless they are of the why-did-the-chicken variety. Banter and whiplash repartee, which Southern women love, leave him puzzled if not downright stunned.

He retreats to conclaves and civic meetings, where he feels such relief that he goes overboard displaying the only kind of masculinity he has. When Wesleys get together, they slap backs, pump hands, and throw each other mock sidewinders in a frenzied search for affection. Lost bear cubs in a sex-conscious woods, they usually manage to break something or cause some sort of damage that gets them thrown out of restaurants and motels, and so once again they are in for another tongue-lashing from For Heaven Sakes.

Wesley is the least horny of the Good Ole Boys. His wife's repeated refusals may have atrophied his sex drive until he does not need very much, and since he is so seldom in the company of women (other than For Heaven Sakes, and the Miss McIlhennys that populate his working life), he seldom experiences those unexpected forms of stimulation that keep other men constantly wound up. One would expect the sexual side of his life to be the least of his worries. Not so, because Wesley spends so much time in the company of large gatherings of drunken men. They are not really horny either, but they can neither admit it nor leave well enough alone. Sooner or later one of them says: "Nooky!" and with this code word Wesley's ludicrous three-legged race is on.

They·decide in a hearty, unanimous vote to go out and "russle up some women." *Nobody* wants any nooky, *nobody* knows what to do with nooky, and *nobody* knows where or how to find nooky, but they go anyway. In a pack. With their hats on.

They hit the best hotel in town, where one of them sees a good-looking woman in the lobby and says: "Now that's what I call nooky!" Only it isn't; it's the president of the Junior League. She has the touch of arrogant confidence that the well-to-do always have, and she damned well knows how to get indignant.

After they get thrown out of the hotel, they hit the taverns, where one of their number manages to buy a beer for a trashy girl and then spills it all over her. As he attempts to dry her off with a napkin, his hand touches her breast, at which precise moment in history her husband walks in. He was looking for her to finish the fight that sent her stomping out of the house, but now he has somebody else to beat up.

The unfortunate Wesley is usually saved by his lodge brothers before he suffers too much damage, but the debacle results in the loss of his fez. Wesley is the kind of man whose wife sews name tags into everything he owns, and so the next day the tavernkeeper calls up For Heaven Sakes and says: "This here's Gentry's Tavern. I got yore husband's hat down here."

When Wesley and his lodge brothers lie to each other about the nooky they have enjoyed, they always create larger-than-life women, Pallas Athenes of the sheets with mythological powers. "She had a clitoris, I swear it got to be 'bout an inch long. . . . I felt her spurt, I swear I did, 'way up inside her. . . . She came just from havin' her tit-ties played with, I didn't have to do another thing!"

For heaven sakes, she *must* have been a goddess.

For women, football is, at best, a thing apart, but it's the Good Ole Boy Jock's whole existence. He is devoted to the big game—in the stadium, on television, and on his car radio. He frequently drives to one game while listening to another, filled with regret that he cannot be in more than one stadium at once. As he drives on, he drowns his sorrows in the beer can that he holds between his legs. He cannot seem to navigate without this aluminum truss and is able to drink one crotch-warmed beer after another with no apparent ill effects.

He seldom says anything to women except "Shhh!"

He is a behind-slapper, but no woman need fear bending over because it is men's behinds that he slaps. Especially on Mondays at the office, when all the Good Ole Boy Jocks re-enact the big game.

When his wife is mad at him, he tells everybody: "She sent me to the showers."

Any male co-worker who does not spend coffee break talking about the great Stretch Malooski's forward pass is a queer.

Any male co-worker who does not know who Stretch Malooski is, is a Communist queer.

Any woman who does not know who Stretch Malooski is, is a woman.

If the inarticulate Stretch Malooski happens to be so brain-damaged that *he* doesn't know who he is, he's a great guy, I mean a real great guy, you know what I mean?

The jock wears baggy pants because he thinks that tight, revealing pants are for queers, yet whenever he is standing in front of a woman he keeps hitching up his falling pants until the crotch seam bisects him and shows the shape of his equipment. If the woman looks—and it is hard to avoid looking because he does this most often in offices when the woman is seated at her desk—that means she "wants it." If he does it again and she looks a second time, that means she "wants it real bad." If she avoids looking and turns her eyes in the only directions open to her (the ceiling, to the side, or behind her), that means she's playing hard to get, and furthermore, that she is frigid—which means that she "needs it real bad."

Because his pants are so baggy, he cannot see the shape of his own equipment, so he keeps touching himself to make sure it's still there. Any woman who happens to be looking his way when he does this is "begging for it."

The only way to escape the interpretive powers of the Good Ole Boy Jock is to come tapping into work with a white cane.

His great concern for a woman's sexual needs is a masquerade because all he ever seems to want is fellatio. It is his prescription for any troubles his men friends have, especially nervous tension or overwork. "What you need is a blow job, ole buddy," he whispers, and then proceeds to tell all about a gal "who really knows how to do it." If he sees a woman purse her lips in thought, he will say: "See? Looka there. She wants a lollipop, only she can't admit it to herself, thass why she keeps doin' her mouth like 'at." Nail-biting, pencil-chewing, and smoking are all "signs" of a woman who is *dying for it*. You don't dare move, and for God's sake don't bring a banana for lunch.

In bed, he absolutely refuses to return the favor because: "You do that to a woman and 'fore you know it she's a Lesbian."

He never returns the logic, either.

The Haut Good Ole Boy is the upper-class Southern man who harbors a vague fear that being rich, prominent, and pictured in the society pages may have tarred him with the brush of foppishness or effeminacy. That's why he deliberately lapses into Good Ole Boyhood from time to time in order to get back to the basics as he sees them.

Like so many Southern men, he uses bad grammar for protective coloration, as did the father of the deb I overheard at a cotillion: "Ain't every day you can present your little ole gal to society."

The difference between the Haut Good Ole Boy and his bas confrere is that they both wear white shirts.

The Haut fastens his collar with a gold button and adds a bow tie for the many full-dress functions he attends. Because these are nearly always woman-oriented events, his facial expression is a mixture of discomfort, resentment, sheepishness, and an indefinable sadness.

He is forever standing around with other Hauts waiting for something important to begin, and to calm his anxieties and bring out his false Good Ole Boyhood he drinks bourbon out of Dixie cups. (I was a grown woman before I realized that these cups were not named after the South.)

At debutante cotillions the paper cups are likely to outnumber the red roses. A trail of them litters all deb functions, indoors or out; they are like the Boy Scout's pebbles dropped to help him make his way back through the woods. If you want to find Haut Good Ole Boys, simply follow the trail of crumpled paper cups until you come upon a group of men dressed like penguins, drinking out of more paper cups.

Like many other types of Good Ole Boys, the Haut is unconsciously trying to overthrow the South's gynecocracy and make the region male.

The Good Ole Boy Who Isn't? He's the Southern intellectual who is uncomfortable with his indoors role. To me he is the most tragic of the Good Ole Boys because his deliberate personality distortion tears him to spiritual pieces. He has a large feminine component in him, and playing the man's man conflicts with his sensitivity. It eventually ruins his creative work, wrecks his love life, and sends him down the alcoholic's drain.

He is a dedicated writer, artist, musician, or professor. Like all such men, he has an intense and sometimes insatiable need for intellectual companionship. It is as important to the creative soul as is air to the lungs, and his deepest instincts tell him that he will shrivel without it. Yet he is forced to maintain a spuriously folksy façade because so many Southerners distrust and scorn intellectuals; he spends years telling his shucks-I'm-not-a *serious*-writer lies until he is literally exhausted by his masquerade.

He is very definitely a woman's man but he is afraid to show it, so he invents a dream-woman whom he puts into all of his novels. She fulfills his yearnings for a "complete" relationship, a woman to whom he can both talk and make love, someone capable of understanding and appreciating his ideas and work—yet wants him as a man, too. He leads a double life, carousing with his buddies at the local tavern and communing with his fictional heroine at the typewriter.

And then, one day, he meets his dream-woman in the flesh.

His sensitive side is overjoyed as his personality is freed with a long whine of release, like a spring that has been tightly coiled. He falls wildly, passionately in love with the woman and keeps saying, over and over again like a chant: "You have a mind as well as a body."

At first the two attributes are equally appealing; both the sex and the conversation are the most fulfilling either party has ever known. But then something happens. The woman begins to notice that the chant has taken on a hollow ring, as though he is trying to convince himself that he does not mind her mind. He sounds increasingly like a little boy whistling his way past the graveyard at midnight.

The pseudo Good Ole Boy knows that something is wrong, but he refuses to analyze it even though analyzing human nature is his business, because he loves and needs the woman too much to admit that she has begun to threaten him. He covers his anxieties with the penultimate compliment: "I enjoy talking to you as much as I enjoy going to bed with you."

He is telling the truth, and therein lies the rub. He has spent so many years playing the Good Ole Boy and pretending that "women are only good for one thing" that he half-believes it despite his better judgment, his secret dreams, and the woman he has found and loved. He feels that he should turn to men for companionship, but here he is, sitting *across the room* from a woman, just talking. The blot on his Good Ole Boy escutcheon spreads, and he begins to panic, which leads him into the ultimate compliment:

"You think like a man!"

Here he is telling the truth, Good Ole Boy-fashion. She does think like a man—i.e., her thoughts interest him. Now he is openly threatened; suddenly, she *is* a man—yet he is sleeping with her as well as talking with her. He enters a distraught state of psychic pseudo homosexuality in which he projects all of his inner rage onto the woman, and the lovers begin to clash.

He must turn her into a woman again, as it were, because—like all Good Ole Boys, even pseudo ones—he cannot cope with any gray areas between the sexes. The relationship enters its cancerous stage; now there are no more chanted compliments, just one chanted Rx: "You need a man to dominate you."

Each pseudo Good Ole Boy kills the thing he loves, but, worse, he also kills his creative talent the moment he refuses to analyze the conflicts the woman has stirred in him. When a creative person, especially a writer, deliberately skirts any issue of the human heart, the process of destruction is likely to be inexorable. It is also likely to be aided by the reaction of the woman involved. Precisely because she indeed has a mind as well as a body, she fights back and refuses to be dominated, and when she turns bitchy the pseudo Good Ole Boy can lie to himself again and say: "She's just like the rest after all." She becomes another woman to escape from, and so he goes down with the other lads to the pub, from whose depths he perpetually bemoans the sameness of women.

*Her* fate is likely to be more interesting. She can be absolutely certain that she will turn up in his next book as the most lethal, saber-toothed she-wolf who ever came down the pike. If she has brown eyes, he will change them to blue; otherwise, there she'll be in all her glory. The plot of the novel will make no sense whatsoever, because its author stayed angry *and* drunk the whole time he was writing his roman à clef—and anyway, it was intended as nothing more than a vehicle of revenge, another way of whistling past the cemetery.

# 8

## "If Mary Lou Gets Married Now, She Won't Be Able to Come Out!"

### or: Today's Belles: Brides and Debutantes

There are many de jure belles left in today's South because bellehood is largely a state of mind, but the de facto belle is getting rare. The belle can no longer be found in one place doing one thing; her milieu used to be the dance floor, and her purpose in life was leading reels. Her bellehood was established the first time a chaperon sighed and said: "I declare, she hasn't sat down once all evening." Nowadays there are no chaperons left, and the demise of these old dragons has cut deeply into bellehood, since they could make or break a girl's reputation with one whispered comment.

The stag line and the dance card have vanished, which means that boys cannot erase each other's names and get into fights. How can you be a belle unless a worshipful young gentleman with tears in his eyes begs you for the fifth waltz? A true belle would promise it to him, just as she promised it to four other worshipful young gentlemen with tears in their eyes, because such calculated errors are guaranteed to cause "scenes"—crucial to bellehood.

A "scene" in the good Southern sense begins when one young gentleman says: "There are ladies present!" and another young gentlemen says: "I think we'd better step outside." These young gentlemen were always soused, which helped immeasurably to ignite the hot tempers that a girl had to ignite in order to be a belle. Nowadays, the young gentlemen may be stoned rather than drunk, in which case they have no wish to fight each other or anybody else.

The really unfailing sign of a belle is that she *exhausts* people. In the old days, a girl could faint, which meant that some man had to pick her up and carry her while two or three others ran hither and yon fetching smelling salts, water, or a litter on which to cart her away. This simply doesn't happen anymore. Passing out from too much straight bourbon is just not as bellelike as fainting from unknown causes, nor is it as fastidious.

Another good way to exhaust people, especially men, was riding sidesaddle. This fetching custom provided the belle with an automatic retinue, because she could not get on or off a horse without help. One man had to run and fetch the mounting block, then take the belle's foot in his hand and heave her up. A second man had to hold the horse so that it would not start off before the belle had draped her right leg around the hook and arranged her flowing skirts attractively. When she was ready, both men gazed up at her in adoration, and one of them—the lucky one—handed her her crop.

Shortly, sidesaddles being the challenge that they were, some member of the belle's retinue had to pick her up out of a ditch and "just carry her in his arms like a baby" to the nearest concerned crowd, where everybody fluttered and fetched. When she came to, they had to get her back up on the horse again because: "She's got spirit, she won't let a little fall stop her."

Retinue-exhausting is hard to manage nowadays. The Southern coed who goes to Atlantic City for the Miss America contest is not really a true belle even though Southern girls have a way of winning this prize; the contestant certainly has a retinue, but she does not exhaust them, they exhaust *her*. This is disgracefully unbellelike.

Many Yankees assume that every Southern coed is a belle, but actually coeds cannot possibly exhaust enough people to qualify. They are too busy exhausting themselves with study, career plans, and worries about the job market. About the best a girl can do is become Homecoming Queen, but many colleges are getting away from this sort of thing, and in any case, riding on the back of a convertible that is moving down East Main Street at a snail's pace is hardly the same as being thrown into a ditch in the middle of a gallop.

As for being a drum majorette—that, too, is exhausting. As many

Dixie coeds have discovered, prancing around half-naked on a freezing day can land them in bed, alone, for a week.

So the de facto belle is going the way of the dodo. Nonetheless, holding to the exhaustion-and-retinue theory, I maintain that there are two belles left.

There comes a time in the lives of a large number of girls when they become belles for a brief period—culminating in what is often referred to as "the happiest day of your life." Then there is another, much smaller, group of girls who become belles for an entire summer. These two groups of young women exhaust the only retinue left: the Woman's Department of their local newspaper.

Today's belles are, therefore, brides and debutantes.

The typical Woman's Department writer vacations in the winter and "goes to pieces" in the summer. She can't schedule things any other way, because summer is bride-and-deb season. She starts drinking on June 1 and stops on or about Labor Day; she doesn't get to the beach once during those three months because she's gained too much weight to appear in public in a bathing suit. Besides, who wants to go to the beach and spend two weeks walking up and down the sand wringing your hands and crying? It's better to do it in the newsroom, where no one pays any attention to you except the men in the Sports Department, who blame it on the "time of the month" and grumble that women have no place on newspapers anyway. In belle season, according to the Sports Department, each of us had an uninterrupted three-month-long pip. That's what it looked like, because somebody always had her head on her desk or was running around wailing: "Oh, if it doesn't stop, I'm just going to die!"

The day I went to pieces I did not walk up and down the floor wringing my hands and crying because I am just not the poor Lucinda type. I *ran* up and down the floor waving my hands and emitting great gulping shrieks of laughter until the Woman's Editor finally gave up and sent me home.

I had been sitting at my desk when the most ordinary, run-of-the-mill bride-elect walked in with her wedding form. By this time I could tell at a glance which kind of bride to get excited over and which kind to take in stride. Some brides exude trouble the moment they come through the door; they are the type known to Southern society reporters as "prominent," and they are invariably mired in deepest egomania. It wafts from them like musk. You know immediately that something dreadful is going to happen, because these are the girls whose weddings never go smoothly. You *know* that you are going to lose their photograph, or that it will end up next to the Zonite ad, and that, in either case, Big Daddy will come charging into the office like a bull.

But the mousy little girl who tiptoed up to my desk was placidity personified. She was obviously not prominent, and I guessed that her headline would be a one-column, 24-point PAIR WED or VOWS SAID. All in all, a routine little bride who would fade from my memory as soon as she left.

She handed me her filled-out questionnaire and photograph (timidly). I thanked her (absently).

"There's something I want to ask you," she whispered. "Would you put in something special about the fact that I'm going to sing at my wedding?"

"Oh? What are you going to sing?"

" 'Because,' 'I Love You Truly,' and 'I'd Rather Have Jesus.' "

As all Southern society reporters will verify, anything, but anything, can happen in the Woman's Department during the merry month of June.

Such as . . .

(Phone rings.)

"Woman's Page, may I help you?"

"Would you be good enough to write about my daughter's feet?"

### FÊTE HELD

was the way we commemorated bridal showers because the word "shower" was considered too frivolous. Nobody ever said why, but it seemed pretty obvious to me: "Shower" triggers visions of tipsy women talking a little dirtier than Southern men think women talk. Since the typesetters had no foreign accent marks, we could not put the circumflex over the first "e" to indicate the proper pronunciation of "fête." It is doubtful that a circumflex would have meant anything to Wilma Lee Creech or Mary Jane Hicks anyway, so most of the brides-elect and their families with whom we dealt talked constantly about "feets."

Shower write-ups averaged about one inch for all but the most lethally prominent engaged girls, and since we received them by the carton throughout the nuptial season, we treated them like fillers and marked them for the printers with "wild," which means: "Stick them in wherever they'll fit in the order of their dates."

Having so many of them and being unable to dummy them in, we never knew exactly when they would appear in the paper, which is why we were always on the phone with hysterically weeping girls and mothers, explaining, in the manner of big-city mayors during race riots: "We cannot guarantee tomorrow absolutely."

Unfortunately, all sections of a newspaper can always use fillers, so sometimes the write-ups did make it in, thought not always on the right page:

> Brown and Williamson is expected to rise to 18½ favors tied in lovers knots and placed in an electric meat grinder with the honoree's engagement ring for a game of "Who's Next?" H. J. DuPlessy, Winston-Salem auctioneer announced. Tobacco prices generally will be in a lovely crystal punch bowl with the Surgeon-General for her coming marriage to Ramsey Huddleton, Jr., affected by a wet growing season."

One of the first things journalism students learn is that a guideline is the first two words of a headline, and that these two words should be written at the top left-hand corner of each page of copy so that the typesetters will get all of the right story with the right headline.

What they are not told is that occasionally it is quite possible for two entirely different stories to have the same guideline, which means that the wrong headline can appear over the right story; or if you prefer, the right headline can appear over the wrong story.

Like this:

TAYLOR VOWS TO FIGHT VD EPIDEMIC
TAYLOR VOWS SPOKEN IN BAPTIST CHURCH

Headline writing, by definition, does not lend itself to romantic allusions, nor is it supposed to—except on a Southern society page in June. Writing bridal headlines is a perilous job on any Southern newspaper because everyone expects something saturated in poesy. Everyone has heard of that legendary headline: MARRIAGE CONSUMMATED IN FIRST METHODIST CHURCH. This is so famous that I am sure it was actually printed during some merry month of June, when society writers below the Smith & Wesson line just aren't thinking straight.

There are certain bridal headlines of mine that my former co-workers will not let me forget:

MR. WEBB TAKES MISS PIERCE
PLIGHT TROTTED
VOWS WED
PAIR SAID
MR. KELSO GIVES DAUGHTER AWAY
MISS DENHAM WEDS AL FRESCO

If worse should come to worst, I could always get a job writing ad copy for silver companies, except that I would rather starve. I hate silver companies. Their brochures turned my co-workers and me into basket cases as we listened to bride-elect after bride-elect babble about their choice of flatware. Two or more engaged girl friends would go downtown together for the purpose of registering their patterns at the jewelry store. As they climbed into the car they began arguing the virtues of "Renaissance Colonial" over "Early American Medici." The argument continued all the way downtown, up and down the parking ramp, in the store, over lunch, and finally it invaded the mad sanctuary of the Woman's Department itself. They stood around arguing in front of *us*, because they assumed us to be experts on the respective popularity of Classic Rose, Damask Rose, Tudor Rose, Stuart Rose, Queen Anne Rose, Buckingham Rose, and Modern Old Rose.

The great silver flip is the Southern bride's most intense preoccupation. She invariably locks horns with her mother and grandmother, and they argue violently throughout the entire engagement period, month after month and in every conceivable place. In the ladies' rooms of Southern department stores, over the sound of flushing toilets, they fuss and fume over silver.

"That looks tacky, Mama, I don't care what you say. All those holes in it. I don't want holes in my silver!" (Pzzzzzzz)

"They're not holes, they're ornate piercin'." (Pzzzzzzz)

(Pzzzzzzz) "I don't care what it's called, Mama, it looks like holes, and I say it's holes! I want Celtic Egyptian! It's got such a traditional contemporary look."

"I don't like that timeless modern business, sugar. I've always said that there's nothin' like the simple elegance of Swedish Da Vinci." (Pzzzzzzz)

I was once caught between a mother and daughter who nearly came to blows in the office and asked me to arbitrate for them.

"What's your pattern?" the mother asked me.

"S&W Cafeteria. I've got eighty-seven covers." (It was true, except I hadn't stolen quite that many.)

The Southern silver fetish sounds mad and is actually quite logical. Dr. Jonathan Latham could not understand why his girl friend was content to sit in a filthy house and polish her clean silver. He should have remembered that it was silver that his forebears stole from Southerners during the Civil War. It was their silver that Southerners took such pains to hide in the well or bury under the smokehouse. They could not risk bringing it out at mealtimes, even when they had something to eat with it, because they never knew when a Union patrol might appear. They had to eat with wooden spoons or with their fingers for years, and such an existence hurt the Southerner's fierce pride and his enjoyment of nicety—for generations.

We of the Woman's Department could empathize with all the silver-tongued orators we had to endure, but that didn't stop us from enjoying a number of private jokes at their expense. One morning, one of our loyal staffers dragged herself through the door and collapsed at her desk. We knew she'd had a big date the night before.

"What did youall do?" we chorused.

"Ornate piercing."

The moment a Southern girl's engagement is announced, she starts to fight with her mother. They do everything but take to the dueling oak with rapiers. If it ever came to that, they would also fight about *what time* the duel should be and *whom to ask* to serve as seconds, because that is the sort of thing they have been fighting about all along.

The typical June bride wants to be married on a Saturday so that she can get her picture in the Sunday paper. This presents an immediate problem because nearly everybody else wants to be married on Saturday for the same reason. There can only be five Saturdays in June at the most, so the first thing they fight about is when they can "get" the church. It all sounds as if they are planning an auto-da-fé.

If the bride has a sister, the honor-attendant argument does not come up because a Southern girl will "do the right thing" even if she loathes her sister. If she does not have one, all hell breaks loose because Mama vetoes her choice of maid of honor. Sally Ann is either too fat, too thin, too pretty, too ugly, or "there's just something about her" that Mama does not like.

Now we have an enraged, white-lipped bride-elect who snarls in measured tones through clenched teeth:

"Sally Ann . . . is . . . my . . . very . . . best . . . friend."

By the time Daddy gets home from work, they are chasing each other through the house shrieking:

"You never did like any of my friends!"

"That whole family's common! They're just common!"

"Sally Ann's mother is wonderful! She's not like you!"

"You're known by the company you keep! I've told you and told you, but you won't listen!"

Next comes the children-in-the-wedding tilt. Mama always wants the youngest flower girl and ring bearer possible because it would look *so cute.*

"I can see that little angel now, just droppin' petals."

"She might drop somethin' else," says the bride-elect. "She's only three years old."

Two hours later:

"I won't have my wedding ruined!"

"It'd break their hearts if we didn't ask them!"

"Suppose Skipper dropped the rings? I'd die! I'd just die! I won't have those brats in my wedding!"

"You're a monster! You're abnormal!"

Then we come to Great-Grandmother's wedding dress, an argument that goes on for so long that the entire house reeks of mothballs because Mama has been running through it holding the precious relic, chasing Daughter, who clutches her copy of *Modern Bride* and refuses to look.

"If she was good enough to leave it to you, you ought—"

"I'm marryin' Bartley, not Vincent Price!"

"You wouldn't have gone to college if it hadn't been for Big Mama! It was her money that paid for it! You don't have any gratitude!"

Mother and daughter have a new, different *big* fight every week, but invariably, throughout the entire engagement period, there is also a running battle over something very minor that may not get settled until the night of the rehearsal, when one or the other finally breaks down and gives in. The little fight keeps cropping up at odd times and ruins the few moments of peace the family knows. Anything can trigger it, even table grace. As Daddy finishes mumbling: "We thank Thee for these fruits of our labor . . ." mother and daughter suddenly look up and eye each other with murderous determination.

As soon as grace is over:

"I still say that fruit punch recipe is—"

"What's wrong with it?"

"Strawberries floatin' in punch? I never heard of anything so tacky."

"It's in *Modern Bride*, and besides, Arabella Buchanan had it at her wedding, and if you're goin' to say the *Buchanans* are tacky, I'm goin' to walk out of this house right this minute and never come back!"

In movies, restaurants, and even in church, mother and daughter keep "the little fight" roiling along for at least three months. You can hear them hissing behind you while you try to concentrate on the spy drama.

"The epergne . . ."

"The bowl . . ."

"The prayer book . . ."

"That awful chandelier . . ."

"Reverend Parker will *not* read 'The Song of Solomon' out loud, I tell you! He's a nice man!"

Just about the only thing mother and daughter do not argue about during the engagement period is the bridegroom. They may not even mention him at all except when they're discussing "his list." Southern gynecocracy has such a field day at nuptial time that everyone forgets why these plans are being made and these fights being fought. Even if a Southern man does not like to go out with the boys, he is forced to do so during his engagement period because this is a time of titans, and all the titans are women. The event is not an approaching marriage but an approaching wedding, an opportunity for yet another regional tug-of-war. Women win it, they yank the South out of male hands and plant their flag. Men must wait for football season to recapture the occupied territory and make women feel de trop.

Thanks to this alienation, some engaged couples break up. The bridegroom gets a foretaste of what life with Mary Lou will be like as he listens to her fight with Mothah. He sees qualities in her that he never knew she had, including greed and hysteria. All the ultrafeminine qualities that the South requires women to have, come tumbling out of her in a mockery of femininity, until Mary Lou starts to seem like a misogynist's parody of her sex. While the stream of inane drivel that comes out of her mouth is driving her fiancé insane, she buries him under a pile of brochures and clippings. When they huddle together on the sofa, it is over an etiquette book, and she makes it clear that she expects him to do something terribly cloddish. If she says it once, she says it a hundred times: "Make sure your pants aren't too short!"

She turns him into the worst sort of Good Ole Boy. He is the enemy now, a male, a member of the army that will win back the South come fall.

All brides crave their moment of glory, but in the South there is a *name* for a woman who dazzles multitudes—a belle. For many Southern girls, a big wedding is the only chance they will ever have to be this legendary creature that all Southern women are supposed to be. A big wedding is much more than a moment of glory; it is a storybook fable come to life.

Because of such intense, deep-seated emotions, the Southern Woman's Department is forced into a nerve-destroying state of eternal vigilance. If one little thing goes wrong with a wedding write-up or photo, panic ensues. Above all, no matter how crowded our pages were with ads, we had to make sure that a wedding account appeared in the paper *the next day*. If it did not, we had to deal with an hysterical mother of the bride.

On the morning after her daughter's wedding, a distraught woman hurled herself through the door and collapsed into our visitor's chair. (As usual, all work immediately ceased in the Sports Department; they loved nothing better than a chance to witness women being silly.)

"Elva phoned me from White Sulphur Springs at the crack of dawn, just crying like a baby, the poor child. My heart ached for her, 'deed it did, it just broke right in two when I heard her poor sobbing little voice. I said, what happened, sugar? Are you sick? and she said,

Mama, the most horrible thing happened, it's just like a nightmare, I just can't believe it. Yesterday at the wedding I was so happy I didn't know what to do, but now I'm lying here wishing I were dead. Those are the very words she said to me," sobbed Mama.

Not a cigar in the Sports Department moved; to a man, they sat motionless, teeth clenched in big grins as they listened.

"Imagine how I felt, when my only daughter calls me from her honeymoon and says she wants to die! Let me tell you, my knees just gave way, 'deed they did. I said, sugar, tell your mama what happened, and she said, Mama, when I saw it I just couldn't believe my eyes. I just started cryin' like I never cried before. Mama, she said, have you ever just stared at something and told yourself it couldn't be true?"

By now there was no sound at all in the entire newsroom except the click of the wire service machines. If the bell had rung, no one would have paid any attention to it. Mama blew her nose and continued.

"She told me, Mama, I just woke up this morning so excited. I had to get it, I just had to, I couldn't wait any longer, so I got dressed."

That did it. . . . Cigars fell out of mouths, and somebody collapsed on his typewriter and hit the return key, which knocked over an entire tray of hot coffee.

"That poor child went down to the *ho*tel lobby at six o'clock in the morning to buy this newspaper so she could read her wedding write-up, and youall didn't put it in! Can youall imagine how that poor child felt when she realized it wasn't in?" Mama shrieked. We tried to keep a straight face, but the men didn't bother, and the hilarity that rocked the newsroom only made matters worse. She wept more loudly than ever and kept yelling: "How would youall feel if you didn't get *yours* in?"

For months thereafter we had to endure a daily exchange with members of the Sports Department, who tiptoed up behind us and whispered: "How do you feel when you realize it's not in? Hee-hee-hee."

The members of the Woman's Department all agreed that from a personal standpoint, we could not conceive of a woman who would get out of bed and leave a brand-new husband—or any man—to go and buy a newspaper at six o'clock in the morning. However, we understood very well why this bride and most of the others we handled would do it. The reason was painfully simple: If the wedding write-up did not appear in the paper the very next day, it meant that they were not *offi-*

*cially married* . There they were, on a honeymoon, in bed with a man, their virginity gone—and not a word in the paper about it.

When I returned to the South a few months ago, I found that much of the fervent heat has gone out of bridal reporting in most big-city dailies. The write-ups seldom contain *gemütlich* descriptions of "Alençon lace . . . Juliet caps . . . cathedral trains . . . chapel veils" nor the endless lists of bridesmaids, ushers, or wedding guests that we had to copy and check with such care. Gone, too, are the splashy 42-point italic headlines that we used for "prominent" brides; the woman's section is more democratic, and there is less difference between the placement, head size, and photo treatment of brides from different walks of life.

I seriously doubt if this means that Southerners are any less interested in walks of life. That would be anthropologically impossible, and besides, I also noticed that today's society reporters *still* cannot bring themselves to come out and say that a man is a farmer. The old way of putting it—"The bridegroom is engaged in farming"—continues to glare out from wedding write-ups.

What the changes do indicate, I think, is a reduction in the feverish passion for marriage that I remember from my newspaper days in the middle and late Sixties. But there are still many journalistic bastions of hymeneal fever in the South—usually in small-town newspapers with more space and fewer brides. These society pages still go into prolix ecstasies about "cascading organza panels softly gathered at the Empire waist," and they continue to record with maniacal thoroughness a complete profile of the flower girl, carefully noting that she is the bride's *third* cousin. Except for the typically Southern obsession with degrees of cousinship, such wedding write-ups can be found in weekly papers throughout America—even in taciturn New England. The reason has nothing to do with either the status of marriage or the inroads of Women's Liberation; it is simply that, given a big fish and a little pond, rambling fluff about *point de Venise* and the mother-of-the-bride's hat is *news*.

As for the larger daily newspapers, they are running devastatingly frank articles on the rape crisis, like every other newspaper in America.

Oh, for the good old days, when I was accused of being a Communist because I would not run a four-column photo of Master Rupert

Hohenzollern Finley in his velvet knee pants, under the headline:
RINGBEARER'S PILLOW USED FOR THREE GENERATIONS.

### DEB BALL LEADER CHOSEN

Miss Royal Stuart Montgomery, daughter of Mr. and
Mrs. Charles Stuart Montgomery IV, has been named leader
of the annual debutante cotillion.

Said Miss Montgomery: "I feel truly humble for the first
time in my life."

Debutanting is the South's way of hanging onto the old image of
the belle. There are debutantes everywhere in Dixie, and a profusion
of balls both large and small. This is another reason why Woman's
Department writers are so nervous; the word "balls" is always cropping
up in headlines, along with the expression "coming out." It is so easy to
write a headline like: LOCAL WOMEN WORK ON RICHMOND BALLS or:
GIRLS WILL COME OUT WITH SCHOOL FRIENDS. Somebody is always
coming out, and there are . . . well, as I said, there are all these *balls*.

The crème de la crème is, of course, Charleston's St. Cecilia Ball,
but there are plenty of lesser ones, and small towns like Shelby, North
Carolina, even have subdeb balls.

The position of deb ball leader is an honorary one, much like the
position Scarlett O'Hara assumed when she led the reel at the Atlanta
bazaar. The only difference being that Scarlett was auctioned off to the
highest bidder—a sensible way to do it but a very un-Southern way that
would have been unheard of had it not been for the war emergency.
If only the South would permit money to buy *anything*, the Woman's
Department would not have to cope with young women like Royal
Montgomery. The position of ball leader would have been undisputed
if cold cash alone had been the deciding factor. The winner would
have been a quiet, introspective heiress whose sole interest and intended profession was archaeology, an interest that her fifteen-million-
dollar trust fund permitted her to pursue.

All she wanted to do in this life was dig holes in what she re-
spectfully called Asia Minor. She was a lovely girl with a straight A average, she had been accepted by Radcliffe, and was the easiest deb to
interview that I ever met. She actually stayed put in the chair in which

she sat at the beginning of the interview. The phone didn't ring *once* the whole time, nor did her mother fall in the door with six shopping bags.

She would have made a nice, calm deb leader, but she never had a chance. However formidable her wealth, her blood was not up to snuff. On her mother's side, she was descended from Carpetbag aristocracy—and she had run afoul of one of those all-powerful little old ladies who stage-manage the Southern debutante scene.

Every good Southern socialite knows the debutante's catechism. She learned it at her mother's knee:

"Mommy, how does God make debutantes?"

"God doesn't make them. Little old ladies in towns all over the state plant seeds in the minds of the sponsoring committee."

"You mean little old ladies make debutantes?"

"Yes. Remember when you grow up to be a big girl, you must never let little old ladies know that you have sex or else you won't be able to come out."

"Can't debutantes have sex, Mommy?"

"Of course they can, darlin'! After all, we're Southerners. It's all right to do it, just don't let little old ladies know you do it."

"I see. Thank you, Mommy."

By the time a girl reaches her eighteenth birthday she knows, as does everyone else, who these little old ladies are. No one ever actually tells her, but she *knows*. They lurk behind their damask draperies, sherry glasses in hand, and keep an eye on all the young girls. Each year, they send in their recommendations to the exclusive club that sponsors the deb ball. If they do not approve of a girl, they issue what amounts to a lettre de cachet.

The archaeologist deb had enjoyed a nice, quiet introspective affair with a classics professor twice her age, and some old lady found out about it. The old lady had been gunning for her anyway, not only because of her Carpetbag blood but because she was a "bluestocking"—a female intellectual in a land of pert, scatterbrained charmers. The old lady decreed that the girl's enormous fortune meant nothing compared with the horrors of blood, brains, and sex scandals, and so refused to approve her as deb leader.

On the other hand, there was Royal Montgomery, who humped like a bunny all over the state, but whose blood was of the bluest. As the

Dear Old Thing explained on the way to the Richard Evelyn Byrd Flying Field, the South is made up of old blood and old money; old blood and new money; new blood and old money; new blood and new money; and that especially revered category, old blood and no money.

The Montgomerys had the oldest blood around and quite a bit of old money, but they were not rich enough to pay for all the things that everyone, especially Royal, considered her birthright. You can go pretty far in the South with a name like Royal Stuart Montgomery. Everyone thinks you have money, or assumes that you used to, and those who know better feel that you ought to. The result of this situation in Royal's case was that everybody identified with her—because not identifying with her would place their own real or imagined birthrights in question, if not in jeopardy. By a process of Southern sociological alchemy that no one could ever quite define but which everyone instinctively understood, Royal became a kind of local Anastasia who turned bankers and credit managers into White Russian émigrés. They were only too happy to lend the Montgomerys whatever they needed with Royal's birthright as collateral.

Royal's behavior was such that she was constantly being rewarded for *not* doing things. When she graduated without incident from a select private high school, she was rewarded with a trip to Europe and her very own American Express card. When she returned from abroad with trunks full of new clothes, she was rewarded with a Lincoln convertible for not also bringing back a diseased Italian husband. When she wrecked the convertible, she was rewarded, for not dying in the crash, with a swimming pool all her own. Her abortion bill ran neck-in-neck with her Montaldo's bill, and rumor had it that the reason she rode sidesaddle was because the hook over which she draped her right leg enabled her to achieve a most pleasant form of stimulation.

The little old ladies adored her because—

"Her family is so prominent!"

"She's descended on *both* sides from Signers!" (Of what? The Declaration of Independence, plus land grants, charters, and every kind of writ imaginable. The Stuarts and Montgomerys had spent three hundred years signing their names, and thanks to Royal's spending habits they were still at it.)

Every time the old ladies got together, they talked about Royal's blood. She was living proof of their intense conviction that "blood tells." The entire Montgomery family, Mama, Daddy, and Baby, looked like Plantagenets fresh from a glittering medieval court. Tall, slim, small-boned, with thick golden-blond hair of the type known as "leonine," they reeked of money that they did not really have. They were "collie-muzzle aristocracy"; everything about them was long, thin, delicate, and slightly quivering. Royal's nostrils flared a lot— particularly when she rode sidesaddle—and that was enough for the little old ladies. She could have had an abortion at the foot of the Confederate monument and they would not have cared.

The deb season kicks off with a round of parties that get bigger and bigger as the long hot summer wears on. Many parties have a "theme" and involve costumes, which is why the girls are photographed doing strange things and wearing clothes that no one would ever associate with a debutante. Someone gives a Moulin Rouge party and all the debs show up dressed as can-can girls and, of course, do the can-can to the questionable efforts of a rock combo playing "Orpheus in Hades." They never hear the society reporter when she repeatedly asks their names because they are all screaming: "Isn't this just the most fun?" and *"Je suis La Goulou!"* When she gets back to the office and tries to write a cutline for the photo, she must try to guess who is who from a line of bloomered bottoms while a member of the Sports Department hangs over her shoulder, chomping on a cigar and saying: "Hee-hee-hee."

Next comes the Casey Jones party, to which all the girls and their cotillion escorts-to-be, known in the South as "marshals," wear striped overalls, red neckerchiefs, and engineer hats.

Another clever cutline is called for. This time it is provided by the entire Sports Department, who chorus in unison: "Debs, won't you blow? Hee-hee-hee."

Then there is the inevitable marina party. When a member of the Sports Department is dropping cigar ashes on the sunburn you got on the docks, chasing around behind debs who were wearing eye patches, bearing live parrots, and forcing one another to walk the plank, there is a terrible temptation to follow the instructions of the Good Ole Boy at your shoulder and write: "Debs are frigging in the rigging, hee-hee-hee."

All of this is par for the course during every deb season, and the Woman's Department is used to it, but nothing could ever compare to the year of Miss Royal. Somehow, she got it into her gorgeous leonine head that just because she had had more affairs than any other girl in the state, she also had to have more parties. Her Praetorian Guard of little old ladies stood ready to honor her, for she was their victory; she represented the Old over the New, morality over decadence, and closed legs over open.

They fought like tigers to give parties for her, and they insisted upon the most flowery, compliment-loaded "pieces" that we—or more likely, *they*—could dream up. They wrote or dictated their "pieces" to us, and they could not call her enough of what they thought were flatering names. Other, more ordinary, debs were easy to handle. We had a standard way of writing up their parties, and any of us could have done it in our sleep. "Miss Nancy Doe was entertained at a tea at the home of Mrs. Vauxhall de Percy McFarlane III. In the receiving line were the debutante's mother. . . ."

Not so for Miss Royal. The old ladies wanted more, and since most of them still talked like the first edition of Roget's *Thesaurus*, they suggested copy that ran something like this:

"Miss Royal Stuart Montgomery, the saucy minx who has so deservedly been named debutante ball leader, filled all with pride as she received like a true belle of the Old South, winsome yet dignified, a lady to her fingertips. . . ."

One morning I arrived at work and found a colleague with her head on her desk. She looked up and croaked:

"Now they want us to call her *hoyden!*"

We all agreed that the word had tomboyish connotations and feared that somebody would charge that we had called Royal a Lesbian. Strictly speaking, it would not have been libelous because rumor had it that she was not all that fussy about her sex partners. She did not have proclivities, she had a vulva.

The parties that the old ladies gave Royal were nothing compared to the ones her family threw, for she was her mother's "ladybug" and her father's "bootsie." They managed to stay financially afloat long enough to give:

—the Royal Mile party, a Scottish history affair to which Royal invited all of the boys with whom she had canoodled and required them to wear kilts. The result was a crush that looked like a reenactment of the battle of Bannockburn. When the guests drove through town on their way to the Montgomery home, a traffic jam ensued; somebody asked a cop if the Black Watch Pipes and Drums were performing in town, and where could you get tickets?

—the Hunt party, which was held at the country club after a near-duel between Mr. Montgomery and the manager, who would not permit Royal to make her grand entrance into the banquet hall on a horse. A compromise was reached, and saddles were draped across the railing that surrounded the dance floor. Everybody had to dress for the hunt and sit on saddles instead of chairs. At the end of the evening, Royal got drunk and rode in anyway, wrecking the bandstand, the mirrors, and the drummer, who was kicked by Lord Bothwell, her skittish mount, The bill for the damage was three times the bill for the party. All the little old ladies said: "Thank heavens Royal wasn't hurt!"

"Special guests included the police," I wrote, but the Woman's Editor deleted it.

All the while such flagrant displays were taking place in honor of Miss Royal, we were also coping with that quintessentially Southern phenomenon, the *poor* debutante. She is the girl whose blood is excellent but whose financial resources are utterly and literally nil. Her family "had money once," as they say in Dixie—"once" meaning pre-1865. The poor debs have few parties, and those are usually modest unless they have relatives who managed to recoup the family fortune post-1865. Great tact is required of the society writer when she describes the functions of poor debs, but her problems pale beside those she encounters when the moneyed debs go on the inevitable economy kick.

Midway through the deb season, the fathers realize just how much everything is costing them, and all but the richest ones promptly raise the roof. They begin stalking through the house behind mother and deb, shouting: "You can't do this! I won't have it, I tell you, I won't! Cut it down immediately!" Southern women, trained to at least pretend concern for the male ego, must now conciliate Daddy, and so somewhere around the first of August they overreact and cut spending down to the bone.

This, more than anything else, finishes off the Woman's Department, which must go on describing parties as if they were still exercises in Babylonian spending even though they no longer are.

Filthy-rich debs do not destroy the Woman's Department. They

are easy to handle; they live in gorgeous mansions, have unlimited resources, buy the best, and hire the, not a, Lester Lanin band. That's
that. Covering their parties is simplicity itself because there are no tactful economy-minded improvisations to write around and yet avoid
writing *about*. Adjectives like "clever," "imaginative," and "original,"
which can blow up in a society writer's face since they hint at budgets,
are not necessary when one is writing about the truly rich. Nor are la-
bored adjectives like "elegant," "tasteful," and "imported"—redun-
dant by definition when one is describing the homes, clothes, and appointments of millionaires.

And so from the first of August until cotillion night, we had to figure out some way to describe the six thousand miles of crepe paper that
Mrs. Montgomery bought in a way that sounded classy. She covered
everything with crepe paper, including Royal herself, for the Greek
Myth party, but we could not allude to the fact that Royal's toga (which
she ripped off at the end of the evening in an imitation of Phryne on
trial) was not made of the finest handwoven linen.

By the time cotillion night rolled around, the members of the
Woman's Department, who had been drowning their sorrows in bourbon all summer, looked like potbellied camp followers who had been
through at least one war, starting with the Spanish-American. One of
my co-workers found her first gray hair and promptly had the hysterics
that she had heroically restrained since the beginning of June. My
cocktail dress would not fit, and I moaned, as Royal had been moaning
all summer, "I don't have a thing to wear!" None of us did; we wondered how much crepe paper Mrs. Montgomery had left, feeling that
she owed it to us, but her husband was in such a pet that she had actually arranged to return the unused portion to the store—this after the
five thousand dollars the Montgomerys had shelled out to repair the
country club.

We put together some navy-blue outfits with full skirts and slunk
through the crowds at the ball scene, writing our last stories of the season. On one of my rounds, I encountered a group of poor debs who
were trying mightily not to look as miserable as I felt. It was obvious
that they were not entirely convinced that blood was all and money was
nothing. Gowns from Stella's Smart Shoppe cannot stand up next to
gowns from Dior's Paris showrooms, and nobody knew it better than
the girls with blue but no green. As usual, I helped with zippers and

buttons, and as I bent down to fix one girl's sash, I saw that it had been very carefully darned. When I looked up, she thanked me with quiet dignity, but her discomfiture was just visible enough to make her iron will wrenchingly touching.

It was easy to tell the poor debs from the others with out even looking at their dresses. Gloves said it all—the rich ones wore white kid and the poor ones white cotton.

When the presentations began, the Woman's Department huddled together in exhaustion in the back of the auditorium, unable to believe that at last we were getting rid of Royal.

"It's over," we whispered to each other. "Imagine. It's actually over."

They came, the words we had been longing to hear:

"Miss Royal Stuart Montgomery!" the MC boomed. "Daughter of Mr. and Mrs. Charles Stuart Montgomery IV!"

Royal floated down the steps with all her natural Plantagenet grace, truly a breathtaking girl for all that she was a study in pathology. It was clear from the bursting pride on Mr. Montgomery's face that she was indeed his "bootsie," despite the sheaf of bills and citations that he had collected over the summer. She did not hold onto the railing as she descended the stairs. Her grace, her confidence, her carriage had the sure impact of a whiplash. Gasps went up from the assembled crowd, and one of them came from me. I realized that the old ladies were right, and so were their adjectives. She *was* saucy, pert, and winsome . . . and she was a belle.

There was a difference between Royal and the so-called swingers of today. There are plenty of sluts, tramps, and whores around now, but how many hoyden minxes? Many of the Seventies swingers merely fantasize what they would like to do; Royal went out and did it. She did everything that it is physically possible to do with one or more partners of both sexes, yet she did it so well, with a style and dash that are sadly missing today. She was a Restoration jade, an Amber come to life— and a lady to her fingertips despite everything.

What America needs are fewer swingers and more royal Southern hussies.

# 9

## "The Poor Thing, I Bet No Man Ever Looked at Her."

### or: Old and Young Maids

Thanks in large measure to Helen Gurley Brown, the American single woman has a more attractive and dashing image than ever before. Yet despite the advent of that Cosmo girl, Southerners are still talking about "old maids" and still saying, "The poor thing, I bet no man ever even looked at her."

Foremost among Southern old maids is, of course, the Poor Thing. Physically, she falls into two types; either her problems are congenital ("The poor thing, she's ugly as homemade sin") or she is simply a mess ("The poor thing, I'd just love to get my hands on her hair").

Psychologically, she falls into two additional subcategories, and here we have an exquisite testimony to Southern flakiness—the Poor Thing may not really be a Poor Thing at all. If she lived in some other part of the country, she would cast off her inferiority complex overnight, but as long as she lives in the South she will languish as one of two types, or maybe even both:

"The poor thing, she's so plain."

"The poor thing, she has no fire."

Thanks to the cult of Southern womanhood, a "plain" woman is one who is *not* riding down Main Street on a purple float with a papier-mâché crown on her head, waving frantically, sobbing with joy, and shrieking: "Hey, how y'all! 'Deed Ah'm just so happy Ah could die!"

127

In the feverishly romantic Southern brain, a woman with "fire" is Miss Royal Montgomery in a black riding habit who takes every fence effortlessly; a crop in her hand, a derringer in her bodice, and murder in her eye. Leaping off her sidesaddle, she *flounces* into the parlor, her spurs striking the lovely old hardwood floors with a fiery clink, and confronts the dissipated but handsome man by the fireplace, crying: "You're the last of the Sutherlands, Jason, and I swore I wouldn't let any of you live!" With that, she grabs her derringer, which is warm from her breasts and faintly redolent of lemon verbena, and empties it into Jason's stomach.

The woman who is constantly flouncing in and out of rooms in a furious temper, throwing things, and slamming doors is so dear to the Southern heart that it matters not at all that she is also hard on Southern nerves. She is part and parcel of the magnolia-drenched gospel, and Southerners do not want to relinquish her *or* her grand exits. To make matters worse, Vivien Leigh, Paulette Goddard, Bette Davis, and Susan Hayward have behaved this way so often on screen that what is romantically termed "high spirits" has become a Southern fixation.

Any girl who does not behave this way occasionally is in danger of becoming a Poor Thing.

The Flounce Plague, that corollary to the Pert Plague, can actually destroy a girl who is naturally quiet and shy. Being quiet and shy was all very well for Melanie Wilkes, who had a naturally kind heart, a sweet disposition, and a minimal sex drive. She also had old blood and old money, which opened social doors for her despite her muted personality. But the average Poor Thing is often forced into a Melaniehood for which she is not really suited by temperment—she decides that if she cannot be dazzling and popular, she can at least be "nice." Because the niceness she adopts does not spring from a truly unselfish heart, the Poor Thing often becomes warped and vicious from long years of slinking behind potted palms and helping with the refreshments.

A bona fide wallflower, she spends most of her life making herself useful. As soon as the dishes start to pile up, the Poor Thing will slink into the kitchen: "I'll just make myself useful and help with these." There, up to her elbows in soapy water, she quickly curdles in self-pity, resulting in a facial expression that inspires everyone to say: "The poor thing, she's not having a good time." Because the Southern unconscious mind still thinks that "having a good time" means leading a reel and causing a few duels in the course of an evening, the Poor Thing's secret fantasies of popularity are outlandishly unrealistic. She sinks further into despondency simply because she never causes a furor that leads to some man's death.

The vicious circle widens with each self-pitying tear that rolls down her cheek and splashes into the sinkful of gummy dishwater before her. Inevitably, because she is not really the Melanie she pretends to be, she becomes a victim of gut-gnawing resentment. Add to this the fact that the Poor Thing stays in kitchens and other places where old ladies on refreshment committees hang out, and you have a preordained situation: She becomes a fink. It is always the Poor Thing in a girls' dorm who gets in with the housemother and tells all she knows—who's drinking, who's screwing, and who left the starch on the bottom of the iron. From free-lance finking she graduates to the girls' honor council and the dormitory standards board, which brings her full circle because the old ladies then say: "The poor thing, none of the other girls like her."

Southern housemothers, notorious for their blind spots, never figure out why nobody likes the Poor Thing. They take other, more popular, girls aside and say: "The poor thing, why don't you invite her to the party?" This puts the popular girl on the spot; although she is "a heartbreaker," she's also supposed to be sweet. The popular girl then feels *guilty*, which forces her into Melaniehood, too. So she invites the Poor Thing to the party.

The Poor Thing comes to the party and spends the evening making herself useful by washing dishes—which gives her a perfect opportunity to peer into the backyard and note who's in the bushes, who's in the pickup truck, and who disappears into the woods and returns covered with grass stains and chigger bites on the backs of her thighs. Having a Poor Thing at a party is as bad as having the dean of women under the bed with a tape recorder.

The Poor Thing being living proof that the Southern romantic dream is not what it has been cracked up to be, she becomes the target of all those who resent having their dreams disproved—which is just about everyone, at one time or another. She depresses people by wearing quilted robes and scuffie-wuffies, a great deal of navy blue, and coats a size too big because she feels an overwhelming urge to hide.

Women resent her because she grays their magnolia-blossom reputation; men because they look at her and wonder: Is this what all the chivalry and gallantry are for?

Sex rears its head in her life, but it invariably results in some ungodly contretemps reminiscent of Joanne Woodward's schoolteacher in *Rachel, Rachel*. She is usually long overdue when she finally has her first experience. She hits age thirty or so and suddenly decides that her hymen is a disgraceful contraband that must be deep-sixed at all costs, so she hurls herself into a disjointed drive to Get Rid of It. By now she is not thinking clearly at all, so she will end up with a goon, a nut, or a sadist. If she had lost her virginity at a sensible age, she would have been able to spot such men. But she didn't—she knows *nothing* about men —so something hair-raising is bound to happen. She may find herself in a sleazy motel where a floating crap game is in progress and not realize that she is supposed to be the "entertainment" for everybody. The motel is, of course, raided, and the Poor Thing goes off to jail with the fellas.

Southern men still believe that homely women are good in bed, out of gratitude to a man who has been kind enough to bother with them. The Poor Thing need not lack lovers, but neither she nor they have a very good time. The self-sacrifice Poor Things feel honorbound to adopt prevents them adopting the creative selfishness that good bed sport demands.

It also makes life hell on everybody else, for there is nothing worse than a *mean* ole Melanie.

The Silly Old Maid, whose prototype is *Gone with the Wind*'s Aunt Pittypat, is still around. Today's version is, necessarily, not quite so innocent. Margaret Mitchell's Aunt Pittypat did have a hazy idea about where babies come from, but her sexual knowledge pretty much ended right there. Today's Silly Old Maid knows that there are homosexuals in our midst, but she can never remember that they are now called gay, so she persists in referring to her womanizing nephews as "gay young bachelors." When they hiss at her: "For Lordsake, Aunt Pitty, hush your mouth!" she becomes "hurt." Her little chin quivers and she pouts, just like her namesake.

Like Queen Victoria, she either does not know or will not admit that women can be homosexuals, too, so she rattles on about that nice roommate her niece Becky has acquired—ignoring the niece's parents, who plant frozen smiles on their faces as Aunt Pitty gets in deeper and deeper: "Isn't it a good thing that they don't have lots of boys around, the way so many girls who live together do?" When Becky's mother stops smiling and starts to cry, Pittypat is stunned. "Why, what did I say? Oh, Law, I'm sorry, truly I am, but what in the world. . . ."

Pitty is still terrified of living alone. Her bogeymen have not changed much, either. There are no more Yankee soldiers around, but there are still plenty of soldiers in the Army-base-dotted South. Her carpetbaggers are now hippie boys with canvas backpacks; she also dreads dope fiends, kidnappers, hijackers, and anybody on a motorcycle. Any and all of these are lumped together in her mind as rapists. Nowadays she can actually bring herself to speak the word—though here again a certain unvanquishable innocence intrudes to throw her off base and into a puzzled ambivalence that frays her peace of mind even more than the original fear of being raped.

Because she knows nothing of abnormal psychology, she is certain that no man would find a fat old lady desirable enough to rape. Yet it has happened, and she knows it. Why? she wonders. Why would a man rape *her*? It is not a question that she can ask anyone, and she would not be caught dead with the sort of reading matter that might explain it, so she goes to a store where nobody knows her and buys a copy of Gerold Frank's *The Boston Strangler*, which she can pass off as a good mystery story should anyone see it in her home. Of course she skips all the "bad" parts, which means that she finishes what little is left of the book in half an hour and is more bewildered than ever.

Dwelling as she does in such a state of confusion, she alternates between paranoid door-bolting and witless chance-taking. Always thinking eight things at once and talking about at least four of them, she traipses out of her apartment without locking *any* of the locks on her door because she just remembered that she forgot to turn off the ignition of her car. When she tries to reenter her building, she cannot get in: Thanks to her pleas, the landlord has just installed an outside lock, and she has forgotten her key. She rushes down the street in a "pet" and looks for some "nice young man" to ask him if he would be good enough to climb through her window and let her in.

I lived in an apartment house in Virginia surrounded by a whole gang of Silly Old Maids, all of whom were frozen in terror over what

Southern women call "a great big black nigra." This particular great big black nigra was a door-to-door salesman. When I returned home one evening, Silly Old Maid #1 met me in the lobby all a-flutter.

"There was a great big black nigra roamin' around here today!"

I went out to the grocery store, where I found a neighbor, Silly Old Maid #2.

"Did you hear that there was a great big black nigra *lurkin'* in our buildin'?"

When I got back from the store, I heard a tap-tap-tapping on my door. I opened it, and there was Silly Old Maid #3, carrying a teargas canister.

"I brought you a teargas fountain pen, honey, 'cause there's a great big black nigra *lyin' in wait* for white women."

The next day he came to my door. I opened it and looked down, and sure enough, there was the great big black nigra in all his glory—a café au lait version of Truman Capote, obviously handpicked by his white sales director so that he would not frighten all the Silly Old Maids who Southern sales directors hope will buy their products.

Nineteenth-century Silly Old Maids were supported by male relatives, but today's Pittypat cannot throw herself on Brother Dear anymore. She has to work somewhere, file a 1040, and manage to remember all the numbers that fill our lives with so much unapplied mathematics. Naturally she gets them all mixed up, and her particular bête noire is the area code. The Dear Old Thing is so used to throwing herself completely on the mercy of others that she will always go through the operator rather than dial direct; the Silly Old Maid, who never had the late Mr. Tazewell to save her from herself, makes disastrous stabs at self-sufficiency. Finding herself connected with Eugene, Oregon, or Boise, Idaho, she screams: "Oh, Law!" to something less than the edification of sturdily independent Westerners, who have not grown up with women who go around screaming: "Oh, Law!"

Neither can Aunt Pittypat remember that Richmond is 703 and Charlotte is 704, though this usually works out quite nicely, thanks to the Southern Wrong Number Syndrome: If one talkative Southerner dials a wrong number and gets another talkative Southerner, it may well be the start of a friendship. When I lived in Raleigh, I got a wrong number from a Silly Old Maid in Charleston, who after ascertaining that I was not her party, began to list all the people in Raleigh she knew. It just so happened that I knew one of them, too, and we had old home week for twenty minutes. As we hung up, we both said simultaneously: "It certainly has been nice talkin' to you. You come see me, you hear?"

Like the original swooning Aunt Pittypat, today's version is as physically robust as an ox. Northern readers of *Gone with the Wind* are often perplexed because Aunt Pittypat never seems any the worse for wear even though she is already sixty at the beginning of the story and lives through a war-torn era. She suffers fire and deprivation, and she is a refugee for a good part of the time, yet she remains fat throughout the entire saga, even during Reconstruction when no one has enough to eat. At the end of the book, she is seventy-two and still going strong despite the fact that her rattled approach to daily living must have taken an inordinate amount of energy.

The Silly Old Maid is robust because she is so self-indulgent. Having no man to pamper you in the South makes a woman feel cheated, so to atone for Fate's cruelty, the Silly Old Maid is unfailingly kind to herself. Somehow, she always manages to get the best piece of steak or the breast of the chicken; when she eats out, she can always convince the waitress to garnish her sandwich with a few extra pickles and potato chips. At home, she gorges herself—and thrives on—all the things that fat old ladies shouldn't eat.

Today's Pittypat can often be found in state government offices, where tenure alone makes her the supervisor of the file room. The girls who work for her pay absolutely no attention to her—which is just as well, since *they* know what they're doing. Her disjointed instructions would wreck the entire filing system if anyone followed them, so her girls just say: "Yes, ma'am," and continue doing whatever it is that Aunt Pittypat just remembered she forgot to tell them to stop doing.

After work, Aunt Pittypat can be found putting herself on the public library's reserve list for the newest Taylor Caldwell novel, *Digestion of God's Iron.*

The carnage of the Civil War created an old maid designated by that Elizabethan pronouncement: "Her heart's in the grave." The South still contains plenty of bereaved single women who lost men to World War II, the Korean conflict, and the Vietnam adventure, but the entombed female heart is "out" now. Women no longer subscribe to such male-invented proofs of love as lifelong mourning. Furthermore, all of the people who could bring themselves to utter empurpled metaphors like "Her heart's in the grave" with a straight face are dead now. (The last time I heard it was from Granny.)

But customs die hard in the South, and Southerners still find it necessary to excuse or rationalize spinsterhood. They have therefore developed a modernized version of Her Heart's in the Grave, known as: "She never got over it."

Got over what? Well, we don't really know because no one ever offers a complete explanation, just vague allusions to "the wreck," "the trial," or "that awful night when . . ."

Recently I arrived somewhat early for a dinner party to which a She Never Got Over It old maid had also been invited. I had never met her, but before she arrived our hostess took me aside and whispered frantically: "Don't say anything about boats or water, you hear? Remember, *no* boats and *no* water."

In this uncertain world of ours, it's nice to know that you can always depend upon Southerners.

The Ready, Willing, and Frantic old maid appeared briefly in *Gone with the Wind* in the person of Honey Wilkes, Ashley's younger sister, who had "a nervously obvious desire to be attractive to every man in sight."

The girl with this problem used to be called boy-crazy. She is now called cock-crazy. The moment she comes into the presence of anything male she goes to pieces, because she is the ultimate victim of the South's commandment: *Thou shalt flirt*. Being "popular with boys" is the watchword of her whole life: She is the daughter of a woman who was never a belle herself, who tries to relive the past through her daughter. Making Mama proud of her is overwhelmingly important to the Frantic Old Maid; terrified that her flirting will not work, aware of Mama sitting over in the corner watching her, she panics and flirts harder . . . and harder . . . and harder. Her smile becomes more and more fixed, her eyes glassier, her giggle higher-pitched, the tilt of her head saucier and saucier. Afraid to finish a sentence for fear that a man will lose interest by the time she's done, she interrupts herself perpetually, forgets all about what she started to say, and rushes on to the next sentence.

When she invariably notices that trapped look of despair come over the faces of the men around her, her behavior becomes truly desperate. If any man says anything at all, she collapses in mirth against him so that he is forced to hold her up. While she is hurling herself around like a human missile, she keeps a rolling weather eye out to see how many other men are present that she has not gotten to yet. As she snuggles hysterically into one man's shoulder, screaming in his ear that she's never heard anything so funny in all her *life*, she is busy peering past his head to see who those four men are over by the fireplace.

Her performance at wedding receptions is especially frenzied, because the hothouse atmosphere of some other girl's love-honor-and-cherish triumph throws her into a state of terror and hopelessness.

Though our blunter age calls her cock-crazy, she really is not. "Boy-crazy" actually suited her much better, for she is terrified of real sex. She has been so thoroughly trained to go after the icing that she loses interest in the cake; she is also afraid that if she "goes all the way" with a "boy," he will lose interest in *her*. She would rather be "popular" than bedded because, in her mind, the two are mutually exclusive.

Sex is simply not her métier. There is something too serious about intercourse; you can't giggle or flirt, and you can't throw yourself into a man's arms because you are already in them. All of which helps explain why this kind of old maid is usually a virgin, which is just as well. She gets so worked up at the mere sight of a man that sex would probably kill her. Her heart would give out, or she would have a convulsion and swallow her tongue.

As time passes, she tries to hang onto her youth by becoming another kind of old maid known as Little Eva. These women, fading from the scene nowadays, nonetheless can still be found—wearing, in their fifties: blond curls in bouncy little coils, hair ribbons, charm bracelets, anklets, and even ballerina slippers. They lie about their age and swear "on a stack of Bibles" that they have absolutely no memory of Pearl Harbor because: "I was just a gleam in my daddy's eye."

By the time she gets to be a Little Eva, the boy-crazy old maid has forgotten her former desperation and now no longer even thinks about getting married. Marriage, after all, is for adults, and she has come to enjoy making mud pies on the playgrounds of her mind.

Little Eva is more fun than a barrel of monkeys, especially in an office. She likes to play games, such as coming up behind people, putting her hands over their eyes, and saying: "Guess who!" She loves to hide something and ask everybody to: "Guess where it is?" As luck would have it, she has a curious tendency to be in charge of either supplies or petty cash, so that when a man requisitions something, she can hold out both fists and offer him a choice.

I once worked in a New Orleans office with a woman of fifty-two who spent her lunch hour playing hopscotch on the multicolored tiles in the corridor. One afternoon, she challenged me to a race to the front door: "Do you remember how to skip? I bet you can't skip as fast as I can. Come on now, on your mark, get set, ready, GO!" Little Evas get their feelings hurt very easily, so I skipped.

The Hoot 'n' Holler old maid is perhaps one of the South's worst casualties. She spends half her life driving back and forth to coin-operated ice machines. She parties constantly—and always pays the bills. Someone is always "coming over," and she has a cat that has been stepped on so many times that he no longer notices it.

This old maid is good ole Lolly, who has a heart of gold. She is so busy befriending people that she never has time to make friends or love with any *one* of them. She has subscribed wholeheartedly to the South's ideal of the self-sacrificing female who "goes out of her way" and "is more than happy" to do anything under the sun for people who never do anything for her. She sees herself as Scarlett's mother, Ellen O'Hara, who could not rest while there was a good deed to be done, sick to be nursed, or hungry to be fed. Of course, Ellen O'Hara had a very rich husband and was also the mistress of a great house— undoubtedly cheering, no matter how many nights she went without sleep in the service of others.

Lolly, on the other hand, has nothing but a Southern myth. The sick she nurses and the hungry she feeds are not her devoted slaves; they are the down-and-outers, the misfits, the losers. Tormented homosexuals bend her ear all night long without once thinking that perhaps she has sexual problems, too—or at the very least, that she has to get up and go to work in the morning.

Everyone takes advantage of good old Lolly, including her poor ole mother who lives with her. Ole Miz Ramsey, the *soundest* of sleepers (for excellent reasons), is wonderfully incurious about all the goings-on in the house and never says anything about it except, maybe: "Honey, who was that?" when ten men show up at midnight with a keg of beer.

Hospitality is sure to be the death of good old Lolly, yet she will not relinquish this Southern ideal either, even if her friends cause her to be evicted or arrested. Her welcome mat is always out: "Just come right over, it's no trouble at all, make yourself right at home." Just fall through the door at any hour of the day or night, and stay as long as you want.

Someone is always crashed down on her well-sprung couch, and ole Miz Ramsey sometimes has her heavy slumber disturbed when Lolly heaves her over toward the wall in order to make room for herself.

"Move over, Mama, I got to sleep with you. I just gave my bed away."

"Who'd you give it to, honey?"

"Bo Garrett. They repossessed all his furniture, and he's got nothin' to sleep on."

Lolly is often a virgin because she is an old-fashioned "good girl," but she performs every other wifely duty for her many strays. She can be found standing over a hot stove or a hot ironing board as she indulges in her own version of promiscuity. She runs a free cafeteria and a free laundry service, and while men may marry a girl who has slept with everybody, they do not marry girls who wash and iron other men's underwear.

The Lollys who are not virgins do not really enjoy sex in a sensual way. To them it is simply a more intimate version of their free-wheeling, catchall maternal instinct. They do it "for him," never for themselves, and when For Him gets married to someone else, Lolly will spend her last nickel on a lovely wedding present. If they need a car for the honeymoon, they can take hers.

On a scale of Southern belles, That Child is the Southern ball. She is permitted to be as masculine as she wishes, and no one will criticize her. Because of this carte blanche, she is the only Southern old maid who survives life with nary a scratch on her psyche.

She is perpetually going off in a cloud of dust and a thunder of hooves as her sweet, fluttery mother shakes her head and laughs indulgently: "I declare, I just don't know what I'm goin' to do with that child."

Whatever her age, she is always referred to by this diminutive. When I covered the Raleigh horse show, I met a That Child of forty-four and her seventy-year-old mother who informed me: "I declare, I just can't get that child off a horse no matter what I do." Apparently, she had long since given up on the dress.

That Child is bluff and hearty if she is over thirty; brave and plucky if she is younger. She takes pleasure in being a courageous and sea-soned victim of all the awful things that horses can do to humans: She has been stepped on, chewed on, kicked in the stomach, scraped off against fences, and thrown like a rag doll into stagnant ponds. What she really enjoys, however, is That Child's foremost status symbol: get-ting her foot caught in the stirrup as she falls from the saddle and being dragged fifty yards or so through dust, gravel, mud, and manure. Such a contretemps always leads to an argument with Mama, who wails: "I just can't get that child to see a doctor no matter what I say!" By the time this argument ends and That Child is carried bodily to the emer-gency room, her broken ankle ("Aw, it's just a scratch") has swollen so badly that the doctor has to cut the boot to get it off.

"Aw, my new boots!"

Like many mannish women, That Child is very easy to get along with. She puts everyone at ease and poses no threats, not even to the flakiest Southern outpatient. Men like her because she is such a relief from the belles, self-rejuvenating virgins, pert plaguers, and town nymphos. They do not have to flirt with her, compliment her, wait on her hand and foot, or go through arch guessing games about what per-fume she is wearing. (It's always manure.)

Women like her because she is no competition in the popularity stakes or any of the other crypto-mating games that the South plays full-tilt. Unlike the Poor Thing, who *cares* that men don't like her, That Child could not care less. Her sole interest is horses, and her free-dom from sexual-image agonies wins her a great deal of respect. Pos-sessing her own kind of dignity, she is perhaps the most invulnerable Southerner of all. She deflects Southern cattiness and disarms all but the most determined female mysoginists simply by being herself.

That Child has an additional cachet that wins her much admir-ation in a region famed for its decorative females. She can *do* something, and she does it magnificently well. She is a really superb equestrienne, which earns her the admiration of all Southerners because riding well is so inarguably aristocratic.

Her sex life, if she has any, is something of a mystery because she keeps it to herself in a land where women are constantly on the telephone swapping sex stories. What ecstasy she experiences while astride her horse is never known; she holds the whole subject of horse-womanship so sacred that she would never besmirch it with such a discussion.

This is her only area of sexual modesty. Thanks to the earthiness that surrounds horsiness, That Child is refreshingly matter-of-fact about sex. She is always talking about mating, sires, dams, which of her mares is in season, and what she plans to do about it. With a crowd of male stable employees she casually observes a hell-for-leather horse mating and discusses the finer points of what is taking place with an utter lack of shyness. She thinks nothing of lifting a mare's tail, studying the condition of the vulva, and calling over to one of her Good Ole Boy pals for a consultation about Flicka's vaginal discharge.

Her attitude toward sex is actually torpid, which is just what the jangly Southern atmosphere needs.

The unmarried Southern woman does not have any Old-Maid-Power, and she has never had any.

The New England old maid is a product of America's cradle of nonconformity. Her region's limitless devotion to rugged individualism long ago resulted in a contrary streak that had no object other than a desire to be different. Miss Prudence Saltmarsh could rasp: "Get married? Any fool can get married. Believe I'll stay single," and win the admiration of every other Yankee square peg. When she began collecting cats and performing odd rituals in her tower room, her fellow Yankees fondly observed: "We Vermonters do what we damn well please." Miss Prudence thus becomes a sterling example of the best of her breed and everyone is very proud of her.

The Irish old maid has much old-maid-power thanks to the status that Catholicism bestows on virginity. It does not matter what she looks like; the uglier she is, the more she is respected—and feared—because if she is truly hideous, she will be credited with hex power in addition to old-maid-power. She thus becomes "Nora the Witch," and her fellow villagers walk a wide path around her, crossing themselves as she goes by. This is status indeed.

The Southern old maid has none of these comforts. She cannot pull a Prudence Saltmarsh because the South does not admire square pegs, particularly female ones. Nor can she follow in the footsteps of Nora the Witch; the Protestant South reserves no special niches for virgins, and while she is required to cast spells, she must do it with feminine allure. There is no room in Dixie for the humpbacked female tinker.

The Southern woman who does not marry is like the Jewish woman who does not marry. The late Miss Sheila Levine who is dead and living in New York would be surprised to know how much she has in common with the late Miss Betty Lee Winfield, who died on the vine in Jessup, Georgia, where she still resides.

# 10

## "He's a Little Funny, but He's Nice."

### or: The Gay Confederation

Homosexual men tend either to leave the South or to move to New Orleans or Atlanta, which is why straight men in smaller towns are always bragging: "We don't have no queers 'round cheer."

The obvious problems that confront the Southern homosexual are conformity and masculinity hangups. A lesser problem but a very important one is Southern liquor laws, which virtually preclude the existence of gay bars. It is still impossible to get liquor-by-the-drink in most of the South. Gay men loathe beer because it is a symbol of the superstraight workingman who has traditionally hated them; they want a martini (straight up), a pink lady, or a grasshopper, but in a region of Baptists and briarhoppers these libations do not officially exist.

The homosexuals who do not emigrate are among the most colorful Southerners of all, and paradoxically, they are also the high-profile variety.

Every obscure hamlet has a homosexual that nobody could miss; a fin de siècle aberration complete with ascot, lisp, falsetto, and flapping wrist. This is Town Fairy. Nobody minds him, and he is no threat to even the worst queer-hater. The reason he isn't is that Southerners believe in heredity, not environment, and Town Fairy is universally considered to be nobody's fault: the Lord did it. Town Fairy's problems are blamed on the fact that he was—are you ready for this?

A change-of-life baby.

This is perhaps the South's neatest sleight of mind, one that cheers both men and women. It strikes a blow of revenge against the all-powerful womb and at the same time credits that infernal organ with even more power—Town Fairy is such that only a magic uterus could produce him.

He is one of the happiest people in the South because there is absolutely no question in anyone's mind about what sex he really is or what he likes to do in bed. He is immune to anxiety and self-doubt, and he gets all the sex he wants—the passive kind—from rednecks and sturdy young bucks in overalls who *do* have anxieties and have to act them out from time to time. He never has to take trips to big cities where there are gay bars he can visit (they would probably ask him to leave anyway), and he never has to worry about his parents' being able to hold up their heads because they were already forty-nine and fifty-six when he was born and their heads have not moved at all for the past ten years.

The women of the town serve as Town Fairy's private bodyguard. Southern women usually adore gay men, who offer a relief from the Hotspur element in Southern heterosexual males. Women also can identify with Town Fairy, in a way, because he behaves like the classic belle every Southern woman wants to be. A straight man who makes a contemptuous allusion to Town Fairy will quickly be told by his wife: "Now don't you bad-mouth him, he's *so* nice even if he is a little funny."

Town Fairy's greatest allies are the little old ladies in the garden club—he adores flowers and can talk about the finer points of horticulture for hours on end. Many such old ladies have lived for years with husbands who are bored by stems and stamens and communicate in grunts, so they overflow with gratitude every time they lay eyes on Town Fairy because he is the only male they know who actually talks to them. Some of these old ladies are sure to be town doyennes with some say-so and power, and Town Fairy's friendship with them does not go unnoticed. It provides him with additional protection.

He reaps another advantage: the old ladies' determined ignorance of the seamier facts of life. Even the most innocent Dear Old Thing knows what Town Fairy is and what he does, but the blue-rinse set simply refuses to think about it. Their blind spots are so calcified that eventually they actually forget that Town Fairy is Town Fairy. They even stop talking about his change-of-life-baby status, until finally, in the serene confines of their minds, he is simply "an only child." Which, of course, explains why he's "a little funny."

Town Fairy, who lives all by himself in a "lovely old house," keeps the roses "just the way poor Ethel would have wanted," say the members of the Calvert Street Garden Club. They are constantly running over to swap cross-fertilizing stories with him, and he addresses their meetings regularly.

God help any man who ever lays a hand on Town Fairy in anger. The ladies of the garden club would take up their pruning shears and call a charge.

Uncle Cary is the aesthete who has taught classics for so long at the little college around the corner that he speaks Alabamese with a Latin accent. Everybody knows he's a brilliant scholar, so there *has* to be something wrong with him. He is protected by his silver-haired-orator appearance and demeanor, which remind Southerners of great statesmen—i.e., those sword-rattling human metaphors who dragged the South into the Civil War. Uncle Cary, who knows good protective coloration when he sees it, heightens this effect by adding a string tie to his ensemble.

He also takes advantage of the difference in the Southern mind between Northern intellectuals and Southern intellectuals. The former are bad 'uns who speak sociology; the latter are good 'uns who speak Latin and Greek exactly as they were spoken three thousand years ago. He takes care to remind the people around him of the heritage of cultured refinement with which the South cowed the Yankees in the 1850's, so he comes off as something of a nineteenth-century patriot— a credit to his race, one might say, except of course no one ever does.

If his apartment contains replicas of classical statues, and if those statues happen to be of naked men, no one minds because he does teach classics, after all. Whenever he appears in anything flowing . . . well, so did the Romans. Uncle Cary can therefore own Japanese kimonos, cloaks, and capes, and no one will point to him and say: "Aw, looka that Goddamn Communist."

Uncle Cary loves "nice things," so he is not particularly anxious to receive visits from his nieces and nephews. Nonetheless, he welcomes the entire family with open arms on major holidays because all of them, including Uncle Cary, are engaged in a silent conspiracy to make everything look "all right." Having a homosexual in the family has the paradoxical effect of making Southerners stick together. If they cut Uncle Cary off, people would know that something was wrong, so his family hurls itself on Uncle Cary and lionizes him.

In addition to saving face, they have other reasons for visiting him. They want to check to see (a) if he's still queer, and (b) if it's starting to "show." Here we have a sterling example of Southern contradiction: The family expects, at one and the same time, to find that Uncle Cary (a) has a lady friend at last, and (b) that something dreadfully Dorian Grayish is happening to him. Perhaps the statue of Michelangelo's "David," which Uncle Cary tactfully hides in the closet for the sake of the children, is starting to shrivel. Perhaps Uncle Cary himself is starting to shrivel or, at the very least, is looking more like Somerset Maugham than he did last Christmas.

The most memorable Uncle Cary I ever knew was a silver-haired gentleman I met in a vet's waiting room. His cat, Octavia, had escaped and "gotten herself" pregnant. She was troubled with a vaginal discharge, so Uncle Cary had to take her to the vet and utter the word "vagina" for what was undoubtedly the first time in his life.

Latin professors do things differently. As the vet told me later, Uncle Cary pointed to Octavia's troubled area and announced, complete with a hard "g": "Her *wageena* is inflamed."

Poor Willis has had homosexual experiences, but he is now neither gay nor straight. The only thing he fingers is the organ at church, because by the time his mother finished with him he was able to identify with nothing but a diminished seventh.

All church organists are not Poor Willises, and all Poor Willises are not church organists, but somewhere along the line these twains do seem to have a way of meeting. Poor Willis's respectability is unquestioned by the townspeople because he never does anything about which they can talk. He may occasionally ejaculate while playing "Onward, Christian Soldiers," but no evidence is ever found because he was taught to clean up after himself years before and he has never forgotten one single thing that Mama ever told him.

The chief characteristic of a Poor Willis is simple bad luck. It is his bad luck, for example, to have had one of those rare Southern good housekeepers for a mother. If he ever summoned the courage to go to bed with a woman, he would give her a towel because towels have always played a vital part in his existence. Mama adored towels and was always handing them out to all members of the male sex with orders to "Clean up!" When Poor Willis was twelve and doing what all twelve-year-old boys do, he was careful to keep a towel in his bed; instead of finding incriminating sheets, Mama found incriminating towels. When she demanded to know what the towel was for, Poor Willis got powerfully confused. Mama wanted him to use towels, yet here she was, furious because he had done just what he was told. He got so nervous about forgetting to hide his towels from her that eventually he no longer remembered the reason for their use.

Poor Willis thereafter became extremely quiet and withdrawn, which worried his father because he was afraid his boy might grow up to be "funny." To ward off this fate, he sent Poor Willis to a military school.

Once he was launched on the road to manhood, there was no stopping the inexorable course of human events. Poor Willis, small and girlish, was sodomized by the entire drum and bugle corps and quickly became, against his wishes, the regimental wife.

To confuse his sexual development even more, he was assigned the duty of cleaning out the cannon after it was shot off every Sunday. To do this he had to stand beside it while it exploded, and then step smartly up to the barrel and swipe it out with a cloth-wrapped broom handle. Thanks to these deafening fanfaronades and the gamy atmosphere of barracks life, Poor Willis developed a fart fetish. Farting excited him, but he got it into his head that only men emitted these bodily ruffles and flourishes. He did not want to be a homosexual, but he could not get excited over women because he had never heard one make such a sound and was positive that they did not do it.

He figured that if he could hear a woman do it just once, his sexual problems would be over and he could live a normal life. He was too naive to go to a prostitute and ask her to pass gas for him, so he sought out the only woman friend he had ever had, a Hoot 'n' Holler old maid of twenty-five (official Southern old-maid cutoff age) named Lolly.

He told her his problem.

"Why, Willis honey, you're just funnin' with me! You mean to tell me that you don't know that women— I don't believe it!"

"I swear, Lolly, it's the honest truth."

"But honey, didn't you ever hear your mama do it?"

"Oh, my Lord! Mama wouldn't, she just wouldn't!"

"Willis darlin', I want to help you, I'm more than happy to do anything I can."

"You're so good, Lolly, you've got a heart of gold. I don't know what I'd do without you for a friend."

"Oh, Willis, you know good and well I'd go out of my way to do anything I could for you. Now listen. You just listen to this."

Willis listened; Willis beamed.

"Oh, Lolly!"

"Didn't I tell you? Now how do you feel?"

"I knew it had to be true, but I just couldn't make myself believe— Oh, Lolly!"

"See? I'm goin' to get you over your troubles if it's the last thing I do. Are you gettin' hard?"

"Well, I'm a tad excited. Maybe if . . . would you mind if I touched myself?"

"You go right ahead and do anything you want, you just make yourself right at home. Now you listen, here it co— Oh! Oh, Law! OH, NO!"

"Oh, Lolly, it's not your fault, it's mine."

"No, it isn't, now don't you blame yourself. You just stay sittin' while I go upstairs and take a shower and change my clothes."

That was the end of Poor Willis's attempt at heterosexuality. He was so traumatized by Lolly's accident that he wanted nothing more to do with either men or women sexually. He went back home and played the organ at church.

Gonad Manqué tends to write novels, either published or unpublished. His mother, who is his major problem, is usually in them.

She and Sonny go everywhere together, just like Violet and Sebastian Venable in *Suddenly, Last Summer*. Fusty, eccentric, and resembling a moneyed Wasp Gypsy, she wears twenty-five scarves at once and always trails filmy bits of chiffon. She takes care to "red up" so that she and Sonny will look as much like a couple as possible. She has a heavy hand with the rouge and shows off her ravaged cleavage in low-cut dresses. Her look is designer-original funkiness, and she reeks of expensive perfume, always one of those morbidly voluptuous scents that, like Salomé, will not give up until something awful happens. Guerlain's Mitsouko leads the list.

There is something fetid about her, like a rain forest in rot. She seems to be a woman designed by Providence to be a tart, but because she inherited money the divine plan was thwarted. She is so Southern Gothic that you expect her to fade into a flashback before your very eyes, which is probably why Sonny became a novelist. In his books, he uses her quite often, hush-hush-sweet-Charlotte-style, to purge himself of his hatred of her.

In *his* flashbacks, she is an eleven-year-old girl who ran off from her grandfather's plantation and went to the carnival. This, Sonny tells us, was the turning point in her life, for she left the plantation as a happy, carefree child and returned in a state of trauma after being buggered by Hector the Strong Man on the merry-go-round (something Gonad Manqué wishes would happen to him).

Like all his flashbacks, this one attempts to answer that Gonad Manqué question: "What terrible thing happened to make her the way she is today?" As the calliope music mounts to a crescendo, the flashback fades back into the present and we find ourselves once more in the presence of this crumbling pile of human female masonry. We stare at her with new eyes, realizing that we are seeing Biloxi's own Miss Havisham, for whom time stopped on that memorable day, the last happy day of her life, when something happened that she was destined never to forget, something that left such an impression on her that she could not get Hector the Strong Man out of her mind. For the last fifty years she has been haunted and obsessed by what he did to her on the merry-go-round, and it is because of this irradicable memory that she has degenerated into a Paris-original thrift-shop houri.

She loved it, and she hasn't had a good buggering since.

Sonny has never had one, which is why he writes the kind of novels he writes. He identifies with Mama the minute he comes near a typewriter. He has rejected the Southern Hotspur version of masculinity, but he hasn't turned queer either, so the result is creepy eroticism on every page. Everything quickly gets impossibly sensitive, aesthetic, ethereal, and opaquely lovely, yet there is a Grand Guignol thread running through it all that results in constant ominous tension, as though something dreadfully beautiful is going to happen at any moment—i.e., the author is going to turn queer.

Reading a Gonad Manqué novel is like listening to "Clair de Lune" played on the bagpipes. Just as the Welsh novelist feels compelled to "lilt," Gonad Manqué feels compelled to *aesthetick*. Gauzy descriptions abound, and everyone has so much insight that they're all half mad. A dying butterfly on the lawn or a fly feasting on cow manure can hurl all the characters into a Southern version of the Proustean agony, where real meanings sell for five cents on the dollar.

The protagonist is a sickly male child who Grows to Maturity, thanks to the events of a traumatic summer. It's always summer in these books, thanks to Gonad Manqué's favorite wishful thinking equation: heat=sweat=blacks=sex=me. The little hero has always been too fragile to play ball with the other boys, so he has developed Sensitivity, which he exercises in his Secret Place, an area of the woods where he goes to be alone.

However, he finds that he is not alone there during the traumatic summer because suddenly his asylum is invaded by inhabitants from the outside world. He starts seeing all sorts of things guaranteed to nudge him into delayed adulthood—copulating couples, fellatio, weeping strangers, sodomy, a black named Raoul staring at a dead fish, fellatio, the town's eighty-year-old doyenne burying a jewelry box, sodomy, more weeping strangers busily castrating themselves, fellatio, a crushed flamingo, and of course, the town idiot busily masturbating.

None of these incidents is ever related to any central event, nor to each other. They are allegories whose sole purpose is to make the little hero's testicles descend. Being a Southern lad who hangs out in woods, he has seen such things before, but now he really sees them because he is starting to become Aware. He is Growing Up.

The climax of his growing awareness comes when he finds a severed ear in his Secret Place, which he promptly puts in the old Bull Durham sack in which he carries the mementos of childhood, like dead butterflies, stuffed insects, and the pennies that closed his grandfather's eyes.

At the end of the novel we find that the severed ear belonged to Raoul, who was lynched for raping a white mill girl named Linthead Lil. This makes the little hero realize at long last that no man is an island and that we are all links in the chain of a common humanity that is sometimes cruel but nonetheless human for all that. Armed with this new and wonderful if vaguely articulated knowledge, and still toting around the now-rotten ear, he goes once more to his Secret Place where he runs into none other than Linthead Lil herself, famed for the carefree complaisance that her IQ of 75 permits her to enjoy.

Lil is Miss Mighty Thighs, that imbecilic earth goddess so favored by the Gonad Manqué novelist because he so loathes women. When the little hero sees her breasts "spill" out of her dress, his "manhood rises." As her mighty thighs engulf him and he "sinks his member into her hot, throbbing secret place"—which is now a touchstone of potency because Raoul was in it—he thinks to himself: "They won't call me Deltaville sissy balls anymore because I'm a man now!"

A Gonad Manqué novel can be spotted instantly by its title—usually something like *The Gossamer Dulcimer*. Also popular are "River of" titles, like *River of Unseen Echoes*. Then there are the "Home in" titles, like *Home in Loneliness*. And, of course, the "Time Is" titles, such as *Time Is a Lost Flute*, though you have to look high and low to find a flute anywhere in the book.

The jacket copy goes: "Caldwell McCready loved the woods. It was his refuge from the adult world that he did not want to enter, the place where he could dream his childhood dreams undisturbed. But things began to happen that summer that thrust Caldwell into the painful world that he dreaded. . . ."

The dedication page is cloaked in mystery because the novel is usually dedicated to Gonad Manqué's secret male love of many years, who, unfortunately, never knew that Gonad Manqué had a lech for him (Gonad Manqué never fully knew it himself):

"To L. H. DeP., who understands," reads the dedication, which is followed by an interminable quotation in classical Greek that nobody understands.

On the title page you will find something that has absolutely nothing to do with anything in—or out of—the book:

Forsooth, good Lord Pluckley, the question's naught but sworn ere birds do send the stickie nectar of mead to trickle down the gullet of Exeter's postillion by the morrow.
   —James Hamilton-Crickie,
   Fourth Viscount of Fenwick Manor
   From *My Gleanings*

An ideal title for Gonad Manqué is one that he is far too sensitive and aesthetic to use:
*My Hip Pocket Smells Like Rotten Ears*

Gonad Manqué can often be found on the faculty of small Southern colleges. He hates the South and constantly runs it down, but somehow he never gets around to leaving and living elsewhere—however fond he may be of talking about how free one can be in New York. It is fortunate for New York women that he never relocates there because they are already saddled with his Yankee counterpart, the Neurotic New York Intellectual, who sits on the edge of the bed with his head in his hands, moaning: "I shouldn't come here on the days that I see my analyst."

Gonad Manqué keeps trying to make it with women, to whom he murmurs sweet but not very obscure nothings, such as: "Get it up for me." There is only one way to do this, and so she does it. This is the only thing that Gonad Manqué wants from her because then he can close his eyes and pretend that she is really L. H. DeP., who understands.

Mama Tried is heterosexual, but you would never know it in a thousand years. His mother is nowhere near as bad as Gonad Manqué's, but she does her best, usually because she cannot castrate her husband and must castrate somebody or else go mad. Her husband is so coarse-grained and insensitive that he is unable to perceive when a woman is after him with a nutcracker; it goes over his head entirely, and his wife eventually reaches such an apex of frustration that she *consciously* sets out to turn her son into a sissy. This being the only thing she can do to make her husband take notice of what she is doing with her days, she does it.

Used to a husband who does not catch on quickly, she does everything but take Sonny to a gay bar in Atlanta. She develops a Little Lord Fauntleroy approach to son-raising early on, which requires Sonny to fight his way through elementary school. He comes home every day beaten to a pulp and carrying the shredded remains of his lovely clothes in his book bag. Daddy responds by teaching him how to box, which causes something in the house to get broken, whereupon Mama screams: "Bulls in the china shop!" and Sonny gets the guilties about being so rough and making her weep.

She teaches her boy to hold her knitting wool, which Daddy grabs out of his hands and throws on the floor. She then tries to thwart Daddy by teaching her son how to feed his baby sister, because Daddy can't very well throw his daughter on the floor. Sonny grows up learning how to be feminine one minute and masculine the next; he doesn't know which one is correct and so he takes turns—which is precisely what he was taught to do at home, only nobody ever figures this out.

He is potent with women, but they hardly ever discover it because they assume he's homosexual. He looks like one, dresses like one, talks like one, does everything like one—except make love like one. He wants women and seeks them out, but when he finds one, she immediately relaxes, tells herself that *this* one is not going to be all over her, and adopts him as a brother. Girls are always running out of bedrooms half-dressed and asking him to "please zip me up," and they think nothing of adjusting their panty hose in his presence. Naturally Mama Tried gets aroused by these incidents and makes a pass, which shocks the girls so terribly that *he* is traumatized by their shock. He sees so many girls plastered up against walls with their eyes widened in incredulity that he comes to feel like a fruity rapist.

Mama Tried is his mother's revenge and his father's countermeasure, all rolled up into one untenable mess. He visits prostitutes a lot and takes up with slatternly tavern maids who have long since stopped being surprised by anything male on two feet. His problems are complicated still further by the fact that women like him very much and seek him out as a buddy, but when he asks them out for what he intends to be a date, they always assume that it's dutch treat and drag out their money when the check arrives.

In a way, Mama Tried is the personification of the South itself: a gynecocracy but an unofficial one, a culture-mad and mannerly receiving line, a male wasteland of raucous taverns and gun-freakery—at one and the same time.

There are many straight but effeminate men in the South, which is why it is so hard to define the Southern gentleman. There is a point at which gallantry and effeminacy meet and become inextricably intertwined in one terribly nice man. Too much gallantry, especially in this day and age, can seem effeminate because it takes on the anachronistic qualities of a minuet. Fussing over women is a risky business; a man who does too much of it becomes simply fussy. Scarlett O'Hara's second husband, Frank Kennedy, was described as fussy and as "an old maid in britches." I daresay his Mama tried, too.

Brooding Beau, a nonpracticing homosexual, is nowhere near as ingratiating as Mama Tried. He gets the way he is because of Southern woman-worship, but unlike the Blue Angel hound, he is too fastidious to seek out a slut. Instead, he seeks out a woman he can be physically intimate with and still worship in that good ole down-home schizoid manner.

He does not pick a self-rejuvenating virgin who goes all the way and then pretends she didn't. No indeed, Brooding Beau picks out somebody even nuttier—that sweet Southern girl best described as an infibulated mare.

She is the idealist who literally dies on the vine. When she is young she insists that she cannot have sex unless she is in love. When she is old enough to realize that some people simply never fall in love, she sets up another ideal: Her sex partner cannot be just anybody, he must be special, outstanding, admired, universally acclaimed, a household word, A GENIUS! When no latter-day Tom Edison shows up and she passes thirty, she avoids sex by finding fault with men. She will *not* go to bed with them because: They mash their peas, they smoke cigars, they crack their knuckles, they scratch their ears—in other words, they have the reek of humanness about them.

By the time she's thirty-five everybody knows that idealism is not her problem. She's just skeered to "do it," thass all.

She is Brooding Beau's best girl because he cannot worship a woman into whose vagina he places his penis, and he is her best beau because she could not "live with herself" if she ever permitted a man to place his penis in her vagina. So they get together.

And in the strangest ways. The infibulated mare will go to any lengths to avoid bona fide copulation, even if it means breaking one of those bizarre laws passed in the Southern colonies in 1710 and never repealed. Her specialties include "abomynable crymes against Nature and the Almyghty in which the Male Membre doth spyll its Seeds upon any parte of the Femayle Corps exceptyng her Organs of Generation."

Her dates are terribly messy, and she requires an overnight bag even though she never stays all night with a man ("I couldn't face myself the next morning"). She has to carry cold cream, several boxes of moistened towelettes, a bottle of witch hazel, and a can of air freshener for the car.

No matter what outlandish substitution she permits Brooding Beau, he will never try to do the normal thing and dishonor her. No matter how near the holy orifice their abominations take them, he will never try to get nearer. Sometimes, during their lubricious activities, his Membre slips and accidentally brushes against the sanctuary, causing the mare to scream: "Don't! Don't!"

"Excuse me," Brooding Beau whispers.

He, too, is an idealist.

Southerners have a genius for psychological alchemy. They know what kind of society they want, and, come what may, they usually manage to get it. If something intolerable simply cannot be changed, driven away, or shot, they will not only tolerate it but take pride in it as well. Conformists to the end, they nonetheless feel affection for any eccentric—which is why they arrange as best they can to look upon homosexuals as "characters." Town Fairy's town is almost proud of him; like the Confederate monument and the new jail, he is pointed out to visitors. "That there's our town fairy," they say fondly.

Uncle Cary gives them the least trouble because he actually is someone to be proud of. Thanks to him, the most illiterate redneck with a gun rack in his pickup truck knows the meaning of that favorite Confederate tombstone inscription, *Dulce et decorum est pro patria mori*. The rednecks like Uncle Cary for this sort of thing and often tell their friends that the "perfesser" himself translated it for them. When Uncle Cary floats down Main Street in his gendarme's cape and tam-o'-shanter, rough tavern types do not see a queer, they see Jeb Stuart with his plume or Longstreet with his flowing, curly locks. Happily for all concerned, the Southern mind is incurably romantic.

Homosexuals who stay in Southern small towns often have money, and Southerners of any class have enough ancien régime in their bones to permit the aristocracy forms of decadence that they would not permit to lesser folk. The moment Gonad Manqué gets his name in print, whether on a book jacket or in an obscure periodical, the women form a guard around him and make him into a pet, so the men who would otherwise loathe him can then shrug him off as just another bee in silly women's bonnets. Any male who addresses a women's club too often is just not worth tormenting; he is no longer a worthy opponent, and besides . . . the women would get mad.

Finally, all homosexuals or crypto homosexuals *seem* to be nice to their mothers whether they hate the old biddies or not. That's why Poor Willis, Mama Tried, and Brooding Beau get handed their final protection: Straight men *know* there is something wrong with these boys, but . . . well, heck, they're good to their mamas. I mean . . . well, heck.

# 11

## The Meouw Corner

### or: The Southern Woman as Friend and Foe

"Ginny is just the tackiest thing."

"She's as homely as a mud fence. It's a good thing she married Winton or else she'd have died on the vine."

"Her face would stop a clock. Winton was her last chance."

"You know what I heard? Jo Ann Buckley said that Grace Bradshaw told Connie Winchester she overheard Caroline Hampton say that Jo Wallace *actually saw* Ginny goin' into a *mo*tel with that tennis bum out at the country club!"

"Well, don't youall tell a soul, but . . . I swear, girls, I'll slit your throat if you tell anybody this . . . *but* Sally Tollimer said Nancy Farrar heard from somebody in Natchez that Ginny was seen in a car with Brad Harnett . . . yes, *Brad Harnett* . . . and furthermore, she was *doin'* him."

"Oh, I just hate and despise that Ginny! She's just so— Why, Ginny! Of all people! We were just talkin' about you. Come right in, 'deed we're so glad to see you, darlin'."

Oppressed people are treacherous for the simple reason that treachery is both a means of survival and a way to curry favor with one's oppressor.

Anyone who lived in the segregated South knows who Big Nigger was. He was usually a preacher—and usually light-skinned—to whom the white pillars of the town turned whenever there was trouble. The request was always the same: "Reverend, we're dependin' on you to talk some sense into your people," which really meant: "Get those Goddamn niggers calmed down!"

Big Nigger, who prided himself on his good diction, replied in his mellifluous fashion: "I shall do everything within my means to impress upon the irresponsible elements who have instigated this unfortunate disturbance that they must learn to appreciate the benefits that have accrued to them under the fine administration of Mayor Billy Bo Petrie," which really meant: "Buzz me, Miss Blue, I'm a credit to my race."

Southern white men could relax and sleep when they knew that Big Nigger was dumping on all the little niggers—because they also knew that a house divided against itself cannot prevail.

The lethal cattiness for which Southern women have long been famed is a product of the same psychology. Any society that demands rigid standards of conduct from certain of its members is bound to make finks out of them. Women in competition with one another for male approval form a natural self-police state; they vie with each other to see who can set the most impossible requirements in the hope that some of their number will fall from grace, thus eliminating some of the competitors.

The most dangerous distaff Southerner is Big Nigger's sister under the skin, the female misogynist. She is a deep-dish, purr-baby-purr, men-can-do-no-wrong, hard-core woman-hater. She is St.-Paul-with-the-pip, and I would rather tussle with a school of sharks on a No-cal diet than cross her path.

She signals her approach by rattling her slave bracelets; she wears anything and everything that dangles, jangles, tinkles, or tangles, and she is perpetually shaking various parts of herself to unknot the counterful of costume jewelry without which she will not make an appearance. She also favors the highest heels she can buy and swears that they are the only comfortable shoes she can put on her feet—"I wear a quad A, and they don't *make* low-heeled styles narrow enough for me," she purrs, and then glances quickly but pointedly at the feet of the woman to whom she is speaking. She initiates girlish show-and-tell sessions after a shopping trip and drags out all her purchases, along with comments like: "Oh, I'm sure they have this in your size. If not, you could aᴕk them to put in a special order. Don't worry about this bow at the hip, it's detachable. See? You can take it right off for a more slimmin' effect. Of course, you wouldn't want a dress with stripes goin' in this direction, but they have the same style in solid navy blue."

Amazingly, men never catch on, never realize that she is filleting every other woman in the room. They are too mesmerized by the worshipful looks that she sends in their direction—the kind of look Jeanette MacDonald used to give Nelson Eddy every time she hit a high C.

A parlor Fascist, this woman is devoted to Southern sexual conformity. Like the antiabolitionists and segregationists before her, she dreads any opening wedge, so naturally she is opposed 1,000 percent to Women's Liberation in any shape or form. Her psychology is that of a harem member battling three thousand other women for the attentions of one pudgy, exhausted, and senile sultan. She would rather take her chances this way than see the end of the harem system—for if the other harem members refused to play or decided the sultan wasn't worth the trouble, how would the female misogynist shine?

Her greatest victims are unattractive women, whom she loathes. Their looks remind her of her own, which prompts that disturbing unspoken question: "How important is it, really, to be pretty?" It is damned important to a woman who has sunk virtually all of her time and energy into it. The South awards so many points for feminine allure that she is terrified lest homely women be praised for *something else*, which is why she belittles any achievements other than sexual ones.

This syndrome lies behind the hatred that so many Southern women expressed for Eleanor Roosevelt. I grew up hearing Granny refer to her as "the buck-toothed wonder," "fish-mouth," "slewfoot Lou," and even, one day when she was in such a rage that she forgot her own ironclad rule: "that nigger-lovin' chromo!" Yet it was not until quite recently that I understood a painful fact: There is a little bit of the Southern misogynist in every Southern woman—including myself. Occasionally, when I look at the coverperson on *Ms.* magazine, I catch myself thinking: "Oh, the poor thing, I bet no man ever looked at her."

When groups of Southern women discuss some unfortunate member of their sisterhood in what purports to be sympathetic understanding, the undercurrent is unmistakable:

"She'd be so attractive if only she'd shave or do *something*. They can get rid of superfluous hair nowadays. I heard about how they pour boilin' wax all over your face, then let it dry, then rip it off. All the hair comes with it. Nothing to it."

"She ought to go to a dermatologist and let him just scrape those acne scars off with sandpaper or something. I was readin' about it the other day, it's something new. It's like that machine they used the time they cleaned the grime off the courthouse. They just go scrape-scrape-scrape all over your face with this machine they have, and it takes everything away."

Southerners don't always dwell in the past. When a woman's looks are at stake, nothing is too progressive. Let the misogynists keep at it long enough, and you may hear something like this:

"I *wish* to heaven she'd go to a bone specialist and let him cut her down. They can do that nowadays, you know, make you any size you want. She takes after her daddy, he was real big, too. All you have to do is tell the doctor what height you want to be, and he saws off your legs and puts them back on again, less however many inches. I was readin' about it the other day, it's a new technique to help gawky girls."

Another lethal Southern lady is the Pill. The quintessence of Pillhood was Scarlett's sister, Suellen O'Hara, who exhibited virtually every characteristic of this pharmacopeopath. Many readers have called Suellen a bitch, but where does that leave Scarlett? There is something admirable and even noble about a true bitch; the Pill has no saving graces whatsoever. Suellen whined, complained, stamped her foot, and stuck out her tongue; she was a sneak, a backbiter, a tattletale, a troublemaker, and she "bridled"—meaning that she put her hands on her hips, shook herself, screwed up her mean little face, and looked around for someone to do her bidding.

Pills, who dwell in a world of jejune spitefulness, love to expend their energy on sniping trivia. If Suellen O'Hara had made the famous God-is-my-witness pledge, it would have gone something like this: "I'm tired of being hungry! You're just tryin' to be *mean* to me! If I don't get enough to eat, I'm going to go in my room and slam the door and throw all my hair ribbons on the floor! That'll show you!"

Unlike the often-admirable—and sexy—bitch, the Pill has a weak character and an inadequate personality, and she is utterly devoid of voluptuous allure. For these reasons, her favorite activity is slitting other women's throats one way or the other. She is a born informer, and her specialty is the sort of pippy-poo espionage that no real bitch would have time for.

I ran head-on into a Pill at the University of Mississippi. Her name was RoseSharon Potts, and she was the president of every organization on campus that had the name "Christ" in its title.

RoseSharon's Baptist eye could spot a bourbon-drinking Episcopalian a mile off. She seemed to *know* that I kept at least one bottle of Virginia Gentleman in the bottom of my laundry hamper at all times. She seemed to *know* that I had taken part in the foray in which the signs reading: HE LIVES! that she had tacked up on all the campus trees were torn down and replaced with signs reading: LET'S PUT THE X BACK IN CHRISTMAS.

Verily, RoseSharon was gunning for me.

One night, I went out and returned to the dorm at three in the morning. It was a hot, sticky, Mississippi night, but true to Granny's teachings, I had worn stockings for my rendezvous because no lady can go barelegged and still remain a lady. Unfortunately, it was so hot in my beau's apartment that I could not get the stockings back on again. The sweat we worked up simply never dried. There was nothing to do but transport the garter belt and stockings in my handbag for the short drive back to the Ole Miss campus and the minute or two it would take me to get upstairs to my room.

As soon as I shoved my bare feet into my shoes I cringed with shame. I felt like a tart. Barelegged! Oh, God, how could I? Now I understood the sense of shame that had made Mama crouch under a slimy pier to smoke. Give Granny a child until it is seven, and it is hers forever.

I could not get back to my room fast enough for fear that someone would see my unladylike legs. I rushed up the dorm steps, but there on the landing stood RoseSharon with her hands on her hips and her mean little mouth screwed up. She looked at my legs, shook herself, and Pilled:

"I think it's just terrible the way you carry on and drink and run around with men and come traipsin' in here half-dressed without even the Christian decency to hide your shame. You think you're so smart but just you wait—I'm goin' to tell the housemother and the dean on you and then you'll be sorry!" (Shake-shake-shake)

"RoseSharon, do you think I can ever be forgiven?"

Her eyes lighted with missionary zeal.

"Anyone can be forgiven! *He* loves us all! If you'll just receive Him into your heart and ask His help . . ."

"How can I do that, RoseSharon?"

The thought of having her own private convert made her shiver with joy.

"You just kneel down right here and pray. I'll pray *with* you!"

We knelt, and I prayed:

"Dear Lord, please ask Granny to forgive me for going bare-legged."

Thanks to my plea for intercession, RoseSharon got it into her head that I was Catholic—which upset her more than anything else I had done.

Despite their cattiness, Southern women often get along beautifully and enjoy each other's company in a way that other women cannot manage. They are the only American women who, bereft of their men, once stood alone together and faced an invading army. This makes for a special closeness in the descendants of those not-so-fragile flowers who greeted a battalion from their front porches with a frigid bow.

Another boost to Southern distaff friendship is something that only men as a rule enjoy in other parts of the country: boozing. I do not mean sherry-cum-bridge or grasshoppers with the girls; all women do that. I mean, oddly enough, exactly what I said—BOOZING.

Settling down to an evening of serious drinking is standard sport for Southern best girl friends. Nobody bothers with cocktail shakers or hors d'oeuvres; the point of it all is to slug down as much bonded bourbon as you can hold. Northern men, particularly Jewish ones, are invariably amazed at how much undiluted hooch the fragile flower can soak up without passing out or getting sick. It's that notorious Wasp blood chemistry, and it results in long hours of uninhibited conversation of the sort that welds people together if it does not make them enemies for life.

Southern women also derive a special closeness from a secret of Southern life that they all share whether or not they actually articulate it: The sexes are psychologically reversed in the South. Underneath the veneer of the Southern male's dominance, he is—so to speak—techy and oversensitive, a fluttery creature who lapses into hysterics whenever his ego is abraded. It is *men* who suffer the famous attacks of the vapors when their self-images are threatened. The Southern woman has actually played oak to his ivy—by humoring him, by letting him know, in effect, that he need not trouble his sweet pretty little head about such vexing matters as his ego, for it is *her* duty to rescue a gentleman in distress.

Thus the Southern woman has acquired enough psychological masculinity to enjoy what the world has always called "male camaraderie." Her girl friends are also her buddies.

Great love can lie between Southern women, and it is sometimes sparked by a soupçon of sensuality. In a region drenched in sexual tension, where flirting is literally an ingrained habit in women who are so sexually competitive that they study every inch of each other's persons, intrasexual awareness is unavoidable. Add to this the Southern woman's proneness to physical affection—what Margaret Mitchell described as "slopping all over each other with sugar"—and there is bound to be a sensual component in many female friendships.

Nothing comes of it, but the feeling remains and it forges a pleasant bond. Your best girl friend takes on ever more sterling qualities in your bourbon-reddened eyes, and you in hers. It is an extra zing, an emotional bonus in the Southern sexual tundra that is far more comforting and fulfilling than what our cold age has so clinically termed "bisexuality." Because she so fears the loss of her femininity, the Southern woman tends to panic at the mere thought of actual Lesbianism; she will very likely decide that if it feels *that* good, it's probably best left undone—a decision that permits her to savor that lost emotional art: yearning. When yearning weaves its way into a friendship, the friendship becomes very sweet indeed.

One of the nicest girl friends a Southern woman can have is the local nymphomaniac. She can be a bit trying at times, but she's worth it. One learns so much.

Every Southern town has a nymph, which is why she is a stock character in novels and movies. Her father keeps a goon squad on his payroll to go out and get her when she escapes to a roadside tavern with six rednecks, but the nymph is always one step ahead of Daddy and usually manages to take on the goon squad. Daddy then has to hire another whole set, and the process starts all over again.

The nymph loves women; her loyalties are completely on the distaff side because she has seen men at their worst. She craves female companionship as a rest cure, for she never gets a chance to *talk* to anyone but members of her own sex. She has a compulsion to confess her iniquities, and since she can't very well tell a man what she did with the several dozen other men who preceded him, she needs lots of girl friends.

The nymph turns parties into guaranteed adventures. Merely popping into the kitchen to get more ice can result in one. There is the nymph, seated on a straight chair and fellatrixing her heart out. Go into a darkened bedroom with a guest's coat, and there she is again. Pretty soon, opening any door turns into a game of the-lady-or-the-tiger. People are always returning to the living room wearing expressions of determined nonchalance, still holding an empty ice bucket or a coat. At some point in the evening, the hostess is forced to stand beside the closed bathroom door and say: ". . . don't go in there just yet."

My favorite nymph came to a party of mine shortly after she had had a baby. At the end of the evening, an innocent out-of-towner who did not know her reputation asked her if he could give her a lift home. He meant just that and no more, but the nymph gave him a regretful smile and said:

"I'm sorry, but my stitches aren't out yet."

Even at its worst, Southern cattiness is not nearly so bad as it seems. When a woman hisses: "I just hate and despise Ginny!" she does not really mean it. She is merely a little irritated at something Ginny said or did, but because the theater lost a Barrymore every time a Southerner decided not to go on the stage, just about anything that comes out of a Southern mouth is bound to be a ringing line. Thanks to this dramatic bent, women rip each other up simply in order to entertain. A good story is so dear to the Southern heart that sometimes we forget all about any hurt we might be inflicting. The idea is to go ahead and tell the story so that your listeners will have a good time—because, after all, slander *is* fascinating.

When the bourbon is flowing and the masculine component gets cranked up, Southern women can be delightfully bawdy, aided by their devotion to the idée fixe that aristocrats are blunt. A good hen party can be truly memorable for a half-tight judgment of the latest *Playgirl* centerfold: "He's all potatoes and no meat." Someone at the party is certain to complain about being either horny or sore, and by the time the evening is over there is no doubt in anyone's mind that the Wife of Bath is alive and well and living in Raleigh, North Carolina.

Dr. Jonathan Latham was roundly shocked by the Southern woman's ribaldry. He met a lovely, patrician creature who extended a gracious invitation to a dinner party. She was cool and self-contained, yet warm and outgoing. Latham did not quite know how she managed to be both, but it was the first Southern conundrum he encountered that he found charming rather than maddening.

The picture she made as she sat at the head of the table deepened his reverence. His hostess, he decided, was the last of the great ladies, an untouchable yet infinitely alluring ice maiden.

Three hours later, watching her sip daintily at her tenth bourbon, Latham was certain he felt a stroke coming on. She still *looked* beautifully aristocratic, she had yet to slur a single word; yet a startling change had come over her personality. Latham's pristine goddess had turned into Tugboat Annie.

"He's a Friday turd at a Saturday market," she was saying. "As for that fartless wonder he married—"

Blessedly, she was interrupted by a male guest who had just arrived —and who, of course, hastened to do the proper Southern thing: pay his respects to his hostess.

Latham watched as the man put his arm around her waist.

"Honey, I sure would like a little pussy."

"So would I," she said, laughing. "Mine's as big as a bucket."

Seeing Latham's horrified expression, she was kind enough to explain: "We went to school together."

What in God's name did that have to do with anything? Latham was still trying to collect himself when she turned to an obviously homosexual novelist.

"I'm trying to think of a title for my new book," he said. "Maybe you can help me."

She could.

"How about *Forever Umber?*" she suggested.

Latham had to sit down. While he was huddled beside a lovely antique desk, she drifted over, smiled sweetly at him, and barreled into one of those flowery preambles that Southerners go through in the cause of etiquette.

"I'm so sorry to disturb you, truly I am, but if you don't mind, would you be good enough to hand me that Goddamn friggin telephone?"

Even when something dreadful happens, the memory of an evening with the girls lingers on in a spirit of affectionate Southern neurosis. One such occasion that I shall always cherish for the rollicking sense of regional identity it gave me was the night at Mary Lou Lassiter's when:

—Jeannie McCanless got drunk and nearly set fire to the curtains with her wildly gesturing cigarette.

—And suddenly, apropos of absolutely nothing, screamed at me: "What size gloves do you wear? Tell me this instant! A lady *always* knows her glove size!"

—Mary Lou served coquilles St. Jacques in shell-shaped dishes, and Jeannie McCanless was so drunk she tried to eat the plate.

—Whereupon Jeannie broke a tooth and blamed Mary Lou.

—Which caused Mary Lou to stop speaking to Jeannie for the rest of the evening, a silence that was broken only at the door when Mary Lou rattled off an automatic: "You come back real soon, you hear, Jeannie?"

—After which Mary Lou's roommate, Jordan Reynolds, took Mary Lou into the kitchen and warned her: "If you keep invitin' that Florence King, there won't be a soul in the Junior League who'll *speak* to you!"

—Whereupon Mary Lou waylaid me upstairs in the bathroom and said: "Please stop twitting Jordan, you know how she gets. Say something about your grandmother being an Upton!"

—Whereupon I descended the stairs to find the elegant Jordan occupying herself with "fine sewing," that is to say, needlepoint. As I passed her, I bent down and said: "Pssst! My grandmother was an Upton."

—Which brought forth Jordan's tightest smile, followed by: "*Most* of the Uptons are lovely people."

You can always depend upon the Southern woman to temper her

unrestrained moments with ladylike touches—even if she manages to become what her father still calls a "hippie." A Richmond acquaintance of mine whose name was Ashton launched such a personality change by selling all of her furniture. She bought a dozen beanbag chairs, piles of pillows, and plunked herself down on the floor in a yoga position with her hair in her eyes. She was determined to divest herself of her Southern upbringing, even to the extent of giving up Episcopalian bourbon for French wine. She refused to have anything to do with the Richmond postdeb set to which she had belonged, and cultivated instead the foreign students at the university—until it became impossible to take three steps in her apartment without bumping into somebody named Krishna or Jesus.

One evening, Ashton invited me to dinner. As usual, she served bread, wine, and cheese on the floor, but the polite foreign students—who had been briefed by the State Department on Southern customs to get them safely through their sojourn in traditionalist Richmond—all waited for their hostess to begin.

Just as she was about to sit down, her current lover, a lusty, free-spirited Norwegian named Thor, decided that he wanted her *that minute*. He grabbed Ashton's arm and started dragging her into the bedroom. Then, as they reached the threshold, she turned around and looked at all her guests holding plates of untouched food.

It must have triggered something in her despite her resolute vow to be un-Southern, because she gave the standard gracious wave and said:

"Would youall be good enough to excuse us while we go fuck? Just go right ahead without me."

# 12

## "I Can't Say That to Him, He's My Daddy."

### or: The Southern Father

The Southern father and the Jewish mother ought to get married. They deserve each other, and they have so much in common.

The chief difference between these famous parents is the way they are handled on the printed page. The Jewish writer of the kvetch school runs the mother down, while the Southern writer of the search-for-the-father school runs the father *up*. Otherwise, the literary parents are virtual twins, for the Southern version features ole Colonel Portnoy, seducing with bourbon instead of sponge cake.

The shadow of the stern, drawling Agamemnon that falls across the Southern novelist's typewriter casts unrelieved gloom on every page. His oppressive presence makes the reader feel that the author writes with one hand in his lap, holding tightly to what he fears Daddy will take away—or already has. The favorite Southern accolade, "If you're half the man your daddy was you'll be all right," haunts the Southern writer and leads him to a compulsive repetition of one multi-generational dynastic novel after another. The "halving" process fills him with fascinated terror, so that he must show a long line of men, each of whom was half as good as the daddy before him, ending with the masochistic autobiographical character—who, by definition, has undergone the most complete mathematical reduction of all.

The more threatened the author, the more ponderous the tome.

166

He likes epic lengths—the better to punish himself—and he is fixated on words like "lineage" and "heritage." If he lines up enough generations of half-as-much characters, he can arrange a symbolic suicide for himself, halving himself all the way out of existence in his Daddy-ridden brain.

Even the best Southern women novelists cannot keep their fingers off those magic keys, f-a-t-h-e-r. Margaret Mitchell gave us not one but two idyllic father-daughter relationships. The healthier was that of Scarlett and Gerald O'Hara; the bond between Rhett Butler and Bonnie gave every promise of becoming a classically sick Electra mess prevented only by the child's untimely death.

But it is the male novelist who is more tormented by Daddy, as we can see in that apocryphal best-seller, *Carmichael's Lament.* . . .

Buck Carmichael was coming home from World War II. As the train slowed, he looked eagerly out the window. Home! He was actually back in Carmichael Junction, the town that his grandfather had founded.

Buck's heart swelled with pride and his throat grew tight, but he forced away the threatening tears and clenched his square jaw until a muscle leaped in his tan cheek. As he continued to stare out the window, familiar landmarks passed before him. Carmichael's Feed & Grain, Carmichael's Hardware, and, on the corner of Main Street, the Carmichael Building! He gazed up at the magnificent five-story structure in awe. Built by his father, Big Buck Carmichael, it had been dedicated to the memory of his grandfather, Old Buck Carmichael.

The building housed the family law firm. Big Buck had sent his son a snapshot of the office door while he was fighting in Italy. Many times, he had taken it out and looked at it as he crouched in foxholes and listened to shells scream overhead. The snapshot had been a great comfort to him while he was fighting for his country. Other soldiers drew comfort from pictures of their wives and sweethearts, but Buck preferred a picture of his father's door.

Now he took the picture from his pocket and looked at it once again. What a door! Even though his grandfather had been dead twenty-five years, the door still bore his name out of honor to his memory. How like his father, Buck thought, to keep Granddaddy's name there. . . . Big Buck had loved Granddaddy.

## CARMICHAEL & CARMICHAEL
Attorneys-at-Law

*Buckley Carmichael, Sr.*
*Buckley Carmichael, Jr.*
*Buckley Carmichael, III*

On the back of the snapshot, Big Buck had written: "I added your name so that you can come to work in the family firm as soon as you get back from the war."

Buck frowned. He was not sure whether he wanted to practice law or not. He had always thought that he would kind of . . . well, like to . . . *write.* He felt his stomach knot with tension, and the muscle in his jaw leaped once more as he clenched his teeth. He had never told his father about his literary ambitions. He didn't dare. He had never let anyone in his family know that while he was in college and later, in the service, he had had a few articles and short stories published. He had always used a pen name, of course—which had reduced his own joy at seeing his work in print. Big Buck would snort with contempt if he knew that his son wanted to be an author! Writing was women's work.

Hell, everybody knew that, Buck told himself, trying to still his shameful ambitions. The South was a man's country, and Southern men left writing to silly women like Ellen Glasgow, Margaret Mitchell, Lillian Smith, Flannery O'Connor, Eudora Welty, Harper Lee, Carson McCullers and Lillian Hellman.

No, he could not become a writer, but did he want to become a lawyer? The knowledge of his indecisiveness shamed him. A man should know what he wanted to do, should have a master plan for his life. His mother had never been able to make up her mind . . . he wondered if he took after her?

It was a frightening possibility, and he prepared to put it out of his mind. God, his jaw muscle hurt! The damn thing had been leaping away in his cheek for years.

No, he decided, there was nothing of his mother in him. He was a Carmichael through and through, the spit of Big Buck, who was the spit of Old Buck, who, in turn, was the spit of the Confederate general whose portrait hung in the parlor.

The train stopped. Buck grabbed his duffel bag and stepped out into the hot sunlight. He quickly looked around at the faces in the station, searching for his father.

He did not have to search far. *Daddy! Daddy!* his heart cried. Big Buck Carmichael stood before him, head and shoulders above everyone else, just as Stonewall Jackson must have stood at Chancellorsville.

Buck swallowed hard. He longed to rush forward and throw himself in his father's arm, to hug and kiss him, but of course he could not. Carmichael men didn't do that sort of thing. Instead, he forced himself to walk foward calmly and greet this man he adored in a manly fashion.

Big Buck held out his huge square hand. As Buck took it, it closed around his own huge square hand like a vise.

"Welcome home, boy," said Big Buck.

"Thank you, sir. It's good to be back." *Daddy! Daddy! Do you really love me the way I love you? You never said you did. I know you do, but if only you would say it. . . . Daddy, please stop squeezing my hand. My jaw hurts bad enough without having a broken hand, too.*

"I'm sorry your mother can't be here to greet you," Big Buck rumbled in his bass drawl. "She went to pieces, and we had to put her away." He shrugged. "You know how women are."

Buck smiled. Joy and inexplicable relief flooded him as it always had whenever his father included him in the fraternity of men.

"Where is she, sir?"

His father's eyes hardened, making Buck tremble.

"Why, up at Carmichael Hill, where else? She's in the new wing I just built."

They got into the car and headed for home. As they approached the road to the estate, Buck gazed up at the tall smokestacks of the Carmichael Mills. His heart skipped a beat at the sight of these symbols of power—Carmichael power! It made him feel proud to be a man whenever he looked at those hard, towering cylinders reaching up to the sky. When he was a boy, the smokestacks had always made him think of his father, and so he loved them.

They passed the stables, and there, frisking in the grass, was Prince Carmichael, the stallion who had sired all their colts. Buck would have to go riding right away. How he had missed it! The feel of all that power between his legs, the biting, acrid smell of sweat, the sweeter one of leather—

Buck leaned forward and gave an involuntary cry of delight as the old homestead came into view.

"Yes," said his father, with quiet pride. "Carmichael Hall."

A few moments later, they were seated in Big Buck's study, a room full of leather sofas and guns, which his mother and sisters were forbidden to enter.

Big Buck went immediately to the sideboard and poured generous glasses of bonded bourbon for them, then sat down in his armchair with a firm, leathery squish.

"You bein' away for four years gave me plenty of time to plan your life, boy."

Buck swallowed. He looked up for a moment at the thirty-foot, full-length oil portrait of Old Buck in an attempt to draw courage from it. As he stared at the stern old man, he remembered how, as a boy, he had crept into this room and walked up and down in front of the portrait, terrified yet fascinated at the way the fierce eyes seemed to follow him.

No, he could not be a writer; he could not disgrace the Carmichael name. His decision made, he breathed easier.

He looked at his father.

"That's mighty good of you, sir. What do you want me to do?"

"Come to work tomorrow. Your desk is waiting for you, and I hired you a secretary. Old Miz Anderson. You remember her, you had her sister for sixth grade. She's one of the few sensible women I ever met, so I picked her for you. She's the kind of woman who belongs in an office."

"Thank you, sir."

"And when you have your first son, we'll add Buckley Carmichael IV to the door the day he's born. That'll be my christenin' present to my grandson."

"I don't know what to say, sir. You're more than generous."

Big Buck smiled the grim, manly smile that always covered his deepest emotions.

"You're my son. I'd do anything for you, boy. Now . . ." he said briskly, clearing his throat, "speakin' of Buckley IV. We've got to have a mother for the boy, so I want you to go ahead a marry Puddyface Castlemaine as soon as possible."

Buck went numb with horror. Puddyface Castlemaine! Oh, no! Not that simpering belle, that spoiled brat, that Goddamned apple of Kincaid Castlemaine's eye! He had known Puddyface all his life and had hated her for every moment of it. When they had been children, she had stuck to his side like a burr and tagged along on his fishing trips even though these were all-boy affairs. His friends had teased him unmercifully, calling him a sissy because he brought a girl along.

Worse, she had always managed to show up on Sunday afternoons and interrupt those precious hours with his father, the only time he could be alone with Big Buck. On Sundays, his father had taken him into the den and closed the door; there, they talked man-talk, guns and politics, and Big Buck told him stories about all the cavalry charges that Carmichael men had led in the Civil War. It was never long before the door burst open and in walked Puddyface, switching her ponytail and smiling pertly while his mother watched from her place behind the stairwell. Damn it! His mother had *arranged* those interruptions, she had connived with Puddyface to drive him and his father apart!

When he got older, Buck's mother had forced him to date her. He had even had to serve as one of Puddyface's marshals at the deb ball. What a dreadful night that had been. As usual, she had thrown a few of her famous temper tantrums whenever something did not suit her. The only thing that had saved him was her total absorption in her father, Kincaid Castlemaine. She had insisted upon dancing practically every dance with her daddy, freeing Buck to get drunk in the parking lot with the other boys, whose dates were also busy dancing with their fathers.

As a child, she had been called "Prettyface" by her father; when she had repeated it after him in her baby voice, it had come out as "Puddyface." From that moment on, everyone called her Puddyface—until neither Buck nor anyone else could remember what her actual name was. She had even been announced at the deb ball as "Miss Puddyface Kincaid Castlemaine."

And she still had the same baby voice. . . . Puddyface Castlemaine was to be the mother of his son! He wanted to die.

His father's sharp voice interrupted his reverie.

"Well? Say something! You're gettin' the prettiest girl in the state and the Castlemaine money besides. Aren't you happy?"

Buck jumped. "Well, sir . . . I can't believe it, that's all."

Big Buck rose and poured them more bourbon, then resumed his seat.

"I want this marriage, son, I want it badly. A union between the Carmichaels and the Castlemaines will enable *my* grandson to own this whole state!"

He leaned forward and spoke with grim urgency.

"You see, boy, my father and Kincaid's father were rivals. I can win that old feud for my father if I can arrange for his great-grandson to inherit all the Castlemaine holdings!"

Then his face sobered. "I promised Old Buck on his deathbed that a Carmichael would triumph over the Castlemaines. It was my duty as his son to do it, and it's your duty as my son to help me. It will be your son's duty to take over the Castlemaine power and keep it intact for *his* son."

A deep thrill of pride swept through Buck. He was part of a master plan, a link in the father-son chain. It meant . . . it meant that his father trusted him! That was love, wasn't it?

"I—don't know what to say, sir. Except, thank you."

Big Buck smiled.

"The wedding is set for the end of the month. It would've been sooner, but Puddyface got the pip. You know how women are."

Big Buck rose and refilled their glasses with bonded bourbon. This time he did not resume his seat but faced the portrait of Old Buck and raised his glass on high.

"Let's drink to him," he said softly.

Buck obediently raised his glass. In unison, the two of them intoned the salute offered only on the most special occasions:

"He was a man!"

How time flies, Buck thought as he rose and poured himself a glass of bourbon. His son, Little Buck, was now three years old. It didn't seem possible that he had been married to Puddyface for three years and nine months. He sighed deeply, recalling how she had taken on about the boy's name. She had become hysterical, screaming from her bed of pain: "If you don't name him after my daddy, I'll set fire to this house! I *promised* my daddy that I'd name his first grandson after him!

Every firstborn son in the Castlemane family has been named Kincaid for generations, and it would kill my daddy to break the pattern!"

As if on cue, Kincaid Castlemaine had rushed into the room.

"Daddy! Daddy! He's bein' *mean* to me, Daddy!"

Buck had watched with disgust as Kincaid knelt beside the bed and took Puddyface into his arms.

"Now, now, Sweet Pea, Daddy's ole Puddyface. Give your daddy a great big hug. Ummmm-hhhh! 'Deed that's the best hug I ever had! Say I missed my daddy while I was havin' my baby. Say I love daddy to the end of the numbers. Say I never want my daddy to leave my side."

She had repeated everything in her babyish voice. Buck shuddered at the memory. Jesus, but she was hung up on her father! Bonnie Blue Butler rides again. . . .

He looked at his watch and decided that he had time for another bourbon before he left for the airport. He drank it down in one swallow, then poured another, savoring its soothing effect on his raw nerves. Thank God he was going on a business trip, he thought. Anything to get away from his wife's voice! Puddyface's shrill nonstop chatter had just about destroyed him. She never shut up! He thought back with pleasure to the one time in his life when he had been free of her. Shortly after her debut, she had gone to study voice at Juilliard. For three whole weeks there had been no Puddyface around to pester him —but then, without warning, she was back. She had collapsed during a singing lesson and screamed herself hoarse. The school had called Kincaid, who blessed them out for making her work too hard and ordered them to put her on the train that very minute. . . .

Now Puddyface no longer sang—she talked. Constantly; an unbroken tour de force of coloratura-range drivel.

Buck poured himself a third double bourbon. Suddenly, for no reason, his old ambition popped into his head. Funny . . . he hadn't thought about writing for so long. He guessed it was remembering Puddyface's onetime career plans that had triggered memories of his own.

As he stared down at the bronze liquid in the glass, he imagined himself as a novelist. Bourbon-to-indent-paragraphs-by, he mused, smiling to himself. If he were a Southern author, he would keep the faith and break up his paragraphs with bourbon. He knew that much about writing, anyhow. It was not cricket to let your characters talk or think too long because readers were put off by big gray blocks of print. A man who was a good writer never let it go on too long, he always . . .

He stopped thinking and went over to the sideboard to pour himself another glass of bourbon, then he resumed his thoughts.

. . . remembered to indent often. Every time a Southern novelist indented, Buck reflected, his characters moved one step closer to alcoholism.

He finished the drink and picked up his briefcase. Puddyface and the boy were waiting to say good-bye to him. He was only too glad to say good-bye to Puddyface, but his son was another matter. He looked at Buckley Kincaid Carmichael. They had compromised on the name to save Carmichael Hall from being reduced to ashes, but the name did not really matter. Little Buck was all Carmichael; the spit of himself. How he loved his son! He longed to pick him up, to give him a hug and a kiss, but he could not bring himself to do it. His jaw muscle leaped as anger and frustration mingled with the forlorn sadness within him. It wasn't right for fathers and sons to fall all over each other like women, he told himself. It was his duty to make a man of the boy, just as his father had made a man of him.

He swallowed and held out his hand.

"Good-bye, son. You're the man of the house now. Look out for things while I'm gone."

As he got into the car and drove off, Buck could not forget the sight of that lost little face staring up at him. His jaw muscle leaped once again, and this time a sudden, fierce resentment stabbed at him.

Hell, he thought. My father didn't slobber all over me, and I survived, didn't I? Let him survive, too. *Why should I give him what I never got?*

When Buck returned home, he found a coy Puddyface and a proud Kincaid Castlemaine seated together on the sofa. Puddyface had her arm through her father's and was pressing her breast against him, as usual.

"We've got news for you," Kincaid said. "Puddyface is goin' to have another baby."

Buck nearly staggered backward at the news. How could she be pregnant? He only slept with her when he was too drunk to know who she was.

He walked slowly over to the sideboard and poured himself a glass of bourbon, then turned to face the two of them. Puddyface switched herself and stuck out her wrist.

"See what Daddy gave me? Another charm for my bracelet! See? Isn't that pretty?"

She rattled the bracelet and waited with an air of challenge for Buck to compliment the gift. Christ, he was so sick of that charm bracelet! She refused to take it off, ever, so that when he slept with her, it always rattled in his ear. Kincaid had given it to her on her fifth birthday and added a charm every year. He also added them for special occasions, such as this, taking care to select a charm that was suitable for whatever was being celebrated.

"See?" she squealed, determined to get a compliment out of him. "It's a tiny gold *baby*. Isn't my daddy sweet to me?"

Buck turned and poured himself another bourbon, then obediently inspected the charm.

"It's real cute." he mumbled.

"Isn't it cute?" Puddyface persisted. "Did you ever see anything sweeter?"

"No, never in my whole life. That's the sweetest charm I ever did see."

Buck had learned his lesson the last time Kincaid had given her a charm. He had been too drunk to take on over it the way she wanted him to, so she had smashed all the gun cabinets with the fire poker. Buck had many reasons for wishing Kincaid dead, but chief among them was that Goddamned charm bracelet. Puddyface's tinkling metallic voice was bad enough; Buck did not know how much longer he could put up with diarrhea of the wrist as well. Kincaid was, unfortunately, healthy and vigorous, and gave every promise of living to a ripe old age. Buck foresaw some thirty more years of charms. Not just to commemorate her birthdays and pregnancies, either. Eventually, there would be a charm for every hot flash. By the time she was fifty, she would be a human lightning rod—which, come to think of it, wasn't a bad idea at all.

A daughter! Buck could not believe his own happiness. Throughout Puddyface's difficult pregnancy, he had told himself that he wanted another son, but now. . . .

He held the pink-blanketed bundle closer. For the first time in his life, he did not feel lonely. At last he had someone he could love freely, someone who would love him back with the same lack of restraint. You didn't have to worry about turning daughters into sissies, and Southern men were supposed to fuss over women! It would be all right . . . at last, it would be all right.

His jaw relaxed, and he broke into a smile.

"Kissypoo," he whispered. "Say I'm my daddy's kissypoo, say I'll never be anybody else's kissypoo except my daddy's, say I'm the sweetest little ole kissypoo in the world."

That's it, he thought happily. That's what we'll call her—Kissypoo Carmichael.

FINIS

# 13

## The Three Fates

### or: Dear Old Things, Rocks, and Dowagers

The Dear Old Thing is a little old lady, the Rock is a big old lady, and the Dowager is a hugh old lady. These adjectives refer chiefly to the spirit rather than the flesh, but it is amazing how often the elderly Southern woman's sobriquet tallies with her physical appearance. The Dear Old Thing is a matchstick figure, the Rock is a Brueghel good wife with a bust like a prow, and the Dowager is after Praxiteles.

All three are faced with the same problem: how to be old in a region that places such a high value on womanly allure. The Three Fates have resolved the problem, each in her own fashion and in accordance with her particular style. Their collective answer is: If you can't be pretty, you might as well cause trouble. In the South, they amount to the same thing.

Dixie has always been firmly under the heel of a Red Cross shoe. Margaret Mitchell had much to say about Atlanta's formidable doyennes, comparing Mrs. Merriwether, Mrs. Meade, and Mrs. Elsing to the Triumvirate of ancient Rome. Things have not changed much; the power that old ladies wield can be phenomenal. Every state legislature contains grandsons and nephews who are thoroughly dominated by determined old battle-axes with a bee in their bonnets. Either they have an outlandish pet project like getting the state to subsidize a worldwide search for Flora MacDonald's snuffbox, or else they beat

177

the drums for a new zoning law in order to wreak havoc and revenge on an old enemy whose house just happens to be in the path of the bulldozers that are already working overtime in their minds.

A stroll down the corridors of any statehouse reveals this liver-spotted grip. There are old ladies all over the place, charging down the hall in full sail, seated like grim reapers in the spectators' gallery—or occupying those two revered thrones: Clerk of the House and Clerk of the Senate.

Enter a legislator's office and you will very likely find a hapless Jaycee on the telephone, trying to get a word in edgewise as he listens to what is obviously an ultimatum.

"Now, Aunt Polly, I can't make a speech about that! Everybody would think I'd lost my mind. But . . . please, Aunt Polly . . . Honey, that's an ex post facto law! We can't pass those. Why don't you just make up with Miz Claiborne instead of tryin' to do her a meanness?"

Southern lawyers endure much from old ladies, who change their wills every time they get mad. Whenever they meet somebody new (or old) that they decide they like, they add another codicil bequeathing a prized possession—completely forgetting that they have already left the same item to a dozen other people. Southern legal secretaries spend an inordinate amount of time taking messages like: "Tell him I don't want Hollis Anne to have Grandmother Devereaux's tea service, to give it to Olivia Morrison instead."

In medicine, the South has evolved the Old Lady Specialist, a GP with enough Arthur Godfrey in him to make him the pet of the blue-rinse sorority. This is a convenient arrangement for the doctor who never wanted to be a doctor in the first place. There are many such in the South, who went into medicine because it was a family tradition, and they are able to salvage their lives and get along quite well, thanks to their aging female patient list.

There is nothing really wrong with most old-lady patients except the ravages of time and a lingering need to be pampered by a man. The Old Lady Specialist can therefore stay drunk if he wishes because he seldom has to do anything important enough to necessitate being sober. He must be able to pat shoulders, call everyone "honey," and tell *slightly* risqué jokes with just the right air of filial roguishness and jaunty gallantry.

If he can do these things, he will acquire an enormous practice because his old ladies will go forth singing his praises to all their friends, vowing that he cured them of whatever it was they wished they had but really didn't. His field of medicine might be called Lipton Teaopathy, but this man is a hero, and the South needs him. As much as it is possible to do so, he keeps the old ladies quiet and happy, which makes life easier on everyone else, especially men. Protecting men from old ladies is an act of mercy in the South: Old ladies never stop trying to have a devastating effect upon the male sex. This is the commandment with which they were raised, and they never forget it.

A devastating effect can be anything from an erection to bleeding ulcers. Old ladies know they can no longer cause erections, so they aim for bleeding ulcers.

The Dear Old Thing is just as sweet as she can be. She can be found sitting on the sidelines at the debutante cotillion, murmuring: "Isn't she pretty?" and you can always depend upon her to be nice to the Avon lady. She buys slews of Avon products that she herself never uses; she puts them away to wrap up as Christmas gifts for the many peripheral people in her life, such as the woman in the dry-cleaning store, the doctor's nurse, and the paper boy's mother. Since the Avon lady is also a peripheral acquaintance, the Dear Old Thing may wrap up a bottle of Avon cologne and give it to the Avon lady.

The next best place to find the Dear Old Thing is at the January white sales, where she buys enough sheets to outfit the Ku Klux Klan. These she also puts away to wrap up as Christmas gifts for important people, like her friends, which is why Dear Old Things keep giving each other sheets for Christmas. These linens are passed around in a circle of gift-giving year after year, until they become threadbare without ever coming near a bed. It is not at all unusual for an absentminded Dear Old Thing to give the same sheets to the absentminded Dear Old Thing who gave them to her the previous year, but since nobody ever remembers anything, nobody is ever insulted.

Linen saleswomen in Southern department stores have to listen to Dear Old Things deplore all the "new" flowered, patterned, and checked sheets that are being manufactured today and compare them unfavorably with the fine old white linen sheets of yesteryear. After they finish calling the new-style sheets *tacky*, they buy a few quires of them—provided they can find their charge plates. Usually they can, after they have dumped out the contents of their handbags on the counter and waded happily through the mess in that archetypal Dear Old Thing search-and-seizure.

Not surprisingly, our little old match girl is a widow. Husbands of Dear Old Things are eulogized on the obit page in tributes that have a curious tendency to begin: "Suddenly, at his home . . . ." Dropping dead is a fate that awaits him, and he seems to know it to judge from the size and type of insurance he buys. His widow never uses the expression "dropped dead" when she describes his passing because it implies that he lived under a strain. She prefers the vaguer: "One minute he was there, and the next minute, when I turned around, he was gone!" Her friends can empathize with this jig-time bereavement because they have experienced it, too, so they reply: "It's better that he didn't suffer." This euphemistic exchange protects the vision of the Southern Way of Life and conceals the fact, known subconsciously to all, that the South's oak-and-ivy marital customs lead to early death from exhaustion for men and scatterbrained helplessness for women.

The average Dear Old Thing has "never worked a day in her life." The rare ones who are employed work as hostesses in restored historical buildings, where they dress in period costumes and run around in circles looking high and low for some priceless objet d'art they are holding in their hands. They project an air of nicey-nice quaintness, pet snuffboxes as if they were puppies, and make visitors feel like mastodons because they rattle on about how terribly breakable everything is.

Sightseers confronted by Dear Old Things are usually too terrified to move: It is obvious that these breathy, trembling guides in lace caps and farthingales would self-destruct in a pile of dusty brocade if anyone took a normal-sized step. Their lectures are incoherent some of the time because they memorize their spiels by heart, stare glassy-eyed at a point on the wall over everyone's head, and then roll brakeless downhill. Should a sightseer have the heart to interrupt with a question, the hostess is shattered, forgets everything, and plunges into a staccato whirlpool in which Lady Jane Grey becomes Mary Tudor, Henry VIII marries Virginia Dare, and Mary, Queen of Scots, emigrates to Virginia where she lives to be ninety-seven.

The most memorable Dear Old Thing I ever came across was Mrs. Lorena Garrison, relict of Randolph Fontaine Garrison, who dropped dead while pacing up and down in front of Mabel's Millinery Shoppe, where Lorena had been cloistered for two hours buying that hat she was to wear on the train that was scheduled to leave in twelve minutes. Randolph was found with his great-grandfather's watch in his hand, still tinkling out its chimey rendition of "My Love Is But a Lassie Yet."

Lorena had spent thirty years building up Rand's shaky ego, which was why he married her. She was considered to be a perfect wife for a man like him because he was so forceful and strong-willed—people said. Once, when he was cited for drunken driving, Lorena rose valiantly to his defense, arguing: "They shouldn't have put those nasty old flares and that police barrier in Rand's way!"

Rand tended to knock over a lot of things because he was usually carrying a load, but Lorena never criticized him for his drinking. "A man's a man for all that," she said, quoting her long line of Scottish ancestors. "Rand's just so big and strong that he demolishes everything. I declare, he's the biggest, sweetest bull in the china shop I ever did see. Why, I wouldn't trust a man who didn't drink a little now and then. I'd be afraid he was one of those sissified morphodites."

Whether she was unconsciously trying to administer the coup de grâce to her ostensibly beloved husband is not known, but we do know that Rand never tried to cut down on his drinking.

Lorena, like most Dear Old Things, did not drink at all. She did, of course, have two glasses of sherry every night before dinner, and she was never known to refuse a *light* bourbon-and-water. She also had enough glasses of champagne at weddings to make her "tiddly," and she eagerly joined in the wassail at Christmas with numerous glasses of eggnog because, after all, even if you don't drink—which she did not —one must be polite on festive occasions. When Bloody Marys took America by storm, Lorena thought it was a fine thing that so many people were getting their vitamin C, essential to good health, so she began having "a nice big glass of tomato juice" every morning for breakfast because the additives of Tabasco and Worcestershire made ordinary old tomato juice taste so much better.

But when her Old Lady Specialist suggested that she "take a little wine for the stomach's sake, honey, ha-ha," Lorena drew herself up and replied: "I don't drink."

Sex-role destruction was a cornerstone of the Garrison marriage. Rand broke feminine things like glasses, vases, and china, while

Lorena set a lot of fires, blew a lot of fuses, and dulled a lot of tools. She broke everything she could lay her hands on if it was something masculine and complicated like machinery or wiring. Immediately following the explosion or crash, she screamed for Rand, who always dropped whatever he was doing—which usually involved a glass—and rushed to her aid. He saved her from herself, repaired whatever she had demolished, and then chided her in that firm but gentle way of his while shaking a finger in her face. "Sugarbunch, how many times do I have to tell you not to throw water on a burning wire?"—to which Lorena would reply: "Oh, I'm just so silly and scatterbrained. I just don't know what I'd do without you."

Unlike so many wives, Lorena never hit the garage door and broke a headlight—for the simple reason that she had never learned to drive. Rand would not hear of her taking lessons. "I'll drive my honeysuckle wherever she needs to go," he said gently but firmly. "It's one of the things a man should do for his wife. Besides, she's so flighty she'd never be able to handle a car."

Lorena agreed: "Women just aren't good drivers." Their compatibility on this subject resulted in a familiar sight: Rand driving around and around the block, hour after hour, while Lorena wandered through the downtown stores with his charge plates clutched in her helpless little hand.

After Rand dropped dead, Lorena found herself bereft of transportation and stranded in her lovely old house, unable to get downtown to continue her daily shopping. She signed up for driving lessons —much against her will and philosophy, of course, but so many of her widowed girl friends were doing it that she joined in. Untold numbers of Dear Old Things follow this pattern, which is why the South is full of little-old-lady menaces. After years spent wrapping themselves around a man, they usually end up wrapping themselves—or other people—around a telephone pole.

As long as Lorena had a male instructor or traffic policeman beside her, she was not afraid, but on her first day out alone after she had gotten her license, she panicked and careened down the middle of a one-way street, shrieking: "Oh, Law! I just can't cope!" From long habit, she threw up her hands in despair, causing her sleeve to catch in the turning knob that Rand had used so manfully during all his years of one-handed, confident driving. The car swung sharply to the right in what would have been a well-executed turn if only she had not hit a stop sign.

She gave up driving and rode the bus, which is how her notorious latter-day career got its start. Today, years after her death, her legend still lingers in the city that she terrorized, where she exchanged her sobriquet of Dear Old Thing for one that has been bestowed on such distaff superstars as Eleanor Roosevelt, Wallis Simpson, and Nell Gwyn: "That woman!"

One sleety day as she and a girl friend were alighting from a bus to hit the white sales, Lorena hit the sidewalk instead. She arose unhurt and all-forgiving, but her friend insisted that the driver had closed the doors too soon, causing her to fall. She talked Lorena into suing the bus company. Lorena at first did not want to do such a thing to the nice bus people, or get that nice young man in trouble, but neither did she want to reject her friend's advice because that would be rude. Besides, her friend was so forceful, just like Rand, and so from long habit she gave in and brought suit. She won a small claim, which she promptly donated to the Animal Rescue League.

For several weeks thereafter she seemed perfectly all right, but then a startling change came over her personality. The die was cast: After a life of passivity and submission to Rand's higher wisdom, she had at last tasted power. And so Lorena went on the warpath. She sought and found injustices wherever she turned—flies in her Cokes, glass in her tuna fish, maggots in her flour; worn steps here, loose carpets there, broken pavement to the right of her, to the left of her, everywhere! Pitfalls, ditches, gulches, ravines! The soup of the day at Walgreen's became a boiling caldron; she was burned, scalded, seared, crisped, shriveled! Scarred for life!

Soon she had so many suits going at once that she became known as "Madame Docket." Merchants dreaded the sight of her wobbly little matchstick figure heading for their stores. They repaired things that they had let go for years, and they spent a fortune on rock salt. The hardware store owner grew rich from his rock-salt and rubber-matting profits, and his joy was so great that he neglected to hold back a few of these precautionary items for himself. He ended up in court on a charge of criminal negligence because Lorena tripped over his SOLD OUT OF ROCK SALT sign and went splat on his slippery threshold.

She still paid her weekly visit to her Old Lady Specialist, but she no longer needed emotional solace from him. He performed far more vital functions for her now, like signing her sheaf of claims that "debilitating shock and tension" had wracked her after she found a cockroach wing in her smothered chicken at Mammy Lou's pancake house.

The doctor humored her at first because, after all, that was his business, but one night after a few drinks at the country club he was heard to make mocking remarks in the men's bar. As Lorena's legal brief put it: "He did maliciously and salaciously state that Plaintiff was suffering from an unfulfilled physical need of an intimate nature, whereupon he demonstrated the nature of said need in an obscene pantomine by striking the bend of his left elbow with the side of his right hand."

This case marked a glorious plateau in Lorena's career of litigious mania. It was her first malpractice suit, and she felt that she had hit the big time. She acquired another doctor and shortly sued him for the injured toe she had sustained in his stirrups.

By now she had learned a great deal about the law. When she fell over a butter churn in Ye Rustick Creamery gourmet dairy shop she told her lawyer: "Issue a subpoena duces tacem. I want that churn in court before they adjourn us sine die." He lost his temper then and shouted that she was non compos mentis, but unfortunately the door was open and everyone in the waiting room heard him, so she sued him for slander.

The thrill of actually suing a lawyer was so orgasmic that she decided to act as her own lawyer from then on. She lost most of her cases because they were Alice-in-Wonderland flights of fancy anyway, but, to everyone's amazement, she also won a few and exhibited a truly awesome knowledge of the law and a ferocious talent for cross-examination. Her courtroom style was flamboyant, and one judge remarked that she reminded him of Sir Edward Marshall Hall.

Inspired by such praise, Lorena decided to go to law school. She scored fourth in the state in the legal aptitude test and carried the results with her everywhere, shaking them in men's faces and snarling: "That'll show youall that women have logical minds!"

She signed up for her courses, but as she was leaving the registrar's office she caught her heel in a loose tile and went rolling down the steps. She arose unhurt and decided that as thrilling as it was to go to law school, it would be even more thrilling to *sue* a law school, so she did.

This coup was too much for her fevered brain, and she began to crack up in earnest. She imagined herself as an English barrister, stole a choir robe from her church, and arranged her white hair in a simulacrum of a QC's wig. She addressed the Bench as "your Lordship" and began her questions to witnesses with: "I put it to you, sir. . . ."

Stopping a Dear Old Thing in the South is like stopping a cow in India. Both go where they damned well please. Southern men were helpless to know what to do about her because she still *looked* like a sweet little old lady. They turned to her only living relative, a nephew, and asked him to have her committed, but when he tried to find a psychiatrist to examine her and sign the papers, every shrink in the state went into hiding. No one would touch her for fear that she would wobble back to the Old Bailey and slap a suit on them.

The reign of terror ended the only way it could. Lorena collapsed in the middle of a summation. On the way to the hospital, a car sideswiped her ambulance, whereupon she did fitfully and with malice aplenty turn her head to the window, murmur: "I'll sue that man," and die.

The Rock is the natural enemy of any newspaper's Woman's Department because she is the publicity chairman of at least six clubs, She is unanimously elected to this position by the other ladies because, as they like to put it: "She's so forceful," a felicitous euphemism that means she has nothing to do with her boundless energies except become the biggest bully in the Pinckney Heights Eastern Star.

Woman's Page staffers can sense when a Rock is on her way to the office. Whenever we heard the elevator door open and shut in a certain way, we stopped working and lifted our heads. When the hallway began to squeak with that rubbery, suction-soled Rock leitmotif, someone would groan, "Oh, God, here she comes!"

All of us had grown up with grandmothers who called Mrs. Roosevelt "She," and now we had many "She's" of our own. There was the Rose Show judge, Mrs. Elizabeth Laburnum, better known as "Yardstick Lizzie" from her habit of prodding everyone in the ribs with the ruler she always carried, which she used to measure stems. She toted this symbol of her office at all times, like a British officer with his swagger stick, even during the winter when there were no rose shows and no stems to measure.

One day, as I was measuring copy with a printer's metal ruler known as a pica stick, Lizzie came in and skidded to a rubbery stop before my desk. She stared, fascinated, her errand forgotten. A smile trembled over her lips; her expression made me think of a child with its nose pressed to a store window, gazing at an animated Christmas display.

"What a lovely ruler," she said, in the quietest voice I had ever heard her use. "I've never seen one like it."

I explained what it was and how it worked. Almost shyly, she asked if she might examine it more closely.

"Where can you buy one of these?" Lizzie asked. "I sure could use one in my profession."

The Woman's Editor and I exchanged glances.

"I have no idea where you can buy them, Mrs. Laburnum," said the editor. "Why don't you just keep that one? You bring us so many good, newsworthy items, it's the very least that we can do to say thank you."

She looked as if she had just won the sweepstakes. She would have forgotten to turn in the item she had brought in if we hadn't reminded her of it. For once, she simply handed over a publicity release without issuing her usual fiats about what size headline she wanted.

After she had squeaked out, happily clutching her new ruler, the editor and I laughed. Then we sat for a moment in a somewhat shamed silence, both of us aware that we had laughed at something and someone that was not funny at all.

"In my *profession*," said the editor. "Dear God . . . no wonder they're such pests."

Rocks, as I learned in my newspaper days, are capable, aggressive women who have never worked outside the home. Frustrated by their club and volunteer work, they seek more outlets by taking on still more of the same. No matter how many gratis activities they take on in their trip around this vicious circle—and some of them have a finger in every pie—they never know the satisfaction of being paid money for their considerable talents, getting raises, climbing up a clearly visible ladder of success. Their triumphs are ephemeral, and their leadership too often bogus, because many of the offices they hold are rotating ones that come to any She who waits.

The Woman's Department staff posed a threat to the most frustrated Rocks. Like all strong personalities, they yearned for power, and they believed we possessed far more than we actually did. We were a group of women with a female boss, a self-contained gynecocracy that resembled their club situations except that we were gainfully employed and had regular by-lines to satisfy our egos. These by-lines constituted the only female names on our pages that stood alone without an honorific. When we wrote about a Rock we had to list her as Mrs. John Parker Laburnum, not Mrs. Elizabeth, but there was no way to tell from our by-lines whether we were married or not. Yet somehow, especially in the South, a female given name and a surname glaring starkly in boldface type managed to seem Spartan, and therefore independent, and therefore unmarried.

Often, Rocks would say: "My, it must be thrillin' to see your name in print." The first time I heard this I could not believe my ears, for who saw her name in print more often than a Rock? It was then that I realized how much these women envied us. My co-workers and I were too young and too unliberated ourselves to realize that we and the Rocks should stick together and be mutually supportive. Instead, we permitted the situation to drive a wedge between us that resulted in what we assumed to be inevitable hostility between clubwomen and newspaperwomen.

In the time-honored manner of thwarted understrappers, Rocks tried to puff up their club duties to make themselves feel important. They tried symbolically to take our jobs away from us by picking up newspaper terms like "deadline," "kill," "cutline," and "jumpline" and using them in a bustling, officious way that was guaranteed to drive us wild, particularly when they got these terms confused and came charging in at one minute to three shouting: "I hope I haven't missed killtime!" Yardstick Lizzie used to barrel through the door, waving one of her novelette-sized notices, crying: "Girls! Get a hopline ready! This is a long piece, and every single word has to get in!"

One day as I was laying out the pages, three Rocks squeaked in and watched in fascination as I wrote "flop" on the back of a photo. They wanted to know what it meant, so I explained that an individual in a photo could not "look off the page" but must face inward, and that two individuals in two separate photos could not appear to be staring at each other. To avoid such instances of bad layout, you had to instruct the engraving department to make a reversed plate by telling them to "flop" the photo.

The Rocks were charmed. They promptly put this revelation on the grapevine, and within a week the Woman's Department was knee-deep in what became known as the Flop Flap.

The lodge ladies came in with photos of Worthy Matron coronations inscribed with "Flip!" "Flap!" "Flick!" and one exquisitely polite and typically Southern notation: "Kindly be good enough to turn me around as I do not wish to stare at anyone." The president of the Iris Society strode proudly in one day, handed me a photo, and shot me a we're-in-the-same-racket-and-speak-the-same-lingo wink. "Just give it a good floppin', honey."

When the Flop Flap finally died down, the Stet Flap immediately took its place because I was caught in the act of writing "Stet!" beside the name of Mrs. Henry Tuck by an intensely curious Rock. Naturally, she asked me what it meant, and without thinking I blurted out the truth: that "stet" means "let stand as is," or, more specifically: "Be careful!"

The Rock frowned quizzically. I sat frozen in terror, wondering if she would catch on, or, worse, that she wouldn't catch on and ask me why the name "Tuck" warranted such extreme caution. After all, I could imagine her saying, it's so easy to spell. . . .

"Well . . ." I began, and then, as is usual when I lie, I overcomplicated things: "The different departments of the paper are having a contest to see who can get a perfect score for spelling proper names correctly."

The Rock brightened and smiled—this sounded like the charity raffles and bingo drives she engineered. Heady with the knowledge that I was reprieved, I babbled on:

"Yes, a contest! The prize is twenty dollars, and we're going to buy a new coffeepot for the Woman's Department if we win, a nice new electric one in a decorator color. Maybe orange! Or yellow! Something bright and cheery!"

I finally managed to shut up. The Rock drew herself into that fire-eating Rock huff that I knew so well and gave me an atta-girl nod.

"Don't you worry 'bout a thing, darlin', youall are goin' to win that prize away from all these ole men!" She darted her head in the general direction of the cigar-littered sports desk, a rattler aiming an expert strike. "I'm goin' to go over everything I turn in with a fine-tooth comb, and I'll tell all my friends to do the same!"

The clubwomen all began to turn in notices with "Stet!" written all over them. When they called up to give us social notes, they spelled their names in ear-shattering tones and then repeated them to make sure we got them right. The most conscientious Rocks were those with difficult names, who proffered apologies along with their meticulous recitations. Mrs. Urquhart waxed nostalgic about a boy named Smith she almost married, then sighed and got down to business.

"U—that's *yew*—r-q as in *cue-u-h-a-r-t*. That's *tee-tee-tee*."

Mrs. Armagh told me how the girls at the bank *never* spelled her name right, then launched each letter at me like a sonorous depth charge.

"A . . . R . . . M . . . A . . . G . . . H ," she tolled. Then: "Stet!"

I was too close to the situation to appreciate the fact that the Rocks were being what had not yet been termed "supportive," and that they, and not we, had been the first to recognize what had not yet been called "sisterhood." I was ashamed to confess to my co-workers what I had said, and I was too busy erasing "Stet!" from the piles of copy that crossed my desk to analyze much of anything. In an attempt to calm the Rocks down, I gathered up my green stamps and redeemed them for a bright-yellow coffeepot, which I took to work and let stand on my desk for a few days so they would get the idea and figure the spelling bee was over.

To divert them further, I showed Mrs. Urquhart how to crop a photo and gave her a cropping wheel all her own in the hope that she would show it to all the other Rocks, who would then forget about "Stet!" and start cropping their own photos. I raided the supply closet for extra cropping wheels so that I would have them ready to pass out; oddly enough, the Rocks didn't roll.

I found out why. Mrs. Urquhart had given her cropping wheel to her grandson. It hadn't done a thing for her, but she *had* been turned on by dummies.

She entered the office in a glow.

"You know that great big ad for the fur coat sale that was on the right-hand side of that blue sheet you were drawin' things on yester-day?" she said. "Well, I opened the paper this mornin', and there was the same ad in the same place, only in the *real* newspaper!"

I could not fathom her childish delight and incredulity. Of course the ad was in the paper in the same place; God help everybody on the second floor if it hadn't been. Then I understood. The thrill lay in having been behind the scenes, witnessing a workaday task while it was still on the drawing boards, and then seeing the finished product. She had acquired a conception of *sustained effort*; everything had clicked in her mind to give her an overall view of how a newspaper comes into being.

She stood before me, fat and frumpy in jersey, her gray hair glued to her head in an obdurate sea of finger waves, gazing at me as though I were the luckiest person she had ever seen.

I felt a rush of pity for her, followed by a warm affection that threatened tears. I forgot my own troubles and invited her to watch while I did that day's layout. It was Saturday morning, and I was making up Monday's pages. We were alone in the newsroom. She pulled up a chair next to mine and watched as I wrote heads, cut lines, and sized photos. I defined terms like "standing head" and "eyebrow"; she repeated them after me eagerly, like a child who loves school and is thrilled by the learning process.

She was particularly fascinated by fillers, saying that she had often wondered why those little three-inch things were stuck here and there throughout the paper. She asked where we got them, if we made them up ourselves, so I showed her the reams of printed fillers that we bought from a syndicate. I showed her how to mark them for setting, and she wrote a couple of 12-point heads for me.

When I wrote "lead out" on a too-short item, I explained what it meant and showed her the only slug I had: my by-line, which I salvaged from the kill rack and put on my key chain. She comprehended "leading out" instantly, nodded, and said: "So the printer puts pieces of metal like this one between the lines to make the space come out right. I always wondered why there were different-size spaces between the lines."

When I finished the dummies, I put them in a suction tube and let her send it up the pipe for me. I told her that the tube made two stops, first the engraving room and then the composing rooms; that the engravers kept the tubes containing photos and sent those containing copy on to the print shop.

She asked a logical question: "How do they know which ones have photos in them and which ones have writing?"

I held out a pneu and a photo and told her to roll it up and send it. In a trice, she had rolled the photo—glossy side out, something that had taken me more than a week to make a habit of.

As she inserted the photo into the tube—so carefully, like someone touching a priceless objet d'art—I could barely keep from crying. So many times in the past I had wished fervently that she would leave, but now I wanted her to stay. I fixed coffee in the now-notorious pot, and we talked for more than an hour. She told me she had never been "a working girl like you." She had married Mr. Urquhart—"a prince among men"—when she was nineteen, shortly after her graduation from the local young ladies' academy. Mr. Urquhart did not believe that wives should work. Not that she had ever needed to, of course, because he was a wonderful provider who would not let her—I held my breath—"lift a finger." She had never *wanted* to work, but. . . .

"I've always liked to put things together, you know—to arrange them and find just the right place for them, the perfect place. That's why I like to make patchwork quilts. My quilts have won prizes for years. I love to figure out the designs in my head, imagine it all, and get a picture of what it's going to look like when it's done. I always see it clearly in my mind, all finished, then I start to piece it together."

How much better, I thought, her layout would have been than my correct but uninspired one. I have no visual aesthetics; I could shove more brides into a page than anyone in the history of the paper, but the page never looked artistic. I fantasized Mrs. Urquhart as the head of the art department on some national magazine, spending her hoarded talent.

I wanted to rescue her somehow; get her a job, or shoot Mr. Urquhart. For a moment I contemplated quitting my job and then begging my boss to give it to her. It was one of the few totally unselfish moments of my life, and I'm grateful to her for opening me up to such a rare emotion. I had one of the linotype operators set her name on a slug and gave it to her for her key chain. The symbolic by-line was the only gesture I could make, the only offering I could extract from the farrago of emotions that I felt whenever I thought of her.

After our Saturday morning together, she never missed a chance to show off in front of her fellow Rocks. Whenever she came by the office and found another one there, she would say something like: "With all the sales goin' on, there'll be so many ads youall won't have room for the eyebrow on Ann Landers's standin' head!"

The Woman's Department was dashed against the worst Rocks when we collected what were genteely called "social notes" for a horrid little column called "The Passing Scene." The column had to be at least ten inches long, so we were always chasing around, wailing: "Oh, God, I've got to have ten inches before three o'clock," which naturally delighted the members of the Sports Department. We had to get on the phone, call Rock after Rock, and ask them if they knew of anybody who was visiting anybody, or anything of a *social* nature. We carefully emphasized "social" to ward off Rocky excursions into sagas of lingering deaths involving somebody who was slowly turning to stone, or being systematically eviscerated by the kind of surgeon found in the pages of *Kings Row*.

Even worse than the phone calls were the written social notes we received from Rock "stringers"—elderly female correspondents tucked away in small country towns. Most of them had no writing experience or talent; they had simply decided that since they were already functioning as town gossips, they could kill two birds with one stone and pick up some change by turning the paper into a clearinghouse for garbled libel.

> Mrs. Clyde Tilly is recuperating at the Vail Hospital with a twenty-pound tumor that was found in her by a benign surgeon swollen to twice the normal size, who also took her gallbladder. She is resting comfortably after losing a complete hysterectomy and receiving guests due to her inflamed female parts, including an Open House this Thursday. She has been visited by her daughter, Mrs. Junior Mims, who came three times after leading a prayer meeting in the hall.

Often Rock stringers sent us women's obituaries in the apparent belief that these rightly belonged in "The Passing Scene." One especially morbid Rock was famed for her Homeric similes:

> The rosy fingers of dawn were reaching through the sky when Mrs. Clarrie Goff, the hardworking one, passed to her reward in the angel-chorusing beyond. She was the widow of Nemo Felton Goff, remembered by all as the accordian-playing soybean farmer.

When I covered the Raleigh writers' conference, I was amazed to find that six of our most incoherent Rock stringers had written epic novels, which they tended to carry around in shopping bags. When word got around that I had sold stories to true confessions magazines, the stringers bore down on me with requests to read their manuscripts and "use your influence to help me get published," as though they thought I regularly swapped puns with Bennett Cerf simply because I had sold *something*. Like so many Rocks, they yearned for meaningful work and had chosen writing because, as they all explained, it was the only work they could do to which their husbands did not object. Why didn't they object? Because writing is something that can be done *at home*.

Thanks to the Southern man's belief that writing is woman's work, an unusually large number of Southern women have a go at it at some time in their lives. They can be found in cities and small country towns all over the South, but their collective story is told in one poignant brush stroke by Tennessee Williams in *Summer and Smoke*, in the scene in which Miss Alma is hostess to the local creative writing club.

Not poignant at all is the galaxy of women writers that the South has produced. We can thank the cult of Southern womanhood, with its emphasis on accomplished, cultured females and Hotspur males, for this stellar list of lady scribes. They, too, obediently worked at home.

Some of the most formidable Rocks that the Woman's Department encountered were the patriotic-society ladies. A typical Daughters chapter is like a typical phys ed class. There are always four or five naturally athletic girls who take it over and dominate everyone in it, who make a pact to throw the ball only to each other, and who never speak to the other class members except to yell: "Get out of the way!"

Most Daughters are lovable old gals who have no interest whatsoever in either politics or jingoistic patriotism. They just want somewhere to go and drink a spot of sherry with other old ladies, to gossip, complain a little, and, after delaying it as long as possible, go back home. Home might be a huge barn of a house in which they live alone and lonely, or a cramped city apartment—cramped not only because it is so small but because it is filled with towering mahogany furniture from less lonely days.

These are the Daughters that the Woman's Department never sees.

Here are the Daughters that no one can avoid:

The Sarah Sandringham Ellsworth chapter met with cookies and punch at the home of Mrs. Yancy Todd yesterday, who served, and Mrs. Slade Moncure who passed out favors. Special guest was Mrs. Albert Galloway, famous writer of books for children on animals, who revealed the fact that the moral fiber of our young people is more dangerous than ever before or since. She deplored the library, which has a copy of *Lady Chatterly's Lover* by Lloyd C. Douglas.

"This book is nothing but fragrant lick toes," said Mrs. Galloway, the heroine, who is an adultress. Her husband resides in a wheelchair from the waist down after the war. When questioned on the floor, the authoress said that everybody was running around in the woods with flowers on unprintable parts, and that the library ought to know better because it is public record that Lloyd C. Douglas has been a Communist dope for years.

The second speaker was the chapter's cause of violence, Mrs. Franklin Wallace, committee chairwoman of same. Mrs. Wallace said that the Communists are trying to entice clergymen and then bore from within. This, she said, is the best way to make anybody lose his religion because it is so much harder to see when it is under cover.

"Many clergymen have had experience right in their churches," said Mrs. Wallace, who feels every clergyman who agrees with her. A large number of them came up afterwards because they want to expose these things.

"Communism causes violence, and then violence causes Communism," she said, describing the enthusiastic agreement of the clergymen, who invited her back for more exploration of these things, which she cleverly calls "church-cleaning," she laughed, and the amused clergymen who also did, too.

Mrs. Wallace then ended, which inspired enthusiastic applause. A resolution was passed praising her unstinting efforts to help the clergy crush the Communists before Christian love is perverted by violent internal boring.

The Daughterly publicity chairman liked to write her own headlines, which gave the Woman's Department such memorable items as:

BORED FROM WITHIN, CLAIMS MRS. WALLACE
LIBRARY WASTES MONEY ON ADULTERY
REDS TOUCH OUR CHILDREN EVERYWHERE

The Ma Joad Rock may not be able to read or write. She says "his'n" and "her'n," uses triple negatives, and in some very isolated parts of the South she still uses a few Elizabethan idioms. Like her namesake, she is a dumpy tower of strength who holds her family together and gets them through every imaginable crisis. Though she thinks nothing of slitting a pig's throat and removing its still-pulsating organs, she has the innate sensitivity that was so exquisitely expressed by Jane Darwell in *The Grapes of Wrath*, in the silent scene in which Ma takes a last look at the precious mementos that she must leave behind.

Like the great lady she is, her name appears in the paper only three times: when she is born, when she marries, and when she dies.

The Southern Dowager is a dying breed. To qualify, a woman must be rich and eccentric, and our era is steadily eroding both. She should also live alone in a huge house on the Battery or in the Fan District, but golden age clubs and urban planning are natural enemies of such solitary splendor.

If you can imagine a woman who would sneer at the members of a golden age club and then proceed to terrorize them with her mere presence, then you know what a bona fide Southern Dowager is. She is too lofty and too much of a rugged individualist to get involved in Rock projects like politics and civic betterment. She would be a dismal failure at anything that requires tact, diplomacy, political savvy, teamwork, cooperation, compromise, and, most of all, a democratic turn of mind.

The Rock is a Roman matron, but the Dowager is a Mandarin empress. The Dear Old Thing wobbles; the Rock bustles; the Dowager glides, stalks, or stumps. She may or may not be tall, but it does not matter because everyone thinks she is. You never know what she is going to say or do next, and you would rather not be around when it happens. That rarely suitable accolade, " a handsome woman," suits her perfectly.

There was a marvelous Dowager in Mississippi when I was in school there. She was so reactionary that she still referred to Germany as Prussia and refused to use a telephone or even have one in her house. When her grandson had one installed for her as a birthday surprise, she ripped it out of the wall and ordered her yardman to chop it up with an ax. She communicated with calling cards.

She was utterly mad in the most imperious way. The democratization of mental illness that has taken place in recent years had led to sans-culottes neurosis, but, just as the Dowager held the line on Prussia and calling cards, she refused to be a traitor to her class by sinking one iota below the level of total lunacy. Like one of Mary McCarthy's characters in *The Group*, she believed that madmen are "the aristocrats of mental illness." The Dowager ruled her madness, however, just as she ruled everything and everybody else. She controlled it, it did not control her. It was a star in her crown, never a bat in her belfry.

She stumped around on a gold-handled cane, accompanied by a devoted black maid who stumped around on a silver-handled one. Everyone was surprised to discover that she had begun paying Social Security for the maid from the moment that act was passed in 1935. Many Southerners neglected to do this for many years. They considered it an insult to their sense of noblesse oblige, which required them to take care of aged servants. Since the Dowager was such a traditionalist, no one could understand why she chose to cooperate with the New Deal, of all things, when she had never cooperated with even one of her fellow Mississippians.

The mystery was solved when the maid had her sixty-second birthday. On the day the first check arrived, they went to the post office. The Dowager opened her box and gave the check to the maid, who nodded grimly and struck a huge kitchen match on the wall. As the check curled up in flames, the Dowager thumped her heavy cane on the floor like a drumroll in a military execution.

Every month the two of them performed this ritual right in the middle of the post office, oblivious to the stares they received.

The sight of a black in the bus station always drove this Dowager into a towering rage. She did not care in the least whether he was in the colored waiting room or the white. She would stump down to the she-riff's office and say: "There's a boy trying to run away. Go get him."

Other Mississippians might get bogged down in the civil rights con-troversy, just as they might be afflicted with mere neuroses, but the Dowager transcended any and all things proletarian. Once, when a liberal Ole Miss professor asked her if she was opposed to integration, she calmly replied: "Indeed I am not, sir. I think it is inexcusable to be opposed to integration. I am opposed to abolition."

She never bothered with flowery Southern manners, and she never smiled. Neither did the maid. People tried to pass the maid off as up-pity and impudent, but they were just as terrified of her as they were of the Dowager. When the maid went to the grocery store, she not only ignored the requisite hee-haw routine that blacks were expected to per-form, she did not even say hello. She stumped in and announced: "My mistress wants the following things." Whoever waited on her grabbed a pencil as quickly as possible.

The maid voted in every election with the Dowager beside her as bodyguard. God help any redneck who tried to stop her or give her a literacy test, or even a dirty look. He would have been skewered on the Dowager's cane.

The maid was *hers*, part of the fiefdom of madness she erected against the outside world that dared to be modern. Just as she forced calling cards with carefully penned messages on a world of telephones, so she forced the anachronism of a devoted black servant into a Mis-sissippi voting booth. It was her way of revenging herself on the entire state for being so déclassé as to get itself embroiled in nonexistent con-troversies like integration. To prove that slavery still existed, she *or-dered* the maid to vote—surely the ne plus ultra of Southern contradiction.

When the two of them arrived at the polling place, the symbol of democracy turned into a Field of the Cloth of Gold. The crowd parted to let them through, and utter silence reigned as they stumped forward together. The Dowager brought out the vassal in everyone; her weapon was her style. She could have commanded boon work and an oath of fealty with a mere glance.

The Southerner's response to this kind of Dowager suggests to me an unconscious yearning to escape the exhausting responsibilities of self-government and "let King George do it." This instinct is germane to human nature, else the world would never have lived so many centuries under royalty, nor invented it in the first place. I think that more and more people in America and throughout the Western world are beginning to feel this way on an unconscious level, in response to the recent spate of scandals and downfalls in democratic governments. They are wondering if we could be any worse off with a monarch, if Charles I was really any worse than Nixon?

We are also witnessing throughout America an increasing boredom, a feeling that life in today's world has become gray, lacking color, pageantry, and style. The human spirit craves plumage, and we are getting less and less of it as time goes on. American politicians in particular always miss this point. We now have a President who once earnestly stated that he was a Ford, not a Lincoln, but the people to whom he was trying to appeal were at the time devouring with happy awe the sight of Gatsby's Düsenberg.

Americans have begun to long for something that Southerners have always longed for and appreciated: a touch of the purple. The more we see of color-me-puce bureaucrats, the more our human spirits crave panache.

When Southerners feel this way, it is called reactionary politics; when other Americans are afflicted with a similar melancholy yearning, it is called a nostalgia kick. If you don't mind, I will ask you to be kind enough to consider the possibility that the rest of America is beginning to catch up with the South. I do not know what the answer is, I only know the problem: The folks next door keep moving into the White House.

# 14

## Way Down Upon the Hudson River

### or: When the Southerner Leaves Home

When you go apartment-hunting in the South you encounter little old ladies who ask you if you use strong drink. In New York you encounter paranoids who wonder if you will commit suicide—not that they care; what they worry about is blood on their fresh paint, a dubious smell in the hallway, or a hole in the awning as you pass through on your way to the sidewalk.

The Southerner who moves to any other part of the country has problems, but the culture shock that attacks the Southerner who moves North is almost indescribable. The first time I looked for an apartment in New York I wound up sobbing hysterically in my hotel room, longing for home.

Mr. Starvoninski met me at the door in his undershirt: "Yeah? Whaddya want?"

I stiffened with Southern hauteur. "I beg your pardon!"

"Whatsa matter, you deaf or sumpin'?"

I stiffened more, giving him a quiver from my Wasp nostrils as I went into a full freeze—the ultimate chastisement.

Mr. Starvoninski did not catch on.

"You smell sumpin', lady? Look, I ain't got all day. Whaddya want already?"

In order to put him in his place and make him feel ashamed of himself, I became icily polite. Incredibly, he didn't catch onto that either. He spat on the floor.

As he showed me the apartment, my throat ached with unshed tears. It wasn't so much that rat trap with a stale piece of cheese in it that I saw on the kitchen floor, but the way Mr. Starvoninski acted—or, rather, didn't act. He was not at all interested in standing around talking about this and that; he was not at all interested in my name; and, worst of all, he did not ask me where I was from. The only words he spoke were not words at all but numbers, such as the amount of rent. He actually told me what the rent was before the first hour was up. I couldn't believe it, he *actually* mentioned money, and so quickly, too.

In the South, you do eventually get around to finding out what the rent is. But both landlord and potential tenant are supposed to pretend sublime disinterest in such matters. The potential tenant pretends that she can pay any price because she has good blood, which the landlord of course realizes because all he has to do is look at her. The landlord pretends that he really does not need to supplement his good-blood income with rents; he inherited all this property and only rents it out in order to control the niceness of the neighborhood by filling his domain with *nice* people.

Southern landlords and potential tenants know that all this is a sham, but they play the game instinctively. And whether you rent the apartment or not, you have had a lovely time talking and dreaming. You have also discovered at least three acquaintances you have in common, and in general have both enjoyed a leisurely opportunity to tell part of your fascinating history to somebody new.

Mr. Starvoninski was not interested in my life. He was concerned with what he thought was my imminent suicide. His manner had upset me so much that I was on the verge of hysterical weeping, and he eyed me suspiciously as he scratched his bare belly.

"Lissen, I don't want no broads around here that're gonna bump 'umselves off. I had a broad in here las' month that filled the bathtub wid water and cut her wrists in it. Flooded the place. Cost me a C note."

I broke down then, but Mr. Starvoninski did not rush to get me a chair or a glass of water. He told me to get lost.

"Dat's what's wrong wid New York, ya know? All these crazy

broads come here to start a new life, and whadda dey do? Dey rent a pad and den dey bump 'umselves off."

Apartment-hunting is only the beginning of the Southern woman's problems in the North. Mr. Starvoninski was my first big problem, but there were any number of additional problems, which, when they were added up, amounted to another Mr. Starvoninski.

—Tipping.

There was a waitress in an Oxford, Mississippi, restaurant named Mrs. Rutherford who had worked there for twenty-five years. No one ever tipped her because she would have been so insulted and hurt that she would have cried her eyes out.

There are no Mrs. Rutherfords in New York.

—Yankee Accents.

Nothing is worse than a cockney whine, but I was used to that. I was more used to what the English in general have long considered the most beautiful, if not the only beautiful, American accent: the Tidewater Virginia with its Scottish-sounding *ou* diphthongs. It is a sussurating burr that sounds upper class even when its owner is not. The extreme Brooklynese accent of dees-dem-dose fame made me feel as though I had somehow stumbled into a movie featuring, *without* music, Damon Runyonesque gangsters and fallen women. Everything got very surreal, and I seemed to be waiting for the movie to end.

The non-Brooklynese accent is not all that bad, if only New Yorkers would stop screaming! Their favorite scream of all is "HEY!" It's "HEY! Whaddya doin'? . . . Where ya' think ya' goin' . . . Whaddya want? . . . HEY! Get outta th' way!"

—The sirens.

Nobody ever turns around with a worried frown and says: "I wonder if that's old Miz Stirling? It's going in the direction of her house, and I heard she was doin' poorly since she broke her hip."

—The refusal to become involved.

It's no wonder that New York is the intellectual mecca of America —New Yorkers never stop reading, no matter what happens. They ignore madmen, singing drunks, women in labor, and they don't even look up to watch a fight. Their ability to concentrate boggles the Southern mind. What, after all, could be more interesting than other people's business?

Whatever they're reading, that's what.

I finally found out why they read so intensely while the world is going to pieces around them. If you look up and catch the madman's eye, you may be the first to get stabbed. If you notice the drunk, he will pick you to throw up on. If you catch the whelping woman's eye, she will beg *you* to call an ambulance or lend her a piece of string. If you catch the fighters' eyes, you will be in the fight before you can say Jack Robinson.

No wonder so many terrible things happened to me on the subway. I was everybody's sweetheart because I kept looking up.

—The literalness of Northern men.

Southern women flirt so automatically that half the time they don't even realize they are doing it. Batting your lashes is a Pavlovian reaction as soon as you say word one to any man, and so is that rapt gaze called "hanging onto his every word." In the South, it's all a game and everyone plays it; there are ways to make it clear that you are serious; you increase or decrease the watts and voltage depending upon how you *really* feel and what, if anything, you want the man to do about it.

Southern men know the difference; Northern men do not (understandably, since Northern women, especially New Yorkers, simply don't carry on in this fashion). When you rattle off a standard Southern thank-you—"Oh, you're just so nice, I don't know what I'd *do* without you!" the Northern man *believes you*! He believes you so much that he follows you home.

By the same token, the Southern man in New York who asks a woman for directions is crushed when she replies: "Two blocks east, turn left, and it's the third or fourth brownstone down."

Ships that pass in the night are not too much of a problem; if a man keeps on following you, you can always throw yourself on a nice policeman and say: "Oh! Thank goodness you're here; I don't know what I'd do without you!" Men that you see every day are another matter; you can't very well call a policeman and sic him on your boss, the sales manager, or the entire mailroom. Once the Northern man is subjected to some Southern-style flirting, he is insatiable. He cannot get enough of it; he wants more and more batted eyes, gasps, and gazes that enshrine him on the spot every time you look at him.

When you go out with a Northern man, his mind is filled with all those belles he has seen emoting on the "Late Late Show," which set him up to expect a hot-blooded, tempestuous, wanton hussy! Here we arrive at Northern self-contradiction. While he expects total abandon from you, he is also very tentative in your company and a little afraid—because he is certain that at any moment you are going to explode and throw something. You are supposed to be a passive geisha with a ferocious temper, as well as a great lady who can't wait to get her pants off. There is no escape from the Southern belle crazy-quilt image no matter where you go.

—On the job.

The first problem is *getting* the job. Northerners, particularly men, think that all Southern women are dumb belles. When they discover that you are not, they get hurt. You have the choice of playing dumb and not getting the job, or playing smart and not getting the job.

Wall Street is the hardest nut to crack because they think you can't add two and two. Lawyers are afraid you will spill the beans on every client's secret affairs the moment you type a confidential letter. The more utilitarian sort of business offices fear that things will not be "colorful and exciting" enough for you, as if every day were a barbecue at Twelve Oaks down in your neck of the woods.

The easiest place to get a job is in publishing, because people who are drawn to this field tend to be more dashing as well as more relaxed, and occasionally more haphazard. They don't mind doing crazy things and taking risks—like hiring Southerners.

They also suspect that you may have some sort of weird Southern literary genius, that something Faulknerian is buried somewhere in your pretty little head.

It is never quite clear just what they have in mind, but it has something to do with the dark side of the Southern moon: Maybe, in a melancholy mood, you will discover an unknown and very melancholy Southern genius and be able to "understand" him and work with him. Maybe you are so tormented, haunted, and full of secret fears that you will be able to hit it off with *any* writer. Maybe you will commit suicide by jumping out of the thirty-fifth-floor window with a just-published book in your arms and they can get some free publicity for it. Whatever it is, they expect the worst, so you're hired.

—Northern women.

They get nervous around Southern women because they think we flirt all the time, which is true. Like Northern men, they don't realize that it's a game, so they feel threatened.

Some of the other things they expect:

· We will come waltzing in three hours late, wearing a long dress.

· We won't allow men to see us eat.

· We will manipulate everybody in record time and have the entire staff at each other's throats.

· We will sleep with the boss.

· We will figure out ways to get other people to do our work because we are lazy.

· We will expect to be waited on hand and foot.

· We will burst into tears at least once a day.

The most annoying thing about Northern women in offices: Whenever a black male employee speaks to a Southern woman, all the Yankee women stop immediately whatever they are doing and watch to see what she does, how she acts, and what she says.

This can be great fun if you can find a black man with a sense of humor well laced with irony—and there are few blacks who have not had the opportunity to develop one. The two of you can put on a real show for the Yankees, complete with "Whu'fo you do dat?" "It don't make no nebbermind," and calling each other "bubba."

—Northern racial attitudes.

Once Northerners get used to having a Southerner around the office, they start to slither up to your desk during coffee breaks to assure you that they, too, are prejudiced.

The typical Yankee opener:

· "I can't tell most people this, but. . . ."

Typical Yankee inquiries:

· "How do you feel when you see one with a white woman? Does it make you sick?"

· "Did you ever see a lynching?"

· "What do you do when one sits down next to you on the subway?"

· "What would you do if you were raped by one?" (The expected answer: "Commit suicide.")

· "What would your father do if you were raped by one?" (The expected answer: "Hunt him down.")

· "What would your brother do if you were raped by one?" (Northerners seem to think that all Southern women have a brother. Often the question is: "What would your brothers do if you were raped by one?" because some Northerners think that every Southern woman has a whole gang of brothers just waiting with a rope.)

The worst thing about prejudice in the North is that many Northerners feel free to throw the word "nigger" around when talking to a Southerner.

"Dear Ann Landers: How can I tell my Southern family that I am moving North?"

Every breakaway story I have heard follows a pattern something like this:

—The announcement of intentions.

"Mary Lou's just goin' to go *hog wild* up there!"

Going hog wild is a Southern code for having sexual intercourse. No one ever admits that Mary Lou might have been getting it regularly at home because everybody knows the North is where bad things happen to nice girls. Northern men cannot be depended on to be gentlemen; they take advantage of nice girls, they don't believe that *any* girl is a nice girl, and, furthermore, they *deliberately* get a nice girl drunk so she'll. . . .

How any Southerner can worry about drunkenness is beyond me. The family knows that Mary Lou has been a devotee of the Gospel According to the Interfraternity Council for four years, but suddenly it is Northern men who are going to get her drunk. The last thing they will admit is that Mary Lou could drink the entire New York National Guard under the table.

—The second stage.

When the family finds that Mary Lou will not be dissuaded by warnings of her moral ruin, they launch the bluestocking argument. She will become a hard-bitten intellectual just like all Yankee women. She will take to wearing black turtleneck sweaters and jeans; she will sit on the floor and *argue* with men!

And not only that, she will need glasses. Why Mary Lou should be cursed with bad vision the moment she crosses the Mason-Dixon line is never explained, but the image of the bespectacled Yankee governess has never quite died.

A woman in publishing whom I know horrified her family when they found out that she had actually finished editing a manuscript while timing her early labor pains. She should have been on her bed of pain, and there she was, timing the assaults on her delicate pelvis and working like a Yankee grind.

—The third stage.

"She'll come back with her tail between her legs, just you wait and see."

Southern pride in defeat knows no defeat. Mary Lou is supposed to be the beatin'est child, but now her family warns her that she'll be just plain *beaten* by Yankee assaults on her energy, her physical strength, her mental health, her emotional endurance, and her patience. Her pertness will wilt.

If this doesn't work, the family steps up its warnings until it sounds as if they expect Mary Lou to come back on a marble slab.

"Somebody'll throw acid in your face, and it'll eat through everything, bones and all. There won't be anything left."

"You don't know who you'll get mixed up with. Some of those criminals don't look like criminals at all. Like in that Marlon Brando movie. They wear tuxedos all the time, but they're criminals just the same and they'll do away with you if they think you know too much."

"You'll be kidnapped, and they'll hypnotize you and turn you into a gunslingin' revolutionary." This Patty Hearst fantasy is actually a modernized version of the old white-slave fear, but the really fascinating part is Southerners worrying about a Southerner becoming a gunslinger.

—Mary Lou's final victory.

If she stays in New York long enough, the family will decide that she is an eccentric, which is the nicest thing any Southerner can say about one of their own.

The Southern woman who moves North often goes crazy over Jewish men. Jewish men also like her. It is a case of chutzpah meeting chutzpah; both have a certain exotic quality, and both are high-profile types from whom others tend to expect unusual behavior. Perhaps the most important thing they have in common is that they are both enigmas to those outside their respective groups. Southerners and Jews regularly puzzle, astound, and enrage other Americans.

After the Southern man's machismo, I found Jewish men a relief and delight. They are definitely the indoor type and would never take a girl down to the town dump to shoot at rats. This is not the Jewish man's idea of a date; he prefers concerts, plays, or dinner in a place that will not erupt into a free-for-all that ends in a shoot-out. The reason he is not macho is that he does not need to be. He enjoys a confident assumption of masculinity based on the simple fact of being born male. He is the only American man who still has an ancient rite of passage at puberty; when he is thirteen, he stands up before a large gathering and announces, "Today I am a man." That's that; he believes it, and so does everyone else. He does not need to spend the rest of his life proving it at every turn.

He is proud of being an intellectual because Jews revere scholarship; Judaic tradition holds it to be a manly duty. And, being comfortable with his urbanity, he does not get sudden urges to take to the woods or get back to the soil.

My own discovery of Jewish men involved a subconscious awareness of certain things that exerted a mystical charm on me. I knew that Jewish men had to cover their heads in the synagogue, and somehow that was comforting because it made them a little like women. I could identify with them in a funny sort of secret way. I also knew Jewish genealogy is traced through the female line; if your mother is Jewish and your father is Gentile, you are Jewish. If it's the other way around, you are not Jewish. In neither case are you *half*-Jewish. This seemed to me like a clear-cut gynecocracy, completely different from the perpetual Southern yin and yang in which women were worshiped and yet patronized, up and yet down, here but not there.

The only time I had any difficulty with Jewish men was when I cooked for them. No matter how "nonreligious" they think they are, they get an odd look on their faces when Shiksabelle makes gravy with pan drippings and milk.

The male Southern expatriate has many of the same problems as the Southern woman, plus a few choice ones of his own.

His "niceness," which includes his soft-spokenness and his gift for pleasant preliminary conversation, are interpreted as weakness. Northerners think they can get the best of him in a hard-driving business deal. "He won't be forceful enough," they say. "He'll let people walk all over him because manners mean more to him than making money."

—Great Yankee expectations.

• "He must have some terrible habit. That's why he left home, because he couldn't do it down there."

• "He must be the black sheep of his family."

• "He'll haul off and shoot somebody at the drop of a hat." (This is *nice?*)

• "He's a mama's boy." (In Portnoy land?)

• "He sits around in a daze." (This is a tangled fantasy consisting of part Thomas Wolfe tortured novelist, part Ashley Wilkes spinning dreams, and a large chunk of the Mint Julep Syndrome that makes Northerners think Southern men never leave the porch.

• "One day, he just won't show up." (The hare-brained image, related to the hair-trigger image.)

• "He'll hire all his crazy cousins." (He won't. Southern clannishness is abstract—talking about blood ties is more usual than doing anything about them.)

• "He'll get the women all stirred up." (True.)

• "What'll we do with him at lunch?" (I have thought about this for years and finally decided that they expect him to order grits and embarrass all the out-of-town clients.)

When a Southern man proves himself to be a good businessman, Northerners change their tune and see him as a reincarnation of the ruthless riverboat gambler who never lost a poker game. Suddenly he acquires magical powers; he knows what cards his opponent holds, he *knows* when his opponent is bluffing, and he himself can outbluff anybody in New York!

Now he is strong, like Rhett Butler. Yankees look up to him as a real man and assume that he is a consummate Don Juan. They ask him about all his women and try to pick his brain for helpful hints on seduction.

Three things no Southerner in the North can avoid:

—The misuse of "youall."

Yankees think they are being awfully cute when they tiptoe up to one lone Southerner and say: "How are youall today?" They cannot get it through their heads that this word is *plural only*. The English language needs two forms of the second person, and Southerners are the only Americans who have both. It is extremely convenient when talking to more than one person at the same time, and to differentiate between the president of a company and the company itself. (My literary agent, for example, is "you," and the William Morris Literary Agency is "youall.") Yankees persist in confusing "youall" with the Runyonesque "youse," which can be either singular or plural.

It is possible to explain the foregoing to Yankees, but it is an utter waste of time to try to explain what determines the frequency of "youall" in an extended conversation. It's a matter of instinct. When talking to two or more people, you establish the plural with a "youall," but it is not necessary to repeat it each time you use a second-person verb. It is repeated when it becomes necessary to reestablish the plural, but I cannot explain when this is. I just know, thass all. Like dancing, it is something that one does without thinking.

—The South-haters.

These charmers are usually flaming Wasp liberals and very often female. They are so liberal it hurts—any minority group member who has the misfortune to tie up with them. Female South-haters harbor a secret yearning to be Christianity's Great White Protestant Goddess, one way or another. One way is a Jewish beau, another way is a hyphenated Catholic beau, and a really superb way is a black beau. This garden of earthly delights likes to bestow herself on a man who will "appreciate" her—she really means "crave."

Miss Blondes-Have-More-Fun must suppress her real hatreds, but she *has* to hate someone to let off steam. The one acceptable hate-object in her lexicon is Southerners—because we're so bigoted.

—That "certain-slant-of-light" depression.

Emily Dickinson could have been a Southerner when she wrote of that inchoate melancholy that strikes on winter afternoons. The febrile attempts of the sun to penetrate the canyons of New York on a bitter-cold day have torn me apart many times. The sense of dichotomy is unbearable and makes a Southerner homesick—not necessarily for the folks back home, whom he may have moved North to get away from, but for lush warmth and an earth of black velvet. The wet richness of the Southern landscape seduces the senses, which may be why outdoor sex is such an ingrained Southern habit. Nothing is more likely to start me screaming like a madwoman than New York in February with its piles of blackened snow full of yellow holes drilled by dogs.

# *15*

## "We're Okay, are Youall Okay?"

### or: The Last Pre-Copernicans

As I walked through the Charlotte airport, I heard an unmistakable voice.

"Oh, Law! Now *where* is my ticket? I just had it one minute ago. It's vanished into thin air!"

It had to be a Dear Old Thing. There was no doubt about it, especially after I heard the full thud of her handbag and the rattle of pill bottles tumbling out and rolling across the floor. Dr. Jonathan Latham wasn't the only one; now *I* was going to meet a Dear Old Thing in the airport. My heart leaped with excitement. My first Dear Old Thing in three years! I hadn't realized how much I missed them.

I turned around—and stared in disbelief.

It was a Dear Old Thing, all right, but she was wearing a pantsuit. Moreover, she was squatting like a Marlboro Man over a campfire, picking up her own junk. There wasn't a male lackey in sight, and she had not even bothered to look for one. Before anyone could help her, she had everything back in her bag *and* had actually found her ticket.

When, a few moments later, my friends arrived, the first thing they said was:

"What's the matter? You look so sad."

Before I could reply, I saw what was obviously a Rock in full sail. *She* wore a pantsuit, too.

210

"Oh, no . . ." I murmured.

As we drove to my friends' house, I saw one woman after another in pantsuits, and many of the women were old. I thought: "If I see a Dowager in one, I'm going to burst into tears." I was wearing a pantsuit, too, but that was different. I was not being logical, I was experiencing the awful realization that the South is changing. I had left it in a fury three years before, after a battle royal with a Good Ole Boy Who Wasn't, vowing that I would never return to such a benighted place. Now I had returned to a South that promised to be much less benighted, and I was ready to cry.

I was to stay a week in Charlotte with two friends, both male. As we entered their house laden down with my suitcases, I halfway hoped that a scandal would erupt. I wanted the neighbors to come snooping around and then spread the word about "the goings-on in that house." But no one even noticed us.

After dinner we watched TV. When the commercial came on, I could not hold back my tears any longer.

"This is my wife. I love her. I love her because she takes good care of herself. . . ."

Suddenly I was sobbing wildly and screaming: "If they're going to sell snake oil, why don't they sell it with style, they way we used to down here!"

The flat, bland voices of the ad couple went on, mawkish, unconvincing, sickeningly lifeless. Like Cyrano, I kept thinking, "Oh, what you could have said!" *Cures anything from loss of manhood to dandruff. Any of you ladies with personal complaints will bloom anew if you take Dr. Towson's tonic. Yes, sir, you can even rub it on your sore back and worm the hound dogs with it.*

I started running up and down the floor in a tearful, frustrated temper. I could think of nothing but the millions of Southern homes into which the ad was beamed, the children, whose Southernness would be diluted if they grew up with *that*.

My friends stared at me, and one of them shouted:

"Oh, Law, Flossie's gone to pieces!"

His dire pronouncement saved the day. That was more like it! I collapsed on the sofa in helpless laughter while the two men stared. They were not, of course, upset; they had grown up with this sort of thing. They simply waited through it until I was calm enough to speak.

"But you see," I choked, "we're the same age. We know about going to pieces, but what about those poor children growing up now who'll never be able to brag about female relatives who went to pieces? I mean, what's the South without going to pieces? Women in pantsuits don't go to pieces—they're liberated!"

Naturally, I started crying again. For the sake of auld lang syne, I even walked up and down the floor and wrung my hands.

"Flossie, are you gettin' the pip?" Jimmy asked me.

That started me giggling. By this time we were all half-tight, so I regaled them with the sage of the pain in my right ovary, an affliction that runs in the family. I was desperate for Southernness in any shape or form. Including bourbon. I downed a pint.

"We're all gettin' old, I reckon," Bill sighed. "I've got prostate trouble."

I stared at him with swollen red eyes, and my head began to tremble just like a Dear Old Thing's.

"You can't have *that*," I said. "That not fair! That's *male* trouble! There's no such thing as male trouble!"

Whereupon, I passed out.

The next day, despite my hangover, things began to look up. I discovered that the ultimate Southern contradiction is *static change*, for when I arrived at the TV studio to talk about this book, the lady interviewer greeted me with:

"Hello, I'm so glad to see you. You look lovely, you really do, but don't you say orgasm. We absolutely can't say orgasm or the switchboard will light up like a Christmas tree."

Thank God, I thought. The good old hung-up South still lives.

I was further cheered at lunch when my old girl friend treated me to a comparative analysis of her mother's and her grandmother's change of life. Warmed to the subject, I told the entire story of my right ovary again while my two male friends calmly ate their lunch.

The pièce de résistance awaited me, for that night I met a more subdued version of Royal Montgomery, a young woman of twenty-five who is a member of the hunt. She had just encountered something shocking and was hardly in the door before she was indignantly regaling us with the story.

"One of the women I ride with buttons her *third button* !" she said, nostrils flaring. Proudly, she stroked her own black melton riding jacket; sure enough, her third button was undone.

"*Everybody* knows you don't button that third button!"

We all listened gravely. It was true: We all knew that you are not supposed to button the third button, but none of us, including the hunt member, could remember why. All we knew was, it is traditional to leave it open.

Thank God, I thought. If the hunt member was only twenty-five, there was still hope that paleolithic thinking would not die out completely. Where else but the South could you find a twenty-five-year-old woman trembling in fury because someone had buttoned a button?

After she had calmed her nerves with four bourbons, we all went out to dinner. Along the way, we picked up a Poor Willis, a H ot 'n' Holler old maid, and some assorted newspaper types. One of the latter was a Northern woman who had been in the South for seven years.

"You know," she said, "I still don't understand what makes you people tick."

I beamed at her.

"You don't?"

"All this 'ma'am' business," she burst out. "Look, I'm a newspaperwoman, right? In a newsroom, there's no sex differences, right? But these guys keep calling me 'ma'am'! And they take forever to say what they've got to say—it's 'if you don't mind' and 'would you be good enough,' and on and on and *on!*"

The hunt member caught my eye, grinned, and said:

"You've got to play the game."

"What game?" asked the Northerner.

"Flirting," the women chorused.

"Ecccck!" she said. "Why does everybody have to *flirt?*"

It was then that I found the elusive key for which I had been searching since my return. It was the key both to the South's past and to its future. Why flirt, indeed? It had nothing to do with sex, since it was meaningless most of the time. Why would anyone spend so much time on such a verbal trapeze? The reason lay in the Southerner's conception of himself.

We are egocentristic, the last pre-Copernicans left. Flirting, like everything else Southerners do, is self-dramatization, a personal form of secession to assure our individuality and our determination to be the center of attention and stand out in the crowd—to make people and events revolve *around us*.

The distraught mother of the bride whose wedding announcement failed to make the paper the next day was a pre-Copernican. It wasn't her daughter's disappointment that motivated her to tell that long-drawn-out story. If her main concern had been for her daughter, she would simply have said: "My daughter's write-up wasn't in. Why not?"

But no. She snatched center stage for herself and performed like a true tragedienne. She wanted the spotlight, she needed to celebrate *herself*. Southerners have always feared centralized government; they also fear, perhaps more, centralized personality. They refuse to "come out of Washington." The sun must revolve around them, not the other way around.

Black Southerners are the same way. The Northern social worker cannot understand why her client launches into an interminable and tangled saga to explain why he lost his job, his wife, his food stamps, his best friend, and his front tooth. She simply wants the facts so that she can approve his application for welfare, but what she gets is an action-packed account in which he is the star of a drama featuring the long-suffering Loretta, a Bible-backed neighbor known variously as "ole badmouth" or "the witchwoman," and of course, the inevitable Donald, who seems to have no connection with anything but who bugaloos through the story just the same.

Pre-Copernicanism as it is practiced in the South has been a successful counteroffensive to the problem of aging. America as a whole has never had the European tradition of splendid old grandes dames, but the South has always been a mecca for old ladies. There, they have *power*. The Dowager is comparable to the hideous old Frenchwoman with a salon full of young male intellectuals. The Rock is reminiscent of England's doggy, buck-toothed, tweed-shrouded country woman who dominates everyone in her trumpeting voice and completely runs the village. As for the Dear Old Thing, she is Ireland's biddy, who bends the priest's ear as she practices her sole form of power: exhaustion.

These old ladies, Southern and foreign, are magnificent in their wreckage, not pitiful in their dotage like the average American senior citizen who is shuttled off to Phoenix. A country without a tradition of redoubtable battle-axes is a country that does not offer its young women any positive images for female old age. Despite all the achievements of the women's movement, it has not solved the problem of old women. The South partially solved it with pre-Copernicanism: by granting self-absorbed old ladies center stage regardless of the occasional consequences. The "golden years" are not really golden at all, but they take on a certain glitter if an old lady can be domineering and powerful.

One of the most valuable products of the South was the old-time dean of women who read etiquette books rather than psychology books. She kept such a close watch over her bevy of belles that they blinked against the sunlight when they emerged from their dorms, like Dr. Manette leaving the Bastille. The maturing young woman *needs* such dragons to lock horns with because when she loses—as young women invariably lost when they crossed swords with these fusty egomaniacs—she gains a model for her own future old age. She realizes that an old lady can be truly awesome and influential. Moreover, she gains a precious insight into the real meaning of the expression "woman's place," because a formidable old lady fills a need in the human soul that harks back to the prepatriarchal times when we all worshiped goddesses.

America has tried mightily to eliminate old ladies entirely by developing the standardized size 10 grandmother who lives in a high-rise, takes trendy courses, attends encounter sessions, perpetually diets, and has affairs. The sleek new granny believes Dr. David Reuben when he tells her to copulate into her eighties, with the result that many aging American females are a figure of contempt (men) and dread (women).

Such women are not pre-Copernicans; they have no sense of self. They would be much better off if they could look forward to inspiring terror in their old age rather than hoping frantically to inspire passion.

Southerners of all classes have always had a resounding pre-Copernican sense of self. Archie Bunker is a Good Old Boy, but he doesn't know it and doesn't refer to himself that way. In his opening duet with Edith, he sings: "Guys like us, we had it made." In the South, guys like that have enjoyed a *name*. The Good Ole Boy has recently been mourned as a vanishing species by writers Paul Hemphill and B. Drummond Ayres, Jr., to name only two eulogists. What they mourn is not the Good Ole Boy per se, but the passing of someone who had a high-profile identity—hard to come by nowadays.

As long as the South does not lose its pre-Copernican swath, it does not matter what incidental changes take place. Yet like every Southerner I have an imp of the perverse; I shall mourn the passing of everything, all the things, I've complained about in this book. And that, ladies and gentlemen, is what it means to be a Southerner.

# Afterword to the New Edition

My publisher's decision to re-issue *Southern Ladies and Gentlemen* proves the power of word-of-mouth advertising.

At the time of its original publication in 1975, I got stacks of fan letters during its two-edition hardback life. They continued coming in steadily through eight paperback editions, but then something strange happened. After the title went out of print in the early eighties, my mail, instead of tapering off, kept coming.

Old readers told me they wanted to read it again, but when they tried to buy another copy they couldn't find it. New readers said they had heard about it, or come across a quotation from it, but when they tried to buy a copy they couldn't find it. The most memorable letter came from a woman who wanted to buy fifty copies for party favors—but couldn't find it.

As time went on, my mail took on a note of desperation that frequently threatened to spill over into hysteria. People wrote me about how they had lent their only copy to a friend and never got it back, described their frustrating experiences with book-find services, asked me to sell them my personal copies, confessed to stealing public library copies—and even, in one case, to xeroxing the library's only remaining circulation copy after discovering that the rest had been scarfed.

A few weeks ago I heard from a woman who said she had read her copy so many times that it fell apart, and now she wants another one, and while she's at it she wants to buy a dozen more for Christmas gifts, but she can't find it anywhere, and the book store told her it was out of print, and she nearly died, so would I please tell her where can she get some?

I answered all of this mail, at first with commiseration because I didn't know what to tell you, but lately with pleasure since learning that a new edition was planned. You made it happen, so before I go any further let me say thank you for your loyalty and enthusiasm, and for the delightful and touching letters that have so often made my day.

Has the South changed in the eighteen years since I wrote *Southern Ladies and Gentlemen?*

Of course. It's always Nixon Agonistes time in the pea patch. The latest New South—the eighth by my count—is coping with another trauma. This time it's the invasion of Damnyuppies whose lust for "relocating" (they never say "move") is turning our gothic paradise into a homogenized Sunbelt.

If Oakland has no *there*, Damnyuppies have no *from.* Whatever ethnic background they once possessed has faded with the geographical and psychological distance they have put between themselves and their origins. Most of them seem to have no distinctive traits, habits, or accents—just master's degrees. Higher education, which bestows mobility, has made Damnyuppies *fromless.* If anyone wishes to say "That's what America's all about," now is the time to say it.

Southerners, perhaps the only Americans still capable of home-sickness, can now experience it without leaving home. Damnyuppies are why Southern towns now have Neighborhood Watch to stamp out the crime that used to be stamped out by watchful neighbors. Damnyuppies are why "Mall" is now capitalized, like Golgotha, and why it has replaced the bus station as a good-ole-boy hangout: the bus station has been torn down to make room for a brand-new "Old Town."

Perpetually searching for instant traditions and the quick 'n' easy identity they call the "New You," Damnyuppies display a paradoxical urge to feed off Southern uniqueness on the one hand, and reject it on the other. Take, for example, their linguistic voyeurism.

If a Southerner makes an idiomatic reference to the subtle regional hierarchies known as "ordinary," "common," and "trash," the Damnyuppie gets that lean hungry look and asks him to explain the difference.

Ever polite, the Southerner complies. "If you got a beat-up ole car in yore yard, but it runs, you're ordinary. If you got a beat-up ole car in yore yard and it won't run, you're common. But if you got *pieces* of a beat-up ole car in yore yard, you're trash."

A few days later, expect to see a letter-to-the-editor pleading for more sensitivity to what Damnyuppies call "socio-economic status."

Damnyuppies secretly fear Southern *excess*, as well they might. In *Colonel Effingham's Raid*, Berry Fleming says that this trait is rooted in topology: lacking the breathtaking scenic views of the New England coast or the mountainous West, we atone for our humble red clay and commonplace sand hills by substituting breathtaking characters.

I think Southern excess is rooted in our earliest history. The Pilgrims got good Indians but we got bad Indians. Our ancestors had bleeding heads—not bleeding hearts—from being scalped. They died like flies of famine—not hunger, famine. They fell victim to madness—not neurosis, madness—from living on the edge of a wilderness as sultry as black velvet and not knowing what might happen next.

The only way to relieve such suspense is to do something outlandish—i.e., *that's* what happened next.

Southerners are no different from anyone else, it's just that we do things that never seem to happen in Nebraska and Connecticut. The only shade of gray we ever produced is the Confederate uniform, and Damnyuppies know it. That is what makes them nervous. They never know what we might do.

"What will the South do?" has ever been the leading question in American political life. What will the South *do* if Lincoln is elected? What will the South *do* if Geraldine Ferraro is nominated? What will the South *do* if Ross Perot runs? The clot of primaries called "Super Tuesday" grew out of the conviction that the South is bound to *do* something, and so, unable to stand the suspense, politicians came up with Super Tuesday to find out what we would *do* before we did it.

Handed the historical role of reacting, we have performed it so well, and with such undiluted joy, that the rest of the country is secretly disappointed whenever we seem to settle down. I am convinced that the reason for the current fascination with earthquakes, hurricanes, and meteors is that the South hasn't *done* anything lately.

The presence of Damnyuppies in our midst has given an interesting new twist to Southern graciousness and hospitality. Now that our towns are being swallowed up by interstate highways and metropolitan areas, a new kind of letter-to-the-editor has been cropping up with suspicious frequency in local newspapers.

They are lavishly worded paeans from grateful commuters who have been saved from various fates by native good samaritans. Stalled motorists get help from farmers and hunters, who stop and fix their cars for them right on the road. One obviously awestruck motorist wrote in praise of a samaritan who drove all the way to NAPA to buy him a new fan belt, drove back and installed it, and refused to accept any payment for his labor. Such letters always end with effusions along the lines of "I didn't think there were people like that left!" and "It proves how much good there is in human nature!"

Well, maybe. Putting aside the possibility that the samaritan was one of those good ole boys who will grab any excuse to go to NAPA, what it proves is the strength of the unreconstructed Southern ego. We simply get a kick out of being gracious when it results in an awestruck non-Southerner. That's why the South is the only place in the world where even the working class practices noblesse oblige.

The sexual and civil rights revolutions have pretty much eliminated the North-toward-home fictive genre in which oversexed and oversensitive young men keep saying, "I've got to get out of this place." Otherwise, Southern writing has not changed much, and neither has my opinion of it.

We still turn out too many plotless doorstoppers "about" three generations of women who sit on the porch and talk.

Our writers continue to clog up their prose with descriptive bulletins from the South's great industrial plant, the ol' factory: the smell of the earth, the smell of smoke, the smell of worms, the church smell, the dawn smell, the night smell, the man smell, and the woman smell, which results in the sex smell, which leads back to the earth smell.

Our regional disease of simileitis still produces sentences that scream *underline me!* Sheila Bosworth's second novel, *Slow Poison*, contains some excellent similes ("the empty chair gave the table a depressing visual effect, like a necklace with a missing stone"), but Bosworth has a tendency to get carried away in a decidedly Southern manner; "her voice hit the porch like flat Coca-Cola" and "her calf muscles twanging like twin ukeleles" say nothing and say it badly.

The most important recent event in Southern literary history was the publication of the sequel to *Gone With the Wind*, Alexandra Ripley's *Scarlett*. Four book editors asked me to review it but I turned them all down. To my way of thinking, writing a sequel to a dead author's novel is the first cousin of plagiarism, and I refuse to read it.

I did review two other spin-offs that say much about which side really won the Civil War.

*Scarlett Greene* by Barbara Ucko is about a Wisconsin couple sunk in a terminal South-toward-home complex. He a timid English major with a yearning for decadence brought on by his Faulkner studies; she a vague malkin whose countless rereadings of *Gone With the Wind* have so loosened her grip on reality that she can do little except quote verbatim page after page of Scarlett-Rhett dialogue.

They meet in the liberal mecca of the University of Wisconsin at Madison. Recognizing each other's fake Southern accents, they realize they are made for each other and decide to get married. They flip a coin to see whether they will live in Mississippi or Georgia, and Georgia wins. They settle in a little town where he becomes a high school English teacher and she produces three children named Scarlett, Melanie, and Leslie before taking to her bed of pain for a career of ladylike ailing.

Intellectual teenager Scarlett is the unpaid drudge in this webby household. While Mama languishes in bed humming "Tara's Theme," Scarlett cooks, cleans, and—to make sure she will never be hungry again—eats. Longing for chivalry but finding instead the sexual revolution, the fat but sensitive Scarlett suffers rejection by one stoned draft dodger after another until she moves up North and has an illegitimate baby by a black man. Presumably this symbolizes a break with her past.

Much worse, in fact, unbelievable, is *The Blue Bicycle* by Régine Deforges, a French novel that borrowed so heavily from the original opus that the Margaret Mitchell Estate sued and won.

The story opens on September 1, 1939, at Montillac, the beloved vineyard of Pierre Delmas, a self-made man married to the aristocratic Isabelle de Montpleynet. They have three daughters; Sabine, Lea, and Laure, all raised by bossy Nanny Ruth. The middle daughter, Lea, is her father's favorite.

Hearing that Laurent d'Argilat, scion of the neighboring vineyard, Roches-Blanches, is going to marry his cousin Camille, Lea rushes off to find her father to ask him if it's true.

It just so happens that Papa has spent the day at Roches-Blanches talking about the impending Nazi invasion of Poland.

"War! War!" Lea cuts in passionately. "I'm fed up with hearing about war."

When Papa verifies the gossip about Laurent and Camille, Lea decides to lay siege to her beloved at the Roches-Blanches garden party the next day.

There Lea meets her hated rival. "Camille was much too ugly for Laurent," she thinks. "How boring it must be to live with someone like her, with her delicate health and her meek ways."

Lea lures Laurent into the greenhouse and confesses her love for him, but he tells her that he must marry Camille because, "We belong to an old family, we're worn out, we need peace and quiet." Furious, Lea kicks a flowerpot and storms out.

In the woods where she goes to calm down she sees "a man leaning against a tree who was watching her with an amused smile."

"Anger becomes you, my beauty," he says. His name is François Tavernier. A gunrunner for the French government, he mocks the impregnability of the Maginot Line and predicts defeat. "But don't you worry your pretty little head about it," he tells her.

War breaks out and Laurent and Camille marry. To spite them, Lea gets engaged to Camille's shy brother, Claude, but just before the wedding she comes down with measles and Claude goes off to training camp where he is accidentally killed during a weapons demonstration.

Dressed in mourning, Lea goes with Camille to Paris to live with a pair of dotty maiden aunts who are shocked when François Tavernier reappears and Lea goes dancing with him. Soon she is the belle of wartime Paris, but then. . . .

"The Germans are coming! The Germans are coming!"

Lea must get back home to Montillac, but she has promised Laurent to look after the pregnant Camille, so François Tavernier steals a car for them and Lea makes her way back south with the writhing Camille and an hysterical maid.

Although we are told over and over that Lea is strong, the Lea we are shown is merely a woman with an exceedingly grumpy disposition whose alleged strength takes the form of voracity at the table and in bed. Her actions have the eery affectlessness of a zonked sex slave; after tussling in the hay with a strapping servant, "she buttoned up her blouse and fell asleep until evening, when she was awakened by the dinner bell." To signal her lubricious intentions to men, "She played with her lower lip, twisting it between thumb and forefinger," a gesture straight out of *Hustler*. Her nanny deplores her strange habit of "getting up in the middle of the night to look at the moon, with her dog. Her mother is at the end of her tether." (Incidentally, no writer with a good ear would put a mother at the end of her tether after mentioning a dog.)

Maybe it's the translation. I hope so, because if Régine Deforges really writes this badly, it's only a matter of time before the Académie Française shoots out her kneecaps. Harlequin-Romance sentences abound ("She felt a strange new feeling welling up in her"); the dialogue is unbelievably trite ("This is madness!"); 1940s French characters use 1980s American buzzwords ("You like that little wimp?" "We love the same things, the same books, the same lifestyle").

But it is François Tavernier who gets the worst line in the book. His parting words to Lea: "Regretfully, I must take leave of you now."

What intrigues me about this novel is that Régine Deforges actually names Margaret Mitchell on the acknowledgments page. She may have done it simply for legal reasons, or it may be just another manifestation of the utter lack of humor she displays throughout the book.

Or it may indicate her subconscious understanding of what is going on.

The *Gone With the Wind* craze will continue. There will be

sequel after sequel and spin-off after spin-off, not because readers secretly glory in its "racism," as the Left believes, but because *Gone With the Wind* is more than just a novel. It's a pantheon of timeless divinities and demigods that the human spirit craves but cannot find in the failed religions of the modern world.

Scarlett is Isis, Astarte, Venus, Helen of Troy; Melanie is Minerva, Diana, Cornelia; Rhett is Hector, Achilles, Odysseus; Ashley is chaste Hypolytus and beset Orestes; and the Tarleton twins are Castor and Pollux.

Catholics got something similar to this from the lives of the saints, but Protestants have been completely deprived of a humanized pantheon. Six thousand years from now, *Gone With the Wind* will be *The Yankiad* and Margaret Mitchell will be Homer.

Who said we lost?

When *Southern Ladies and Gentlemen* first came out, women's magazines kept asking me to do some version of the perennially popular article, "Are Southern Women Sexier?" It's a terribly hard article to write because the answer is yes, so I was glad when feminism put a damper on the subject.

My relief was short-lived; the next perennial to grab the mags was "Has Feminism Changed the Southern Woman?" The way to write this one is to mix the words *choice*, *alternatives*, and *options* with the words *tradition*, *family values*, and *femininity*, and then stir.

A better question might be: Has feminism become eerily Southern in ways that that no one, least of all feminists, thought possible? To find out, let's look at the most frequently quoted passage in *Southern Ladies and Gentlemen*:

"The Southern woman is required to be frigid, passionate, sweet, bitchy, stoic and scatterbrained—all at the same time. Her problems spring from the fact that she succeeds."

Nowadays that's called Having It All.

The Dixification of feminism has also revived Lucinda the Frail, she of the "delicate parts" and high-strung nerves, who only weighed ninety pounds on her wedding day and whom the wind could have blown away.

In recent years, feminists have exhibited a distinctly Southern dislike of strong healthy specimens of womanhood. They're forever ransacking history in search of "role models," but they always seem to ignore the fine strapping girls and focus on the kind who fit my grandmother's definition of a good movie: "She dies in the end."

Take, for example, their virtual blackout of Eleanor of Acquitaine, Queen of France and England, who lived to be eighty-two in the twelfth century, sans mammograms, sans Pap smears, sans everything. You would think such an indestructible old rip would do feminist historians proud, but they avoid her like the plagues and poxes she never caught and instead crank out scholarly papers about the welts and weals of Fredegund of Thuringia, dead at seventeen, a victim of medieval diaper rash whose chastity belt killed her.

The same attitude prevails in the area of mental health. The women's studies crowd has snubbed Charlotte Corday, the slip of a girl with nerves of steel who single-handedly conceived and carried out the assassination of Jean-Paul Marat during the French Revolution, and then behaved like such a brick on the scaffold that the executioner, infuriated by her unfeminine stoicism, slapped the face of her guillotined head.

But feminists, like Southerners, don't cotton to female bricks. They much prefer nervous wrecks like Alice James, or those frayed women writers like Jean Stafford who, in the words of one critic, "read her glowing reviews behind locked doors at Payne Whitney." Charlotte Corday stabbed a white European male in his bathtub without turning a hair, but feminist biographers want nothing to do with her. They would rather write about women who have, as genteel Southern ladies used to say proudly, "one nervous breakdown after another."

Woman as picture-of-health had a brief fad during the early years of feminism, when Ashley Montague's *The Natural Superiority of Women* was still in print and there was no one else to quote. For a while feminists crowed that women live longer than men and endure pain and cold temperatures better, but they soon began to sound hollow and dispirited, if not downright bored, by all this female vigor. They were discovering what Southern women had known all along: if you can't say "The doctor told her husband not to *bother* her," you're not having fun yet.

Rescue came in the form of an updated version of good old-fashioned "female trouble": the abortion debate, the crisis over the dangers of the Pill, the crisis over the dangers of IUDs, the crisis over the dangers of synthetic estrogen, and the crisis over the dangers of silicone breast implants.

This was more like it. Lucinda the Frail, hemmed in by Southern modesty, had to be content with laying a guilt trip on *one* man in the privacy of her bedroom, but the New Lucindas could wear down whole panels of men-the-beasts in televised congressional hearings.

As the trapped congressmen listened to women recite the history of their lumps and describe in detail how it feels to be a vessel of leaking, seeping, dripping silicone, their faces took on the sheepish resentment that a Southern woman instantly recognizes and calls "That Look"—when we see it, we know that what we're doing to men is working.

Illness as female metaphor was taking root in the congressmen's minds. Like many a Southern man before them, they were wondering if woman's physical weakness really does imply spiritual strength; wondering if a compensating Nature really does drain all the health from woman's body and transfer it to her soul; wondering if the fragile female really is morally superior to the sturdy male.

This is feminism in the armor of Melanie Wilkes: "She never had any strength, she never had anything but heart."

Female invalidism, real or simulated, has had a much too long and successful history to pick up its chaise longue and go quietly into the feminist night. Illness is to women what "fear-grinning" is to baboons: a way to disarm dangerous Alpha males. If women are once again instinctively using illness as protective coloration, it is a subconscious way of saying that sexual equality is getting them down and they want their moral superiority back.

That the New Lucindas seem to be placing special emphasis on pelvic and mammary disorders should come as no surprise. After all, as I wrote in *Southern Ladies and Gentlemen*: "When you think about it, there is nothing more feminine than female trouble."

Well, the hot flash has joined the Union, hasn't it? Look around you, as Marilyn French kept saying in *The Women's Room*. Baby Boomer feminists have discovered the menopause; they call it the "Big M" and they have placed it "on the agenda."

Gail Sheehy has expanded her *Vanity Fair* menopause article into a book, *The Silent Passage*, joining Germaine Greer's *The Change* in what is being called an "exploding genre."

Manhattan social worker Joyce Morrill runs a menopause seminar.

Medical writer Alice Goodman organized a menopause conference in Woodstock, New York, that gained so much media attention that she now calls herself the "Menopause Queen."

Associate professor Phyllis Kernoff Mansfield of Pennsylvania State University has no secrets from her co-workers: "I announce my hot flashes based on my commitment to demystify this whole event. What makes the event so negative is the secrecy about it."

Janine O'Leary Cobb, a Montreal sociologist, started a menopause newsletter called "A Friend Indeed" because she could find no information on the subject, and wanted to "stamp out the stigma."

The journalist, Elizabeth Hickey, chimes in: "Until recently, menopause stayed hidden"; it "got Mom's silent treatment." But Edith Bunker brought it out of the closet, says Hickey, and now " 'I'm Having a Hot Flash!' is becoming a female political statement."

Once again the progressive South has led benighted Yankees into the sunshine of a brave new world. From the canyons of Manhattan, over the hills of Woodstock, through the halls of Penn State, feminists are singing, "Oh, Law! I'm just burnin' up!"

In the late seventies, *Southern Ladies and Gentlemen* was optioned by television producer Linda Bloodworth. Nothing came of the option but plenty came of the producer, who is now Linda Bloodworth-Thomason of Billary Enterprises.

If Jimmy Carter is a frustrated good ole boy, Bill Clinton is a pseudo-good ole boy, though in some respects he's a bona fide specimen.

Gennifer Flowers told *Penthouse* that he's, er, oral, and I believe her. What she may not understand is that she was merely a substitute for the real thing: food.

As he eats his way into William Howard Taft's custom-made bathtub, alarmed pundits will trot out all sorts of Freudian theories and Rabelaisian allusions to explain why he's digging his grave with his teeth, but the truth is very simple. To a Southern Baptist, eating is the only sensual pleasure that is not a sin. Gluttony is one of the Seven Deadly Sins but they're Catholic so they don't count. The low-church groaning board has driven out the high-church groaning bed, and every good ole boy knows the path to righteousness.

Then there's the South's other oral tradition: talking. As Clinton continues losing his voice, going hoarse at closer and closer intervals until it's completely and permanently gone and we really *need* the manic sign-language lady that Democrats always include on the dais, remember that good ole boys are America's original wonks. They always have an encyclopedic knowledge of something or other—guns, cars, Civil War cavalry strategy—and hold forth on it until there isn't an unglazed eye in the house.

If Southern men talk a lot, remember they have spent three hundred years explaining the South to the rest of the country. First they had to explain slavery, then segregation, then their objections to the civil rights movement, and now backpedaling former firebrands like James J. Kilpatrick are explaining what it means to have "mellowed." Given three centuries of men talking the hind legs off a mule, the end result was bound to be Bill Clinton.

His various oral traditions aside, Clinton does not seem very Southern to me. For one thing, Bubba don't hug other men; he greets his friends by punching them in the heart in a perfect simulacrum of CPR. To Clinton's oft-repeated campaign priority, "I think it's important to touch as many of the American people as we can," Bubba replies, "Sheesh."

No one else in the Clinton family strikes me as particularly Southern, either; something about each of them falls short of the mark and strikes a hybrid note. Mama Virginia Kelley *ought* to look lke Belle Watling, *could* look like Belle Watling, and on good days *almost* looks like Belle Watling, but when all is said and done she looks like Everymadam—especially the ones from Terre Haute who crop up in the novels of James Jones.

Brother Roger is a dead cert to make Billy Carter seem in retrospect to have been as polished as Lord Chesterfield, but Roger's final disgrace, whatever it is, will happen in a nightclub, not a gas station. The heart of a true Southern ne'er-do-well beats under the bib of his overalls; Roger's beats under a cover charge.

Hillary, of course, is from Chicago, which may explain what really drives her—not Yuppie careerism, but the knowledge that she's a Yankee wife. Living for years in full awareness that people are saying "Why couldn't he have married one of our girls?" has been known to do terrible things to Northern women, and it looks as if it's happened again.

The least Southern-seeming member of the Clinton family is the one who is turning the rest of America into one big South. The jokes—and even op-eds—about Chelsea's lack of pulchritude sound exactly like a catty Southern belle sighing, "The poor thing, I bet no man will *evuh* look at her."

It may be for the best that Bill Clinton has shed much of his Southernness. I say this because he was a posthumous child. An illegitimate child, knowing that somewhere there lives a man who is his father, can comfort himself with endless fantasies of proud reunions. But a posthumous child is thwarted by the knowledge that his father vanished from the face of the earth before his own existence began: he *wasn't* before I *was*. It's the difference between desertion and bereftness, and growing up in Big Daddy country can only make it worse.

Let's hope Clinton has shed enough Southernness to escape the implications in our darkling compliment: "If you're half the man your Daddy was you'll be all right."

Do I regret anything I wrote in *Southern Ladies and Gentlemen?* Yes, I do, and I will close these remarks with an apology.

I played a sizable role in the good-ole-boy craze that swept America after *Southern Ladies and Gentlemen* came out, though Billy Carter's advent on the national scene a year later probably had more to do with it. In any event, a few years ago the North Carolina sociologist John Shelton Reed noted, "Explaining what good ole boys were soon became a lucrative sideline for Southern writers," and then went on to quote from my extensive good-ole-boy-ana.

I did not fully appreciate the good ole boy when I wrote *Southern Ladies and Gentlemen*; consequently, my analysis of him tended at times to be overcritical and tart. He can try a woman's soul when she's young and still has that swing he wants in his backyard, but now that I am over the hill and sexual tension is a thing of the past, I have become his biggest fan and most passionate defender, able at last to see him as he sees himself: the only man left in America who says words like "honor" and "pride" without smirking.

*Also by Florence King...*

*Confessions of a Failed Southern Lady*

"A stunning book, a masterpiece."

—*Los Angeles Times*

*Confessions of a Failed Southern Lady* is Florence King's classic memoir of her upbringing in an eccentric Southern family, told with all the uproarious wit and gusto that has made her one of the most admired writers in the country. Florence may have been a disappointment to her Granny, whose dream of rearing a Perfect Southern Lady would never quite be fulfilled. But after all, as Florence reminds us, "no matter which sex I went to bed with, I never smoked on the street."

"An outrageous commentator on men, women, and other sources of amusement, particularly the Southern variety....Florence King never loses her warmth, her humor, or her ability to be delighted by life's inherent contradictions."

—*Chicago Sun-Times*

"Miss King, who lives in Virginia, is among the few writers who can make you laugh and gasp out loud....She is a social commentator who wipes away the thick-as-molasses layers of Southern sham....Write on, Miss King."

—*Chattanooga Times*

"The damndest adventures in autobiographical hilarity to come down the pike in recent years....She is a Bombeck with bite, a female Art Buchwald with Southern sass, an A-one original American humorist down to her wicked, wicked bones."

—Susan Brownmiller

"She leaves more Old South traditions in shreds than Gen. William T. Sherman....*Confessions of a Failed Southern Lady* should appeal to all belles, Southern or not, failed or not."

—*Atlanta Journal-Constitution*